CLINICAL HYPNOSIS WITH CHILDREN

Edited by

William C. Wester II, Ed.D., ABPP, ABPH
Donald J. O'Grady, Ph.D., ABPP

D0146859

BRUNNER/MAZEL, Publishers ● **New York**

Library of Congress Cataloging-in-Publication Data

Clinical hypnosis with children / edited by William C. Wester II,
  Donald J. O'Grady.
      p. cm.
  Includes bibliographical references and index.
  ISBN 0-87630-605-9
  1. Hypnotism—Therapeutic use. 2. Child psychotherapy.
I. Wester, William C. II. O'Grady, Donald J.
  [DNLM: 1. Child Psychology. 2. Hypnosis—in infancy & childhood.
3. Hypnosis—methods. WM 415 C6417]
RE505.H86C55 1990
618.92'89162—dc20
DNLM/DLC   90-15157
for Library of Congress   CIP

Published by
BRUNNER/MAZEL, Inc.
19 Union Square West
New York, New York 10003

Designed by Tere LoPrete

Manufactured in the United States of America

10 9 8 7 6 5 4 3 2 1

To my wife, Betty, and my children, William, Lori, and Scott, whose support, encouragement, advice, and love have given me the inner strength required to complete this book.

WILLIAM C. WESTER II

To my children, Erin and Michael, who have enriched my life as a father, psychologist, and hypnotherapist beyond their imaginations. Also, I thank Helen Berry for being my mentor in intellectual pursuits.

DONALD J. O'GRADY

Contents

Contributors

Franz Baumann, M.D.
Department of Pediatrics
San Francisco Children's Hospital
Private Practice
Past President and Fellow
American Society of Clinical Hypnosis
San Francisco, California

Gary R. Elkins, Ph.D.
Scott and White Clinic
Texas A&M University College of Medicine
Temple, Texas

Susan R. Eppley, Ed.D.
Senior Vice President
Behavioral Science Center, Inc.
Private Practice
Cincinnati, Ohio

Charles G. Guyer II, Ed.D.
Clinical Associate Professor
School of Medicine
University of North Carolina at Chapel Hill
Private Practice
Greensboro, North Carolina

Claudia Hoffmann, Ed.D.
Staff Psychologist
Department of Child Psychiatry and Psychology
Children's Hospital Medical Center
Cincinnati, Ohio

Richard P. Kluft, M.D.
Clinical Professor of Psychiatry
Temple University School of Medicine
Philadelphia, Pennsylvania

Leora Kuttner, Ph.D.
Clinical Psychologist
Pain Management Service
B.C. Children's Hospital
Vancouver, Canada
Department of Pediatrics
University of British Columbia
Vancouver, Canada

Steven J. Lynn, Ph.D.
Professor of Psychology
Ohio University
Athens, Ohio

Donald J. O'Grady, Ph.D.
Professor of Clinical Pediatrics
University of Cincinnati College of Medicine
Director, Psychology Service
Department of Child Psychiatry and Psychology
Children's Hospital Medical Center
Cincinnati, Ohio

Adam Plotnick, M.A.
Ph.D. Candidate in Clinical Psychology
University of Cincinnati
Cincinnati, Ohio

Judith W. Rhue, Ph.D.
Associate Professor of Family Medicine
Ohio University College of Osteopathic Medicine
Athens, Ohio

Janet R. Schultz, Ph.D.
Associate Professor of Clinical Pediatrics (Psychology)
University of Cincinnati College of Medicine
Cincinnati, Ohio

Moshe S. Torem, M.D.
Chairman
Professor of Psychiatry
Northeastern Ohio Universities
College of Medicine
Akron, Ohio

Valerie Wall, Ph.D.
Clinical Psychologist
Private Practice
Seattle, Washington

William C. Wester II, Ed.D.
President/Senior Psychologist
Behavioral Science Center, Inc.
Clinical Professor, Wright State University
School of Professional Psychology
Private Practice
Cincinnati, Ohio

Martin H. Young, Ph.D.
Associate Professor of Pediatrics
Director of Developmental and
Behavioral Consultation Program
University of Massachusetts Medical School
Worcester, Massachusetts

Foreword

A spoonful of sugar makes
the medicine go down in
the most delightful way

from *Mary Poppins*

These words could be the childhood fantasy of song or the introduction of hypnotic communications to the medical or psychological needs of a child. Children have long been regarded as good responders to hypnosis and hypnotic interventions with trancelike states common to their experience. Antecedent conditions are found in childhood play, fantasy, imaginary playmates, and much of the unfolding drama of the developing child. The affective and fantasy experiences of children's literature are blended together to engage and absorb the child into his or her inner world, away from considerations of reality. This blending is reflective of trancelike states, often shifting the child's thought process away from secondary processes to more primitive modes of cognition in which almost anything is suggestible or possible. Josephine Hilgard (1979) has proposed that most of the variables suggestive of hypnotic responsiveness in the adult have their precursors in the creative, affective, and play experiences of childhood. From this it follows that practitioners of medical and psychological services to a pediatric population would want to express their interventions in a language and cognitive style that are appropriate for the inner world of the child.

Clinical Hypnosis with Children is the third comprehensive text edited by Dr. Wester, with Dr. O'Grady coediting this volume. It is devoted exclusively to hypnosis and the specialized needs of children. The first book, published in 1984 and coedited with Dr. Alexander Smith, and the second, published in 1987, contain chapters and case material about hypnosis and the medical, psychological, and dental needs of adults. This third volume begins with an introduction to children with attention to their responsiveness and the special considerations required by this population. Unit Two presents eight chapters on psychological applications, which include two chapters on hypnotic interventions with early-childhood trauma and sexually abused children. Unit Three has four chapters devoted to medical applications commonly seen in medical practice.

As with the first volume, the theoretical and experimental foundations are

xiii

examined, psychopathological states are explained, and various specialized techniques of inductions and therapeutic applications are presented. Case histories are utilized to involve the reader in the moment-to-moment movement of the hypnotic encounter. As with the previous two volumes, the editors have drawn from clinicians who are well known for their work with children and their expertise in hypnosis. Any clinician who desires a comprehensive reference will appreciate the authors' efforts at integrating hypnosis into their own specialty of pediatric treatment. Whether one is a seasoned clinician or just beginning to work with children and hypnosis, this book, and the up-to-date references with each chapter, will be invaluable resource material. Drs. Wester and O'Grady have been careful to select appropriate topics with a continued emphasis on the multidisciplinary approach in acknowledgment of the diversity of clinical backgrounds of those practitioners who deliver services to children.

No population of people requires as much special care and consideration as do children. Fordyce (1988) has proposed two questions that all clinicians are well advised to keep in mind especially in working with children who are still in the process of developing their own internal constructions of reality. These questions—which are derived from the need to maintain a self-supervisory capacity and reflect a sensitivity to the ongoing process of any treatment—are: What am I teaching my patients by what I say and do? What is my patient learning? Throughout this book, the reader will continually encounter each author's special response to these questions within his or her respective area of expertise.

It is an honor to have been asked to introduce *Clinical Hypnosis with Children* to the professional community with special interests in children. This is an outstanding addition to the professional literature on both hypnosis and children. Together with the two previous volumes, it will afford clinicians a rich set of resources to expand their competence in and mastery of the uses of hypnosis. As my father wrote in a text he gave to me many years ago, "Read and learn." I would only add, "Enjoy and appreciate."

—— THOMAS W. WALL, Ph.D., ABPH
President American Society of Clinical Hypnosis, 1990–1991
Diplomate in Clinical Hypnosis
American Board of Psychological Hypnosis

REFERENCES

Fordyce, W. (1988). Pain and suffering. *American Psychologist, 43*(4), 276-283.
Hilgard, J. (1979). *Personality and hypnosis: A study of imaginative involvement.* Chicago: University of Chicago Press.

Introduction

THE PERFECT PLACE

If I'm scared or intense,
Or I feel like everyone is leaving me in suspense,
I go to the perfect place.

The perfect place may be cold or hot.
The perfect place may be an old grungy lot.
I go to the perfect place.

The perfect place puts me at ease,
And you can keep it safe without any keys.
I go to the perfect place.

I can have it with me wherever I go.
I keep it inside where nobody knows.
I go to the perfect place.

It can always be different or always the same,
And sometimes I play it like a silly game.
I go to the perfect place.

If I want to relax or go to sleep,
I just think of the perfect place and I don't count sheep.
I go to the perfect place.

Katie Wheelright

The above poem was written in 1988 by Katie Wheelright, then a 10-year-old girl, who was repeatedly hospitalized for treatment of Crohn's disease, a painful, inflammatory bowel disorder. She learned the value of self-hypnosis well, and her poem demonstrates one of the factors that motivates hypnotherapists who work with children—the richness of children's imaginations. Children constitute perhaps the best group of hypnotic subjects, and hypnotherapy can benefit many children with emotional and physical problems (Crasilneck & Hall, 1985).

Hypnosis under various names has been used for as long as records have been kept. Suggestive therapy is probably the oldest of all therapeutic methods. Using hypnotic techniques with children also dates back to ancient times. Accounts of children responding to various healing methods based on faith and suggestion are recorded in both the Old and the New Testament (Olness & Gardner, 1988), and Margaret Mead (1949) has described how children from primitive cultures experienced hypnotic trance phenomena in a variety of tribal rites and ceremonies. Tinterow (1970) reports that the 18th-century Austrian physician Franz Anton Mesmer (1734–1815) used animal magnetism to cure children and adolescents, as well as adults.

Baldwin (1891) is credited with the first publication specifically relating to child hypnotherapy when his article entitled ''Suggestion in Infancy'' appeared in *Science*. The field of hypnosis has undergone many fluctuations in terms of interest, practice, and research. The practice of child hypnotherapy had basically come to a halt by 1900 and it remained dormant until the 1950s (Olness & Gardner, 1988). Then there was a glimmer of renewed interest in the field with the publication of Ambrose's (1961) book entitled *Hypnotherapy with Children*.

Even though scientific articles began to be seen in many of the professional journals, there was no major treatise on the topic of child hypnotherapy until 1981 when Gardner and Olness wrote *Hypnosis and Hypnotherapy with Children*; a second edition was revised and published in 1988.

Our multi-authored book is intended to reflect not only the diverse uses of hypnosis in the treatment of children, but also different views of what is necessary and sufficient for effective hypnotherapy. We are well aware of the slow progress in validating the effectiveness of clinical hypnosis with children. Alternative explanations are often readily apparent, and confidence in generalizing positive findings across patient groups, settings, and conditions continues to be easily threatened.

These chapters, however, suggest some progress in integrating hypnosis into specialized treatment settings where clinicians and investigators are likely to be working together with larger samples of children with a wide range of problems. It is to be hoped that these child and adolescent health providers will be encouraged by the authors here to include the study and application of hypnosis in their particular area of expertise in the care of children.

REFERENCES

Ambrose, G. (1961). *Hypnotherapy with children* (2nd ed.). London: Staples.

Baldwin, J. M. (1891). Suggestions in infancy. *Science, 17,* 113-117.

Crasilneck, H. B., & Hall, J. A. (1985). *Clinical hypnosis: Principles and applications* (2nd ed.). New York: Grune & Stratton.

Mead, M. (1949). *Male and female: A study of the sexes in a changing world.* New York: William Morrow.

Olness, K., & Gardner, G. (1988). *Hypnosis and hypnotherapy with children* (2nd ed.). Philadelphia: Grune & Stratton.

Tinterow, M. M. (1970). *Foundations of hypnosis: From Mesmer to Freud.* Springfield, IL: Charles C. Thomas.

Acknowledgments

We have many people to thank for their hidden efforts in helping this work become possible. Certainly, our families deserve medals for their patience and their endurance of our frustrations, discouragements, and bruised pride when we found ourselves slowing down. We owe a sincere thanks to our typist, Norma Malecki; to Kathy Kessler and Janet Schultz, Ph.D., for their editorial assistance; and to the people from Brunner/Mazel Publishers, particularly Natalie Gilman, our managing editor, who have been most helpful and cordial. We are privileged to have been chosen by Brunner/Mazel to publish this work.

WILLIAM C. WESTER II, ED.D.
DONALD J. O'GRADY, PH.D.

PART I

INTRODUCTION TO HYPNOSIS WITH CHILDREN

1 Developmental Considerations in the Use of Hypnosis with Children

Valerie Wall, Ph.D.

When working with children, the health-care provider is continually confronted with the issue of determining the most effective strategy based on medical and psychological need as well as developmental level. It is to developmental considerations, rather than specific problems presented for treatment, that this chapter is addressed. How does a practitioner determine what level of distraction, hypnosis, or metaphor would be useful? Are there guidelines, not only theoretical but in current empirical literature, that could direct choices and assist in providing more effective hypnotic interventions? How does one determine the success of interventions? These questions need to be held in the forefront of our thinking if we are to make the best use of hypnotic strategies as primary or adjunctive therapy and improve our own capacity to "think through" the needs of the patient.

Developmental level refers to a broad range of physical, cognitive, linguistic, emotional, and social stages. Of these elements, the ones raised for consideration here will be cognitive, emotional, and language development as it is in these areas that hypnotic strategies interact to provide the most therapeutic benefit—whether the outcome is viewed as mainly psychological or physical. Hypnosis is, in part, a vehicle by which we allow patients to transform cognitive or language-coded information into a physical or emotional response (Bowers, 1977). Thus, if interventions are to be effective, they must be made at the level at which the patient has processing competency.

Developmental theories, from which stages of development are conceptualized, emphasize behaviorism, intrapsychic process, or cognitive/learning

3

process (Langer, 1969; Maier, 1978). While hypnotic interventions often seek a behavioral change as an outcome, they assume an internal cognitive, linguistic, and/or emotional processing modality as the vehicle by which change is executed. This is generally described as an internal focusing of attention or concentration allowing for therapeutically specific input, which is translated into observable outcome (Gardner & Olness, 1981). Thus, it is the theory and research in the development of these internal modalities that provide the professional with the basis for forming strategies aimed at the capacities of children of various ages across a wide spectrum of presenting problems.

The most prominent theorist in cognitive development is Piaget, whose theoretical model will be used in the current discussion. His postulations as to the sequence of cognitive stages have been subjected to extensive clinical research regarding their validity sequentially and in the age frames proposed. Currently, research in the area of linguistics is shedding light on the language capacities of children aged 2–12 years, which go beyond Piaget's originally proposed limitations. Although few developmental language theories exist outside of Chomsky's (1975) "deep structure" concepts or Vygotsky's (1978) socially based acquisition model, the most recent studies appear to work well into a cognitive model of development and will be approached as such.

Piaget's work does not speak directly to emotional or intrapsychic development, and his theory is primarily one of discontinuity. This is distinct from the work of theorists such as Freud or Erik Erikson, which is based on energic shifting and control. Freud's work was the basis for the neo-Freudian formulations of Erikson, who expanded on the role of the ego in interaction with social and environmental influence, and who accumulated large amounts of clinically illustrative anecdotal data with children (Coles, 1970). While theories conceptualizing psychological or emotional growth rely on energic internal shifting, Piaget roots his theory in embryology and the belief that the structures he describes are biologically present in the being. He proposes a discontinuity of development that grows out of the introduction of new information to the individual and the eventual ability to build new structures to accommodate the information. These changes are viewed as qualitatively distinct, with each requiring the structures of the previous stage to be fully stabilized in order adequately to develop the next. Piaget's theory is compatible with and supplementary to psychoanalytic theory and vice versa (Maier, 1978). According to Wolfe (1960):

Despite their methodological differences and divergent goals, the two methods may complement each other in providing a comprehensive picture of the developmental process, each supplying that data in those areas where the other is deficient. (pp. 11–12)

As Charles Odier (1956) has observed:

The strongest aspect of the Freudian psychoanalytic doctrine is the weakest of Piaget's doctrine and vice versa . . . comparing the evaluation of the individual to a river, I should say that Freud with his psychoanalytic approach and Piaget both ascended it to its source but each from his own bank. By definition, this parallelism condemned them never to meet. (p. 32)

Erikson's model, which provides the basis for the current discussion of social/emotional development, is linked with Piaget's findings by Erikson, as if each of them were "weaving with different strands the same cloth of development" (Evans, 1969). It is with this intertwining of cognition, language, and emotion that hypnotherapy interacts. And it is to the varying stages of abilities and needs that the child hypnotherapist must be attuned.

DEVELOPMENTAL STAGES AND HYPNOTHERAPEUTIC STRATEGIES

Both Piaget and Erikson propose that the "completion" of a phase or stage provides the opportunity for internal or structural redefinition and thereby furthers continued growth. In this aspect, both models are heterostatic, rather than homeostatic or focused on a return to a previous state of equilibrium. *Equilibration* for Piaget and *positive adaptation* for Erikson introduce ways of creating new interactions, not solutions that maintain existing structures (Erikson, 1974, 1977; Elkind, 1978; Inhelder, de Capron, & Cornu-Wells, 1987). Linguistics or language research draws heavily on Piagetian concepts and provides the clinical "bridge" into language usage by developmental phase necessary for formulation of hypnotherapeutic strategies. In all three contexts, the criteria for attainment of a new phase are congruent. For Erikson (1963), it is crucial that each stage reach positive adaptation prior to entering the next, as "the strength acquired at any stage is tested by the necessity to transcend it in such a way that the individual can takes chances in the next stage with what was most vulnerably precious in the previous one" (p. 263).

As with Erikson, Piaget also posits stage criteria. These include (1) qualitative changes or leaps in cognitive content, (2) the inclusion of prior cognitive structures in subsequent stages, and (3) an overall integration of the structures of each stage. Growth occurs through the preparatory phase in which the appearance of the upcoming stage shift is sporadically given and the consolidation phase in which the stage criteria are met (Brainerd, 1978). The universality of the invariant nature of stage progression is reflected in the assumptions of Piaget, Erikson, and linguistic researchers.

Linguistics research asks directly the questions generated by the issues of children's ability to comprehend and produce metaphors at various ages. The complexity of definitional issues is readily apparent as researchers work to operatinalize "metaphorical understanding" into measurable and generalizable concepts (Reyna, 1986). For use with hypnosis and ease in summarizing the literature, Vosniadou's (1987) definition will be employed:

> Metaphors are meaningful statements that communicate something about a concept by comparing it or juxtaposing it to a similar concept from a different conventional category. . . . first, the two concepts must be based on some perceptible similarity, otherwise, the statement would be an anomaly. . . . second, the two concepts must belong to different conventional categories, otherwise the statement would represent literal comparison, not metaphor (p. 871)

It is important in defining and utilizing metaphors with children that we do not simply apply the "child-as-a-smaller-adult" way of thinking. Children are beginning categorization by the process of finding similarities, which allows the use of existing knowledge in understanding new information, as in Piaget's preparatory period. They are, as Keil (1986) points out, "universal novices" who may lack information in a domain well within their competence of understanding. This makes children distinctly different from adults in the amount and breadth of material with which they work. However, as novices, once they begin the use of a domain, they readily share information across new items in the domain. The difficulty in understanding comprehension ability in children has led some researchers to conclude that metaphorical comprehension is not present until adolescence—the time at which Piaget's theory postulates the beginning of formal cognitive operations (Marti, 1986). However, more current work that allows for play enactment rather than paraphrasing of metaphors in the young child has shown children of 3.5 to 5 years of age to possess metaphoric understanding. This is especially true when similarities are based on perceptual/physical similarity (Brown et al., 1986; Vosniadou, 1987).

In the following discussion of developmental phases, theory and research will be focused on clinical practice and types of hypnotic techniques or metaphors employed. The phases and suggestions for intervention strategies are summarized in Table 1.1.

TABLE 1-1. Developmental Stages and Hypnotic Interventions

Age, Years	Piaget	Erikson	Linguistic Research	Hypnotic Interventions
0	0–2 years Sensorimotor thought	0–1 year Stage I Trust vs. mistrust	0–2 years Not investigated	Rocking, patting, stroking, repetitious auditory input such as singing or rhyming, visual distraction with toys or presentation of familiar toy to hold
1				
2				
3	2–7 years Preoperational thought	1–3 years Stage II Autonomy vs. shame and doubt	2–6/7 years Metaphors possible if tied to perceptual stimuli (visual) "Because" relationships understood	Use of visual/movement stimulation while giving language input. e.g., talk through a puppet
4				Use of "because" causality in stories
5		3–5 years Stage III. Initiative vs. guilt		Story telling
6	(includes intuitive thought in 5–7-year-old		"if" relationships developing, more complex perceptual metaphors possible	Stories with "because" and "if" possible at 6–7 years
7	7 years to puberty	6 years to puberty Stage IV		Eye-closure techniques more comfortable (over age 5)
8				
9			Increasing capacity to use internal representations of acts and activities	
10	Concrete Operational thought	Industry vs. inferiority		Arm rigidity: e.g., oak tree
11			Use child's area of knowledge Concrete thinking observed	Eye fixation (on hand, coin, wall, spot) Arm lowering
12			Ability to recognize and use voice intonation to interpret meaning	Special/favorite places Listening to music Favorite physical activities or sports Magic carpet Cloud car
13	Adolescence	Adolescence Stage V Identity vs. identity confusion	Egocentrism may be a function of increased cognitive awareness and the new ability to think about oneself relative to peers and to think about thinking	Adult induction methods Naturalistic/permissive methods allowing for patient control while setting internal boundaries; e.g., safe room or space
14	Formal Operational thought			Favorite sport
15				Use of physically based inductions
16				Use of more abstract, less consciously aware metaphor
17			Inductive and hypothetico-deductive reasoning increases into early 20s	
18				
19				
20	Not Investigated	Three adult stages	Not reported here	

PHASE I. SENSORIMOTOR PERIOD
(BIRTH TO 2 YEARS, APPROXIMATELY)

The initial sensorimotor phase ranges from birth to approximately 2 years of age and includes six stages, which cluster about the six areas of cognitive contents delineated by Piaget. This phase corresponds to Erikson's first stage and a portion of the second stage as defined by age. In the Piagetian substage, it is interesting to note a major "leap" in ability at approximately one year between the fourth and fifth sensorimotor substage. It is at this point that Piaget posits the ability of the child to create totally new patterns of behavior designed to influence his or her environment. This is the same age at which Erikson posits the beginning of the second stage of development, which is heavily focused on developing autonomy and resolving conflicts with the environment caused by the child's increasing ability to initiate environmental interaction. Thus, while Piaget's sensorimotor phase as a whole does not correspond in age range to the first stage of Erikson, it does recognize the same shift in competence and interactional behavior.

During the first year of life, the child is moving from the primitive ability to imitate toward independent behavior. It is during this year, according to Erikson, that the social and emotional development of the child leads toward a reciprocally trusting relationship with the primary caregiver and yields a sense of hope and faith in those more powerful than oneself. In the cognitive domain, the child initially displays primary circular reactions that are more like reflex actions and demonstrates little differentiation between himself or herself and the primary caregiver. During the first half of the first year, secondary circular reactions appear in which behaviors learned more or less by chance are observed. The tertiary circular reactions that allow the child to create totally novel patterns of behavior with systematic variations appear in the beginning of the second year. The difficulty with Piaget's estimates is that they seem to confuse infant performance with competence. More current research suggests that early infant imitation is thoughtful in that it differentiates behavior and is responsive to some variance in cueing (Brainerd, 1978). Thus, the child is more capable than Piaget assumed and may at some level be making more decisions about the environment and the effects of interacting with it than his theory suggests.

Also developing in the second year of life are the "hand-in-hand" concepts of time and object permanence. The new infant appears to have no concept of time as an objective thing. Thus, behavioral sequences may show some reflexive quality, but beyond this, sequencing appears nonsignificant. By the second year of life, the child begins to make internal representations of time, such as past events and events not so far in the past. It is also at this time that the infant begins to show searching behavior when an object is covered or removed. As the infant develops some past, present, and future orientation, he or she also appears to develop the ability to hold an image more constant in memory and attempts to find the lost object.

Another, extremely powerful event occurring during this period is the development of the construct of causality. As delineated by Piaget, this becomes a clinically crucial issue when interacting with injured children or perhaps when later working with older children who were injured or abused during this early period. By causality Piaget means the relatively simple capacity to anticipate what consequences will follow from a certain cause. In adults, mature causality consists of the two aspects of psychological and physical causality. Psychological refers to volition or will and physical to more objective cause-and-effect relations. The sensorimotor precursor of psychological causality is *dynamism*, which represents the infant's understanding that internal feelings somehow produce external behaviors. The precursor of physical causality is *phenomenalism*, which is the primitive belief that any two events occurring close together in time must be causally linked. Piaget believes that dynamism and phenomenalism are undifferentiated at birth and that the main task of causal development during the sensorimotor period is to develop a dual system. This theory posits that the first months of life are a time of "magic" when cause–effect relations are believed to be produced by internal psychological processes. The development of secondary circular reactions allows the child to begin to separate the two forms of causality. Tertiary reactions allow the child to begin to be aware that some events occur totally separate from the child or the child's control and wishes.

On the basis of this model and the necessity of developing a sense of trust and autonomy during this age as proposed by Erikson, it becomes clear that in interacting with very young children (preverbal), we need to exercise some caution in providing them with self-controlling techniques that may be beyond their understanding. Techniques that are too sophisticated may cause the child to decide that the technique is the cause of the hurt or to attribute causality to the therapist's voice or some other event in proximity to an injury rather than to experience a sense of mastery. Because the issue of trust is paramount, it appears that simple distractions are probably best with this age group, as are the more traditional comforting behaviors of an external adult. In formulating treatment strategies for an emotionally disturbed child with damage that occurred at a very young age, we need to look carefully at the patient's belief that he or she is, in fact, the cause of the event—that is, the inability to distinguish internal feeling, external event, and proximity. The intervention strategies given in Table 1.1 for this age group are designed to hold the child's attention outside of himself or herself rather than to promote a sense of internal control over an event.

PHASE II. PREOPERATIONAL PERIOD
(EARLY CHILDHOOD—2 TO 7 YEARS)

The preoperational phase of cognitive development encompasses the completion of the second and third Eriksonian stages. During stage II, autonomy in the sense of protecting oneself from rivals, or territoriality, is developed. The child's ability to develop a sense of autonomy—standing on one's own with minimal conflict from shame and doubt—combines with the continuing development of hope from stage I to provide a lasting sense of self-control without loss of self-esteem. This stage is decisive for the ratio of love and hate, cooperation and willfulness, freedom of self-expression and its suppression. Stage III, which begins at approximately 3 years of age and goes through age 5, is a time during which the child establishes a sense of *initiative* or enthusiasm for exploring and being the aggressor toward the world and new discoveries, rather than clinging to the autonomy of stage II. During this stage, the superego gains vital importance, and if it remains too infantile or moralistic, can be uncompromising in the production of guilt relative to the child's exploration. The child must split his or her infantile instincts—which previously provided for growth, self-protection, or discovery and continue to allow for growth and exuberance—from a parental mode that will increase self-observation, guidance, and punishment. The infantile moralism of guilt must be balanced with more mature initiative and incorporation. This balance is viewed by Erikson as one of the most deeply rooted aspects of human development.

More changes occur in the child's life during the preoperational years than at any other comparable portion of the life span. The most obvious are in the child's social environment: the child's range of peer contacts broadens, school entry occurs, systematic instruction in linguistics and abstract symbols begins, and parental expectations shift to encourage independent and self-care skills. Cognitive development during this period is characterized by several important contents and an equally important *absence*: the absence of mental operations, which are defined as the internalized representations of an action. Perception, memory, and imagery, which take place at all ages, are not mental operations for Piaget, as they can occur more passively without intervening interpretation. Mental operations require that concepts include reversibility, either in the form of *negation*, in which an operation can be carried out in the opposite direction from whence it came, or in the form of *compensation*, in which an operation is negated by carrying out a second operation negating the first. For example, if a child says, "My mother got mad because I threw the jam jar on the floor," a negation would be, "Then your mother would not get angry if you did not throw the jam jar on the floor." A compensatory concept would be an application of a solution such as, "If the jam is on the floor, what would happen if you got a rag and wiped it up—would your mother still be angry?" The preoperational child has difficulty solving this problem and tends to respond with such ideas as, "She made me so mad that I did it," or "She made me do it by asking me to put it away," and not applying a reversible logical system to the event. The development of decentering remains quite limited, leading rapidly to frustration and a pursuant need for treatment strategies that allow the child to "see" the point of view of another as if it were the child's own.

Egocentrism is the most commonly discussed content of this period. For Piaget, egocentrism does not imply selfishness. It is, instead, a dimension concerned with the extent to which children view themselves as the center of reality. Any behavior suggesting that children are preoccupied with themselves or are unconcerned about things going on around them may be termed egocentric, that is, any behavior suggesting that children have trouble distinguishing what "I" think or feel from what "you" think or feel. As the process of decentering gradually causes the child to differentiate the perspective of self from that of others, the child becomes more prepared to enter "concrete operations"—the next developmental period.

Also apparent in this stage is the immature and continuing development of a concept of *causality*. In the adult, causality is normally linked to the two forms of "why," which refer to the effects of doing something or the cause behind it. In preoperational children, the two are not differentiated and "why" questions address both issues simultaneously. The results of this nondifferentiated "why" can be a confusing response pattern from the child when the adult attempts to answer the child's "why?" The child at this age also appears to believe that every event occurs as the result of a specific cause and seems unable to accept the view that some events simply are accidental or "chance" occurrences—reality is manufactured according to some divine or grand set of blueprints.

Current language or linguistic research has attempted to observe the young child's ability to produce and comprehend metaphoric communications. As Keil (1986) and Vosniadou (1987) point out, attempts to study actual competence must use tasks within the child's domain of information and processing skill. Keil has noted that the "collapsing of categories" reprted in 5- to 7-year-olds is not equivalent to metaphorical understanding. However, children do comprehend and produce metaphor, especially when aided by nonverbal input. Dent (1987) found that the 2- to 3-year-old child was able to produce and comprehend metaphors tied to perceptual input, such as a fireworks display being described as "flowers." More complex metaphors, based on visual input and movement, were observed in 5- to 6-year-olds, for example, an ice skater compared to a needle on a record.

The young child appears to become less perceptually tied into the thinking process as he or she develops toward concrete operational functioning. This is observed in responses to visual input and in the ability to express more abstract forms of causality. In the former instance, Sparks and Cantor (1986) found that 3- to 5-year old preoperational children express low physical/emotional arousal in anticipation of an exiting visual presentation and high arousal during the event, whereas 9-year-old concrete operational children express more anticipatory arousal and lower arousal during presentation.

This shifting from perceptual dependence to internal functioning represents the developing cognitive capacity for internal representation. Byrnes and Duff (1986) found a significant improvement between the ages of 3 and 4 years in children's ability to express causality in "if" speech forms. Beginning at the upper-2-year age, most children could explain and use "because" forms of causality. However, younger children overextended this pattern into stories requiring "if" relationships. The increasing sophistication of the young child in using these two forms of causality runs parallel to the gradual shifting away from dependence on perceptual cueing.

Several studies have attempted to ascertain how the development of cognition in the young child influences emotional development. Kemper and Edward (1986) and Pillow (1988) have found that the development of causality relates to a shift from passive (external) to active (internal) perceptions of control and interactional influence on the environment. In other words, very young children may attribute cause by proximity but do not perceive that they can interact with and interpret the environment themselves. The latter requires internal representation, which develops over the preoperational period.*

Hypnotherapy with the preoperational child needs to address competencies, both cognitive and emotional. The child is seeking gradually to establish a sense of control and mastery. Much of the child's functioning is perceptually based. Thus, the "apparent hesitancy" to close their eyes in order to image often is observed in young children. These children rapidly cross perceptual modalities and are able to do so fluidly with their eyes open. Strategies allowing for this eye-open fluidity are highly successful. Talking to the child through a toy or puppet, using toy figures to tell stories and create new approaches, pretending a favorite activity, or seeing something that the child likes on a television screen allows the child to represent the needed intervention externally. Remembering to use "because" rather than "if" logic can increase the impact of a strategy. For example, if a child is receiving a medical procedure such as an injection, say, "Your arm will feel

---

*For readers interested, Lane and Schwartz (1987) have extended this discussion into a cognitive-developmental theory as applied to psychopathology.

numb *because* of the fun we are having playing hide and seek now" rather than "*If* you keep on having fun playing hide and seek, your arm will stay numb." While both apparently convey similar ideas, they are understood differently.

As the child progresses to the 5- to 7-year age range, eye-closure techniques using favorite places, TV watching, games, activities, and more developed metaphors in the forms of stories can be employed. At this age, the child is moving into the age of high hypnotizability often referred to in children. As children prepare for and enter "concrete operations," their internal representation capacity materializes and they continue to maintain cross-modality fluidity, allowing for excellent and rapid response to hypnotic techniques.

CONCRETE OPERATIONAL PHASE: MIDDLE CHILDHOOD (APPROXIMATELY AGE SEVEN TO PUBERTY)

The Piagetian concrete operational phase encompasses Erikson's stage IV—industry versus inferiority. This stage is different from the preceding ones in that it does not represent the arduous conflict of moving from an inner upheaval or strife to a new outer mastery. It is a latency period or quiet before the onset of puberty when the earlier drives reappear in new combination. Erikson (1963) describes this stage as follows:

> With the oncoming latency period, the normally advanced child forgets, or rather sublimates, the necessity to "make" people by direct attack or to become papa and mama in a hurry: he now learns to win recognition by producing things. He has mastered the ambulatory field and the organ modes. He has experienced a sense of finality regarding the fact that there is no workable future within the womb of his family, and thus becomes ready to apply himself to given skills and tasks, which go far beyond the mere playful expression of his organ modes or the pleasure of the function of his limbs. He develops a sense of industry, i.e., he adjusts himself to the inorganic laws of the tool world. (p. 259)

The child at this age is receiving some form of systematized instruction. This occurs across cultures, whether at school or in group customs or apprenticeships. All is preparatory for the technology required in adult life. As the child becomes more skilled in the technology presented, the virtue of formal competency or methodological performance arises. This flows naturally into the societal ritualizations of work and vocation. However, the unsuccessful child may not develop a sense of identification with them and the technology offered through instruction. Yet, there is another, and potentially more dangerous, ritualized structure: the child may identify too strongly with his or her work and that "which works" becomes a yardstick for being worthwhile.

It is during this age that mastery becomes a more readily available motivator in the treatment alliance. The child now possesses the internal mental operations and the external physical performance skills to achieve successful interaction with and mastery over the environment.

For Piaget, this is by far the most important period. The bulk of his writing and research is centered on the contents of the concrete operational child. This is the last of the transitional periods before mature operational intelligence emerges. At this level, the child uses operational thought, but it must be tied to concrete realities, as opposed to later mature operations that are freed from concrete ties and can also function on a purely abstract or hypothetical level. There are two major categories of concrete operations: logico-arithmetic operations, which process discrete data, and spatial operations, which process continuous data. Logico-arithmetic operations include the contents of conservation, relations of ordering, and classification, which refers to the relations of membership or belonging. Spatial operations are the contents of Euclidean geometry; projection, which allows us to localize and order objects and to determine distances from one another; and topology, which allows pure categorical information with no description of localization or distance between objects.

Studies of metaphor comprehension in the concrete operational child consistently demonstrate the ability of this age group to comprehend and use the concepts of consequence and order (French, 1988), attributional and relational metaphors (Gentner, 1988), and voice intonation to determine emphasis and meaning (Holdgrafer & Campbell, 1986). In each instance, the need to enter the child's domain in a concrete format rather than with more abstract lexicon is emphasized.

Psychologically, the child at this age is much more able to follow the type of hypnotic inductions frequently used that involve imagination and visual imagery to avert pain and bring about therapeutic growth. However, metaphorical work that relies too heavily on the abstract can be difficult for this child and may not be grasped. Thus, hypnotically speaking, this child continues to need more concrete imagery with clear linkage to observed effect. Children at this age do very well with biofeedback devices. However, the effect of biofeedback training may not hold up well over long-term follow-up. It would be predicted that a child at this age would not transfer from a concrete method to a more abstract representaton of it (i.e., continue biofeedback training effects independently over time), as hypothetical reasoning is required to translate the effect achieved with a mechanical device into self-mastery. One would predict, based on Piaget's model, that this child would be more successful, over time, with direct hypnotic training as cause and effect can be immediately tied—using the less mature logic of proximity and magical thinking, as well as the concrete ability to say, "This works because when I do it I feel a difference," without having the intermediary of a machine. As can be seen from the inductions for this age group in Table 1-1, each involves a known activity or a response based on a physiologically predictable outcome, for example, hands coming together, eyes closing as a result of fixation. In other words, the child increases mastery while remaining connected to concrete processes or images.

FORMAL OPERATION PHASE: PUBERTY THROUGH ADULTHOOD (BEGINNING AT APPROXIMATELY 12 YEARS)

With the beginning of formal operational thought, the child, now adolescent, is faced with the issue of establishing identity anew. Psychologically, the conflicts of earlier years are refought with the artificial use of well-meaning people as adversaries and the raising of idols and ideals. As described by Erikson, the ego now plays a greatly expanded role of selection and integration as the adolescent searches for continuity among friends and the social environment. The ego identity of this age is the "accrued confidence that the inner sameness and continuity prepared in the past are matched by the sameness and continuity of one's meaning for others, as evidenced in the tangible promise of career" (Erikson, 1963, p. 261).

While Erikson sees adolescence as a time of identity diffusion and alignments that produce considerable turmoil, Piaget does not subscribe to the trouble-and-turmoil school of thought. He accentuates the positive features of this period—namely, the appearance of formal operations. These operations begin to appear in early adolescence and are attained at approximately 15 years of age. Hypothetico-deductive reasoning emerges, along with a frequently overlooked weakness in this type of reasoning: our conclusions are true only if our premises are secure. No wonder parents often feel trapped between their adolescent's conclusion and logic and the assumptions underlying them, and this is particularly so with early adolescents. Inductive thought also appears in this stage, which allows reasoning from specific facts to general principles. Gradual increases in these capacities throughout adolescence and into the early 20s have been observed by Brown et al. (1986) and Wing and Scholniek (1968). Formal operations provide for truly abstract reasoning. The individual becomes capable of thinking about such ideas as thought, identity, and a wide variety of more academic and scientific endeavors. It is at this age that we begin to employ hypnotic techniques more similar to those used with older adults—the concept of metaphorical connection becomes more salient and the door is open to many of the indirect techniques discussed relative to adult practice. The child has decentered sufficiently to move away from the concrete and is able to benefit from both direct and indirect treatment strategies and to observe and report on the phenomena experiences.

Hudson and Gray (1986) suggest that adolescent egocentrism, as observed in striving for identity, may well be a function of emerging formal operations. The ability to consider abstractly the effect that one has on others or the validity of one's own thought processes appears to generate worry about appearances to others. This is a central theme when working with adolescents, especially hypnotically. Particular concern and empathy for their newly found self-awareness need to be maintained in order to assess their true thoughts and feelings and to respect their need to maintain control externally while they seek internal reanchoring.

SUMMARY

The theoretical constructs presented outline the viewpoints of Erikson, Piaget, and linguistic researchers. These concepts provide insight into the emotional, cognitive, and linguistic capabilities and needs of children across varying age ranges. It is the understanding gained through knowledge of developmental levels in childhood that allows the practitioner in hypnosis to formulate and utilize interventions at their most effective and constructive level and to provide maximum therapeutic benefit to the patient.

REFERENCES

Bowers, K. S. (1977). Hypnosis: An informational approach. *Annals of the New York Academy of Science, 296*, 222–237.

Brainerd, C. J. (1978). *Piaget's theory of intelligence*. Englewood Cliffs, NJ: Prentice-Hall.

Brown, A. L., Cane, M. J., & Echols, C. H. (1986). Young children's mental models determine analogical transfer across problems with a common goal structure. *Cognitive Development, 1*(2), 103–121.

Brown, J. M., O'Keefe, J., Sanders, S. H., & Baker, B. (1986). Developmental changes in children's cognition to stressful and painful situations. *Journal of Pediatric Psychology, 11*(3), 343–357.

Byrnes, J. P., & Duff, M. A. (1988). Young children's comprehension and production of causal expressions. *Child Study Journal, 18*(2), 101–119.

Chomsky, N. (1975). *Reflections on language*. New York: Pantheon.

Coles, R. (1970). *Erik H. Erikson: The growth of his work*. Boston: Little, Brown & Co.

Dent, C. H. (1987). Developmental studies of perception and metaphor: The twain shall meet. *Metaphor and Symbolic Activity, 2*(1), 53–71.

Elkind, D. (1978). *The child's reality: Three developmental themes.* Hillsdale, NJ: Erlbaum.

Erikson, E. H. (1963). *Childhood and society* (2nd ed.). New York: Norton.

Erikson, E. H. (1974). *Dimensions of a new identity: Jefferson lectures.* New York: Norton.

Erikson, E. H. (1977). *Toys and reasons: Stages in the ritualization of experience.* New York: Norton.

Evans, R. I. (1969). *Dialogue with Erik Erikson.* New York: Dutton.

French, L. A. (1988). The development of children's understanding of "because" and "so." *Journal of Experimental Child Psychology, 45*(2), 262–279.

Gardner, G., & Olness, K. (1981). *Hypnosis and hypnotherapy with children.* New York: Grune & Stratton.

Gentner, D. (1988). Metaphor as structure mapping. The relational shift. *Child Development, 59*(1), 47–59.

Holdgrafer, G., & Campbell, T. F. (1986). Children's comprehension of intonation as a marker for discourse topic collaboration. *Applied Psycholinguistics, 7*(4), 373–384.

Hudson, L. M., & Gray, W. M. (1986). Formal operations, the imaginary audience and the personal fable. *Adolescence, 21*(84), 751–765.

Inhelder, B., de Capron, D., & Cornu-Wells, A. (1987). *Piaget today.* Hillsdale, NJ: Erlbaum.

Keil, F. (1986). Conceptual domains and the acquisition of metaphor. *Cognitive Development, 1*(1), 73–96.

Kemper, S., & Edward, L. L. (1986). Children's expression of causality and their construction of narratives. *Topics in Language Disorders, 7*(1), 11–20.

Lane, R. D., & Schwartz, G. E. (1987). Levels of emotional awareness: A cognitive-developmental theory and its application to psychopathology. *American Journal of Psychiatry, 144*(2), 133–143.

Langer, J. (1969). *Theories of development.* San Francisco: Holt, Rinehart & Winston.

Maier, H. W. (1978). *Three theories of child development.* New York: Harper & Row.

Marti, E. (1986). First metaphors in children: A new hypothesis. *Communication and Cognition, 19*(3-4), 337–346.

Odier, C. (1956). *Anxiety and magic thinking.* New York: International Universities Press.

Pillow, B. H. (1988). The development of children's beliefs about the mental world. *Merrill-Palmer Quarterly, 34*(1), 1–32.

Reyna, V. F. (1986). Metaphor and associated phenomena: Specifying the boundaries of psychological inquiry. *Metaphor and Symbolic Activity, 1*(4), 271–290.

Sparks, G. G., & Canton, J. (1986). Developmental differences in fright responses to a television program depicting a character transformation. *Journal of Broadcasting and Electronic Media, 30*(3), 309–323.

Vosniadou, S. (1987). Children and metaphors. *Child Development, 58*(3), 870–885.

Vygotsky, L. S. (1978). *Mind in society: The development of higher psychological processes.* Cambridge, MA: Harvard University Press.

Wing, C. S., & Scholniek, E. K. (1986). Understanding the language of reasoning: Cognitive, linguistic, and developmental influences. *Journal of Psycholinguistic Research, 15*(5), 383–401.

Wolfe, P. H. (1960). The developmental psychologies of Jean Piaget and psychoanalysis. *Psychological Monographs, 2.*

2 Hypnotic Responsiveness in Children

Adam B. Plotnick, M.A.

Donald J. O'Grady, Ph.D.

Hypnosis has been shown to be an effective treatment modality for a number of childhood disorders (Olness & Gardner, 1988), and several studies have demonstrated that children are more hypnotically responsive than adults (Barber & Calverley, 1963; Morgan & Hilgard, 1973). Nevertheless, relatively few studies have focused on the correlates of childhood hypnotic responsiveness (Allen, 1985; LeBaron, Zeltzer, & Fanurik, 1988; Plotnick, Payne, & O'Grady, in press), the relationship between childhood hypnotic responsiveness and treatment outcome (Hilgard & LeBaron, 1982; Hilgard & Morgan, 1978), or the assessment of childhood hypnotic ability in clinical settings. These issues will be reviewed in this chapter, and the usefulness of incorporating assessment procedures into hypnotherapy with children will be illustrated by case examples.

ASSESSING HYPNOTIC RESPONSIVENESS

Hypnotic responsiveness scales are used to measure an individual's hypnotic talent (Hilgard, 1965). The advantages of these instruments are that they permit the assessment of a broad range of hypnotic behaviors and hypnotic dimensions, including low-frequency behaviors; require relatively little time to administer, score, and interpret; facilitate the gathering of normative data; and are readily quantifiable.

Numerous hypnotic responsiveness scales have been developed in the past 30 years. However, the development of measures intended specifically for children has lagged significantly behind. This lag is surprising considering the proliferation of published reports that describe the successful use of hypnosis for the treatment of a wide variety of childhood and adolescent problems (Olness & Gardner, 1988).

The Development of Hypnotic Susceptibility Scales

Owing to some dissatisfaction with early hypnotizability scales, especially the skewed distributions resulting from their use, the lack of alternative forms, inadequate norms, and a lack of evidence about what items should be included, a number of investigators set about constructing improved scales (Hilgard, 1965). Beginning in the late 1950s, E. Hilgard and A. Weitzenhoffer started work on a series of hypnotic responsiveness scales that are now known as the Stanford scales.

The Stanford Hypnotic Susceptibility Scales, Forms A and B (SHSS: A and B), developed by Weitzenhoffer and Hilgard (1959), were the first such scales to be published. Their initial norms were based on 124 university-student subjects. The two forms emphasize ideomotor-type items (postural sway, eye closure, hand lowering, arm rigidity), and they are essentially equivalent, permitting before-and-after studies. A third form, the Stanford Hypnotic Susceptibility Scale, Form C (SHSS: C), also developed by Weitzenhoffer and Hilgard (1962), was added next. It was published with norms from 203 university-student subjects. The content of the items on this scale is somewhat richer than of those on the SHSS: A and B, with more cognitive-type material (hallucinations, dreams, age regression).

Although the Stanford Hypnotic Susceptibility Scales are valuable in research where the assessment of responses in several specific areas may be essential, investigators (Hilgard & Hilgard, 1979) noted that these scales might be too long and cumbersome for routine clinical use. This concern led to the development of Morgan and Hilgard's (1973) five-item Stanford Hypnotic Clinical Scale for Adults (SHCA: A), as well as Spiegel and Spiegel's (1978) two-item Hypnotic Induction Profile (HIP) and the single-item Stanford Hypnotic Arm Levitation Induction and Test (SHALIT) developed by E. Hilgard, Crawford, and Wert (1979). Hilgard (Hilgard et al., 1979) has noted that the new scales have the advantages of brevity and scoring convenience. He cautions, however, that very brief scales have limited clinical usefulness in ''that they do not sample a sufficiently wide range of hypnotic behavior to guide therapy in the manner in which a slightly longer scale can'' (p. 121).

The Children's Hypnotic Susceptibility Scale

London's (1962, 1963) Children's Hypnotic Susceptibility Scale (CHSS) is a two-part scale designed especially for children. Part I of the scale is comparable to Form A of the SHSS; it is a 12-item scale with items chosen to parallel those of SHSS: A, although adaptations have been made in order to ease its use with children. Part II consists of items that were originally part of the depth scale developed at Stanford, most of which are now found in Form C or in Forms I and II of the Stanford Profile Scales (Weitzenhoffer & Hilgard, 1967). Each item is presented as a four-point scale (0–3), convertible to a plus or minus scale by considering scores of 2–3 to be plus and 0–1 to be minus. London believes that it is important to record qualitative observations in addition to quantitative ones, and provision is made on the scoring forms for doing this.

The CHSS presents a child with ideomotor and cognitive items, and each item yields three susceptibility scores: an overt behavior (CHSS: OB) scale indicates how well a child's responses overtly comply with a suggestion; a subjective involvement (CHSS: SI) scale indicates how much the child's behavior seemed to reflect partial or deep involvement; and a total (CHSS: TOT) scale is a weighted combination of CHSS: OB and CHSS: SI scales obtained by multiplying the two scales on each item and then summing the product.

Part I of the CHSS requires approximately 20 minutes of actual testing time, and if a child is generally unresponsive, it may not be desirable to go on to Part II. The remaining items of Part II typically require about 30 minutes to administer (London, 1962). The reliability of the hypnotic scales is high, and a one-week retest on the CHSS yielded a reliability of 0.78 for the CHSS total scale (London & Cooper, 1969).

The Stanford Hypnotic Clinical Scale for Children

Using the SHCS as a model, Morgan and Hilgard (1978/1979) constructed the Stanford Hypnotic Clinical Scale for Children (SHCS: C) specifically for clinical use. The SHCS: C requires approximately 20 minutes to administer and consists of seven items: hand lowering, arm rigidity, an auditory hallucination, a positive visual halluncination, a dream, age regression, and a posthypnotic suggestion to reenter hypnosis at a hand-clap signal. The SHCS: C comes in two forms, one for children ages 6–16 and one for children aged 4–8 years. An eye-closure relaxation is used for older children, and an imagination induction is used for the younger group. The difference in inductions reflects the preference of younger children for keeping their eyes open during hypnosis. Although the SHCS: C is currently used in clinical settings, it is difficult to make psychometric comparisons between the SHCS: C and other measures of hypnotic responsiveness (i.e., CHSS and SHCS: A) because normative data, beyond the original sample of 182 children (aged 4–16 years), have not been reported in the literature.

Unfortunately, the SHCS: C does not directly assess subjective involvement in the hypnotic experience. This makes it difficult for clinicians and researchers to determine whether children tested with the SHCS: C are experiencing scale items as "real" and involuntary or are simply conforming behaviorally to suggestions made by a researcher or clinician. Moreover, subsequent studies reveal that the SHCS: C's ability to distinguish children with high hypnotic responsiveness from those with average hypnotic ability is limited because the distribution of susceptibility scores tends to be negatively skewed (LeBaron et al., 1988). Because of this characteristic, the scale has relatively low power to discriminate children of moderate hypnotic ability from those of high hypnotizability.

Recognizing these limitations, Zeltzer and LeBaron (1984) modified Morgan and Hilgard's (1978/1979) scale by including an involuntariness report for each item, which they labeled a realness scale, and adding two items (negative visual hallucination and posthypnotic amnesia) that they anticipated would normalize the distribution and make the scale more able to distinguish average from high responders. In a recent evaluation of Zeltzer and LeBaron's revised scale (Plotnick, Payne, & O'Grady, 1989), the retention of the item for posthypnotic amnesia was supported, but doubts were raised about the usefulness of the negative visual halluncination. Moreover, while the realness scale correlated rather highly with the more traditional objective-behavior scale, the fact that the mean for the observed-behavior scale was significantly higher than the mean for the realness scale and that realness scores produce a greater separation between high- and low-scoring subjects lends support to the continued use of the separate scales (Plotnick et al., 1989). A copy of both the CHSS and SHCS: C can be found in the appendixes of Olness and Gardner's (1988) *Hypnosis and Hypnotherapy with Children*.

CORRELATES OF HYPNOTIC RESPONSIVENESS IN CHILDREN

The Role of Age in the Development of Hypnotic Ability

The relationship between age and hypnotic responsibility is complex. As Olness and Gardner (1988) note, most normative studies have concluded that hypnotic ability is limited in children below the age of 3, achieves its apex during the middle childhood years of 7–14, and then decreases somewhat in adolescence, remaining stable through midlife before decreasing again in the older population.

In a normative study by Morgan and Hilgard (1973) of hypnotic responsiveness in 1,232 subjects, ranging in age from 5 to 78 years, based on a modified SHSS: A, a peak in hypnotic ability was found in preadolescence, with a gradual decline thereafter. Data from a more recent study, based on the SHCS: C, led to comparable conclusions regarding the heightened hypnotic ability of children (Morgan & Hilgard, 1978/1979).

Personality Correlates of Hypnotic Ability

Research during the past 30 years has attempted to clarify the nature of hypnotic responsiveness by examining related personality traits and cognitive abilities. A partial list of these characteristics includes social desirability (Hilgard, 1979), acquiescence (Lee-Teng, 1965), involvement in fantasy play (Sutcliffe, Perry, & Sheehan, 1970), role playing (Sarbin & Coe, 1972), absorption (Tellegen & Atkinson, 1974), dissociative ability (Hilgard, 1977), childhood punishment (Nash, Lynn, & Givens, 1984), and attitudes toward hypnosis (Spanos, Brett, Menary, & Cross, 1987).

Some studies of hypnotic ability in children suggest that correlates may parallel those reported for adults (Allen, 1985; LeBaron et al., 1988; Plotnick et al., in press). Nevertheless, research with children is much less extensive. This limitation seems to be influenced by the negative mystique often associated with hypnosis, making parents reluctant to allow their children to participate in hypnosis research (Plotnick et al., in press).

Until recently, much of the information concerning the correlates of hypnotic responsiveness in children was inferred from retrospective studies that relied on adult recollections of childhood interests and behaviors. (Hilgard, 1979). Hence, data coming directly from measurements made during childhood are still needed.

In the following sections, we will discuss the relationships between genetics and parent–child interactions, absorption and imagery vividness, and involvement in fantasy play and the construct of childhood hypnotic responsiveness. Where possible, comparisons are made between findings with adults and children.

The Role of Genetics and Parent–Child Interactions

A study by Morgan (Morgan, Hilgard, & Davert, 1970) suggests that there might be a genetic contribution to hypnotic responsiveness. In a study of 140 pairs of twins aged 5–22, hypnotic susceptibility in monozygotic twins was found to be significantly related for both males and females. In contrast, no significant relationship was found for dizygotic twins or for sibling non-twin pairs. Nonetheless, there was a low but significant relationship between mean parent and mean child susceptibility. In addition, a positive correlation was found between personality resemblance and hypnotic responsiveness for either-sex child and like-sex parent. No such interaction existed for either-sex child and the opposite-sex parent. These results were interpreted as suggesting an environmental contribution to hypnotizability, based mainly on identification with the like-sex parent and modeling of that parent's behavior.

In a longitudinal study by Nowlis (1969), a stern, restrictive, and punitive home environment at the time the children were in kindergarten was related to high hypnotizability when the children reached the 12th grade in high school. Cooper and London (1976) concurrently studied parent–child relationships and childhood hypnotic responsiveness. Parents of highly hypnotizable children tended to rate themselves as stricter and more anxious and impatient than the parents of low hypnotizable children. In her extensive study of personality and hypnosis, J. Hilgard (1979) similarly found that following imaginative involvements, the next most powerful predictor of adult hypnotic ability was severity of punishment in childhood. She hypothesized that punishment tended to elicit a conformity factor characterized by conflict-reducing acquiescence to parental authority based on trust and parental identification.

The Role of Absorption and Imagery Vividness

Tellegen and Atkinson (1974) have defined absorption as a disposition for having episodes of "total" attention that fully engage one's representational (i.e., perceptual, enactive, imaginative, ideational) resources. "This kind of attentional functioning is believed to result in a heightened sense of the reality of the attentional object, imperviousness to distracting events, and an altered state of reality in general, including an emphatically altered sense of self" (p. 268).

Using the Tellegen Absorption Scale (TAS; Tellegen & Atkinson, 1974), a scale designed to assess absorption in various everyday experiences, Tellegen and Atkinson found that the absorption score on the TAS was significantly correlated with hypnotic responsiveness scores on a modified version of Shor and Orne's (1962) Harvard Group Scale of Hypnotic Susceptibility (HGSHS). Based on this finding, Tellegen and Atkinson (1974) concluded that absorption represents an essential component of hypnotic susceptibility and to some extent "it is possible to view hypnotic phenomena as an experiential and behavioral manifestation of . . . the imaginative, enactive, and self-altering representation of an attentional object" (p. 276). This result was recently replicated by Crawford (1982) in a multidimensional investigation of hypnotizability, daydreaming styles, imagery vividness, and absorption measured by the TAS and hypnotic ability measured by SHSS: A and B (Weitzenhoffer & Hilgard, 1959).

Similar research with children is limited. Nevertheless, recent studies by Allen (1985) and Plotnick and associates (in press) suggest that absorption in imaginative involvements and imagery vividness are also related to hypnotic ability in children. Using data from 61 children between the ages of 8 and 12, Allen (1985) found a significant positive correlation between absorption and imagery vividness, measured by the absorption and visual imagery scales from the Children's Fantasy Inventory (CFI: A and V; Rosenfeld, Huesmann, Eron, & Torney-Purta, 1982). Similarly, in a more recent study using data from 42 children between the ages of 7 and 13, Plotnick and associates (in press) obtained results suggesting that a significant positive relationship exists between the capacity for absorption and imagery vividness and hypnotic ability in children.

The Role of Fantasy Play

In addition to the roles of absorption and imagery vividness, involvement in fantasy play has been investigated as a possible correlate of hypnotic responsiveness. A predisposition toward imaginative involvement has been described as representing a "fantasy-prone personality" (Wilson & Barber, 1983), and results from studies in this area suggest that, at least in the realm of adult behavior and adult recollections of past interests and activities, there is a relationship between involvement in fantasy play and hypnotic ability (Wilson & Barber, 1981).

LeBaron (LeBaron et al., 1988) conducted two studies to assess the relationship between hypnotic susceptibility in children and the extent of involvement in fantasy-related activities during early childhood. The SHCS: C and a structured interview scale based on previous work by Singer (1973) were given to 30 medical patients aged 6–18 years in the first study and to 37 healthy children aged 6–12 years from a school population in the second study. In both studies, hypnotic ability correlated moderately with extent of involvement in fantasy-related activity. These results are consistent with the findings of Allen (1985) and Plotnick and associates (in press) that highly hypnotizable children tend to engage in significantly more fantasy play than children with low hypnotic ability, suggesting that there is at least a moderate relationship between an orientation toward fantasy and hypnotic ability in children.

CHILDHOOD HYPNOTIC RESPONSIVENESS AND
TREATMENT OUTCOME

Hypnotic responsiveness has been measured in clinical studies with adults. Results have been mixed as hypnotic ability appears to be related to treatment outcome for some clinical problems but not for others (Wadden & Anderton, 1982). Spinhoven (1987), in his extensive review of hypnosis and behavior therapy, concluded that the relationship between hypnotic responsiveness and treatment outcome is stronger for pain and anxiety than for addictive or habit disorders. Whether this conclusion is possible with children is unclear because of insufficient data.

In a study of 131 asthmatic patients aged 8–73 years, Collison (1975) found that the ability to go into a deep trance was the best predictor of improvement in asthma treated with hypnosis. Similarly, in a study of 34 patients ranging in age from 4 to 19 years, J. Hilgard and Morgan (1978) found that children with cancer who scored in the medium or high range on the SHCS: C were able to achieve substantial reductions in pain and anxiety while those with low scores failed to improve. In a more recent study with 24 children and adolescents with cancer, J. Hilgard and LeBaron (1982) likewise found that patients who scored high in hypnotizability (5–7) on the SHCS: C generally experienced greater reductions in pain than those patients who achieved a low hypnotizability score (0–4).

Smith, Womack, and Chen (1989) did not find any evidence that hypnotizability, as defined by performance on the SHCS: C, was a factor in the successful outcome of a headache-treatment program that included relaxation and mental imagery but no formal hypnotic induction. Smith and colleagues note that this scale's relatively low power to discriminate children of moderate hypnotic ability from those of high hypnotizability might have confounded their data. Hence, further studies with improved measures (e.g., SHCS: C-R) are needed to clarify the relationship between hypnotic responsiveness and clinical outcome in pediatric populations. Moreover, studies comparing hypnotic treatment with other approaches will need to measure all groups in hypnotic responsiveness in order to clarify the role of hypnosis in treatment outcome.

Assessing Hypnotic Ability in Clinical Settings

As Hilgard and Hilgard (1979) note, many clinicians "believe that the measurement of hypnotic responsiveness by standardized scales is unnecessary or inimical to hypnotherapy" (p. 137). There is a long-held assumption that hypnotizability is unrelated to treatment outcome (Wadden & Anderton,

1982), and clinicians often consider standardized scales too lengthy, intrusive, and irrelevant to the demands and patterns that prevail in clinical work (Sacerdote, 1982). In fact, a survey of 45 workshop faculty members at a recent meeting of the American Society of Clinical Hypnosis indicated that two thirds of the respondents did not use any tests of hypnotic susceptibility (Cohen, 1989). Nonetheless, as E. Hilgard (1982) observes, "If the practice of hypnosis and hypnotherapy is to be based on scientific findings . . . some standards of measurement necessarily have to be applied" (p. 394).

Pettinati (1982) suggests that there are several reasons why clinicians generally have not been concerned about the relationship between hypnotic ability and treatment outcome. First, many clinicians believe that anyone can be hypnotized and so can benefit from hypnotherapy. Second, while a number of clinicians acknowledge that individuals differ in their hypnotic ability, they argue that therapeutic gains can be obtained even when the client has minimum levels of hypnotic ability. And finally, some clinicians fear that the measurement of hypnotic responsiveness will have negative effects. Although there is little evidence for this (Frankel, 1978/1979), the concern stems from the belief that if the hypnotist exposes the patient to failure by presenting suggestions that are too difficult, rapport may be damaged and expectancy effects might be diminished.

While the concerns discussed above have some merit, they can be overcome with a little extra preparation on the part of the clinician. For example, a sense of failure can be prevented by a good preliminary discussion with the patient of what it means to evaluate hypnotic ability (Frankel, 1978/1979). Moreover, while this might not be feasible for all clinicians, therapists could avoid possible contamination of a patient's hypnotic capacity by having an independent hypnotist perform the evaluation (Pettinati, 1982).

Frankel (1978/1979) notes that the assessment of an individual's hypnotic ability can be useful in the clarification of the patient's diagnosis and gives clinicians information about hypnotic skills that are already established and that can be further developed and incorporated into individual treatment plans. In addition, while many clients do not initially experience all of the hypnotic phenomena assessed by hypnotic-responsiveness scales, considerable research suggests that most can learn to become adequate hypnotic subjects with practice and repeated exposure to hypnotic suggestions (Diamond, 1977; Perry, 1977). Thus, hypnotizability scales have the added utility of providing clients with practice in developing hypnotic skills while fostering the development of realistic expectations about hypnosis and reinforcing the notion that hypnosis is under their control (Golden, Dowd, & Friedberg, 1987).

In our practice, we use the Stanford Clinical Scales with all patients being considered for hypnotherapy. The concerns about the use of scales being too time consuming, setting up negative expectations owing to failure of some items, or inhibiting rapport because of formality and artificiality are realistic, but can be overcome. The therapist can present the scale in a positive context of helping understand the child or adolescent's "use of imagination," to explore the "best possible treatment approach for them." Often, the use of the scale gives the child a "warm-up" or rehearsal that can decrease performance anxiety. Failure of an item is usually not a problem if the purpose of exploring individual differences is explained to the child. Children seem comfortable "experimenting" with their imaginations first before applying what they often learn from the experience.

With regard to time constraints and excessive formality, if the 20 minutes or so required to do a Stanford Clinical Scale is viewed not only as measurement, but also as a time for the child to learn about hypnosis, the formality and artificiality become less relevant. We have also found that the use of proved, standard induction procedures from the scales reduces therapists' idiosyncrasies or lapses in giving the child the full experience of a hypnotic induction that he or she might build on later.

Case Examples

Finally, two case examples illustrate the benefits of assessing hypnotic responsiveness for both the clarification of diagnosis and treatment planning. Bowers and LeBaron (1986) give some excellent examples of how knowledge of the patient's hypnotizability can clarify the diagnosis. Hence, the finding of low hypnotizability in a supposedly phobic or multiple-personality patient would lead one to consider other diagnostic possibilities (Frankel, 1974).

The case of V.P. illustrates the benefits of finding moderately low hypnotizability in an allegedly phobic 5-year-old boy. V.P. was referred by his pediatrician and mother because of great difficulty in getting him to cooperate in his weekly bilateral allergy shots. He had a history of being hospitalized for asthma, and the injections were felt to be most important. Although descriptions of his behavior suggested some phobic features to his uncooperative behavior, the finding of moderately low (four out of seven on the SHCS: C) responsiveness suggested other diagnostic possibilities. Subsequently, his profile on the Personality Inventory for Children showed a higher elevation on the scale associated with noncompliant, oppositional behavior than on the anxiety scale. Plans for treatment then were revised to include an increased component of reinforcement training for the parents in dealing with the noncompliant child. Hypnosis was used in addition, but his modest imagery ability was augmented by using props, such as a wooden toy soldier suggested by him to help his arms "feel like wood" before the injections.

Treatment was successful over a three-month period and subsequent two-year follow-up.

Similarly, noting the presence of high hypnotizability in the absence of responsiveness to therapeutic suggestions can be useful for diagnostic and treatment purposes. R.B. was an 11-year-old boy with sickle cell anemia referred for possible use of hypnosis in pain relief. He scored high on the SHCS: C (seven out of seven) and reported experiences indicating good absorption in imagination and vivid imagery. He was not, however, interested in applying his skills to the pain episodes. Rather, he appeared to prefer to be hospitalized to receive medication and nursing care, and perhaps to avoid a difficult home situation and school failure. Without the measurement of hypnotic responsiveness, the patient's lack of progress might mistakenly have been attributed to low hypnotic responsiveness rather than to some secondary gain from his symptoms. Treatment plans were then revised to decrease the secondary gain and to increase the benefits of participating more responsibly at home and school.

SUMMARY AND CONCLUSIONS

This chapter reiterates the conclusion that children are generally more hypnotically responsive than adults. In addition, it appears from the few studies to date that the components of hypnotic responsiveness are similar for children and adults. The confirmation of the importance of hypnotic ability for treatment success is much slower in coming, owing to the limited empirical studies that have been done with children. It is too early to say whether the finding of differential effects for volitional versus nonvolitional disorders seen with adults will be substantiated in children. At the current rate of empirical studies with children, progress will continue to be very slow. The recruiting and training of clinical investigators in this endeavor are sorely needed.

Finally, the controversy regarding the value of measuring hypnotic responsiveness in the clinical context also seems likely to be ongoing. Investigators of therapeutic outcome involving hypnosis will likely measure hypnotic responsiveness more often, not only in those patients receiving hypnotic inductions, but in control groups as well. Its routine use in clinical settings, however, seems rare. The bias in this chapter is obviously toward encouraging such routine use. It is hoped that more clinicians will find the measures useful for a better understanding of their individual patients, as well as for more efficient and effective treatment planning.

REFERENCES

Allen, D. (1985). Hypnotic responsiveness in children. (Doctoral Dissertation, University of Wyoming, 1985). *Dissertation Abstracts International, 46,* 2451–B.

Barber, T. (1965). Measuring "hypnotic-like" suggestibility with and without "hypnotic induction"; psychometric properties, norms, and variables influencing response to the Barber Suggestibility Scale (BSS). *Psychological Reports, 16,* 809–844.

Barber, T., & Calverley, D. (1963). "Hypnotic-like" suggestibility in children and adults. *Journal of Abnormal and Social Psychology, 66,* 589–597.

Bowers, K. (1981). Has the sun set on the Stanford scales? *American Journal of Clinical Hypnosis, 24,* 79–87.

Bowers, K. (1983). *Hypnosis for the seriously curious* (2nd ed.). New York: Norton.

Bowers, K., & LeBaron, S. (1986). Hypnosis and hypnotizability: Implications for clinical intervention. *Hospital and Community Psychiatry, 37,* 457–467.

Cedercreutz, C. (1978). Hypnotic treatment of 100 cases of migraine. In F. Frankel & H. Zamansky (Eds.), *Hypnosis at its bicentennial* (pp. 255–259). New York: Plenum.

Cedercreutz, C., Laheenmaki, R., & Tulikoura, J. (1976). Hypnotic treatment of headache and vertigo in skull injured patients. *International Journal of Clinical and Experimental Hypnosis, 24,* 195–201.

Cohen, S. (1989). Clinical uses of hypnotizability. *American Journal of Clinical Hypnosis, 32,* 4–9.

Collison, D. (1975). Which asthmatic patients should be treated by hypnotherapy? *Medical Journal of Australia, 1,* 776–781.

Cooper, L., & London, P. (1976). Children's hypnotic susceptibility, personality, and EEG patterns. *International Journal of Clinical and Experimental Hypnosis, 24,* 140–148.

Crawford, H. (1982). Hypnotizability, daydreaming styles, imagery vividness, and absorption: a multidimensional study. *Journal of Personality and Social Psychology, 42,* 915–926.

Diamond, M. (1977). Hypnotizability is modifiable: An alternative approach. *International Journal of Clinical and Experimental Hypnosis, 25,* 147–166.

Frankel, F. H. (1974). Trance capacity and the genesis of phobic behavior. *Archives of General Psychiatry, 31,* 261–263.

Frankel, F. (1978/1979). Scales measuring hypnotic responsivity: A clinical perspective. *American Journal of Hypnosis, 21,* 208–218.

Golden, W., Dowd, E., & Friedberg, F. (1987). *Hypnotherapy: A modern approach.* New York: Pergamon.

Hilgard, E. (1965). *The experience of hypnosis.* New York: Harcourt Brace Jovanovitch.

Hilgard, E. (1977). *Divided consciousness.* New York: Wiley.

Hilgard, E. (1982). Hypnotic susceptibility and implications for measurement. *International Journal of Clinical and Experimental Hypnosis, 30,* 394–403.

Hilgard, E., Crawford, H., & Wert, A. (1979). The Stanford Hypnotic Arm Levitation Induction and Test (SHALIT): A six-minute hypnotic induction and measurement scale. *International Journal of Clinical and Experimental Hypnosis, 27,* 111–124.

Hilgard, E., & Hilgard, J. (1975). *Hypnosis in the relief of pain*. Los Altos, CA: William Kaufmann.

Hilgard, J. (1979). *Personality and hypnosis: A study of imaginative involvement*. Chicago: University of Chicago Press.

Hilgard, J., & Hilgard, E. (1979). Assessing hypnotic responsiveness in a clinical setting: A multi-item clinical scale and its advantages over single-item scales. *International Journal of Clinical and Experimental Hypnosis, 27*, 134–150.

Hilgard, J., & LeBaron, S. (1982). Relief of anxiety and pain in children and adolescents with cancer: Quantitative measures and clinical observations. *International Journal of Clinical and Experimental Hypnosis, 30*, 417–442.

Hilgard, J., & Morgan, A. (1978). Treatment of anxiety and pain in childhood cancer through hypnosis. In F. Frankel & H. Zamansky (Eds.), *Hypnosis at its bicentennial* (pp. 281–287). New York: Plenum.

LeBaron, S., Zeltzer, L., & Fanurik, D. (1988). Imaginative involvement and hypnotic susceptibility in childhood. *International Journal of Clinical and Experimental Hypnosis, 36*, 284–295.

Lee-Teng, E. (1965). Trance susceptibility, induction-susceptibility, and acquiescence as factors in hypnotic performance. *Journal of Abnormal Psychology, 70*, 383–389.

London, P. (1962). Hypnosis in children: An experimental approach. *International Journal of Clinical and Experimental Hypnosis, 10*, 79–91.

London, P. (1963). *Children's Hypnotic Susceptibility Scale*. Palo Alto, CA: Consulting Psychologists Press.

London, P., & Cooper, L. (1969). Norms of hypnotic responsiveness in children. *Developmental Psychology, 1*, 113–124.

Maher-Loughnan, G., McDonald, N., Mason, A., & Fry, L. (1962). Controlled trial of hypnosis in the symptomatic treatment of asthma. *British Journal of Medicine, 5301*, 371–376.

Morgan, A., & Hilgard, E. (1973). Age differences in susceptibility to hypnosis. *International Journal of Clinical and Experimental Hypnosis, 21*, 78–85.

Morgan, A., Hilgard, E., & Davert, E. (1970). The heritability of hypnotic susceptibility of twins: A preliminary report. *Behavioral Genetics, 1*, 213–224.

Morgan, A., & Hilgard, J. (1978/1979). The Stanford Hypnotic Clinical Scale for Children. *American Journal of Clinical Hypnosis, 21*, 148–155.

Nash, M., Lynn, S., & Givens, D. (1984). Adult hypnotic susceptibility, childhood punishments, and child abuse. *International Journal of Clinical and Experimental Hypnosis, 32*, 6–11.

Nowlis, D. (1969). The child-rearing antecedents of hypnotic susceptibility and of naturally occurring hypnotic-like experience. *International Journal of Clinical and Experimental Hypnosis, 17*, 109–120.

Olness, K., & Gardner, G. (1988). *Hypnosis and hypnotherapy with children* (2nd ed.). New York: Grune & Stratton.

Palmer, R., & Field, P. (1968). Visual imagery and susceptibility to hypnosis. *Journal of Consulting and Clinical Psychology, 32*, 456–461.

Perry, C. (1977). Is hypnosis modifiable? *International Journal of Clinical and Experimental Hypnosis, 25*, 125–146.

Perry, C., Gelfand, R., & Marcovitch, P. (1979). The relevance of hypnotic susceptibility in the clinical context. *Journal of Abnormal Psychology, 88,* 592–603.

Pettinati, H. (1982). Measuring hypnotherapy in psychotic patients. *International Journal of Clinical and Experimental Hypnosis, 30,* 404–416.

Plotnick, A., Payne, P., & O'Grady, J. (1989). *The Stanford Hypnotic Clinical Scale for Children—Revised: An evaluation.* Manuscript submitted for publication.

Plotnick, A., Payne, P., & O'Grady, J. (in press). Correlates of hypnotizability in children: Absorption, vividness of imagery, fantasy play, and social desirability. *American Journal of Clinical Hypnosis.*

Rosenfeld, E., Huesmann, L., Eron, L., & Torney-Purta, J. (1982). Measuring patterns of fantasy behavior in children. *Journal of Personality and Social Psychology, 42,* 347–366.

Sacerdote, P. (1982). A non-statistical dissertation about hypnotizability scales and clinical goals: Comparison with individualized induction and deepening procedures. *International Journal of Clinical and Experimental Hypnosis, 30,* 354–376.

Sarbin, T., & Coe, W. (1972). *Hypnosis: A social psychological analysis of influence communication.* New York: Holt, Rinehart & Winston.

Shor, R., & Orne, E. (1962). *Harvard Group Scale of Hypnotic Susceptibility.* Palo Alto, CA: Consulting Psychologists Press.

Sinclair-Gieben, A., & Chalmers, D. (1959). Evaluation of treatment of warts by hypnosis. *Lancet, 2,* 480–482.

Singer, J. (1973). *The child's world of make-believe: Experimental studies of imaginative play.* New York: Academic Press.

Smith, M., Womack, W., & Chen, A. (1989). Hypnotizability does not predict outcome of behavioral treatment in pediatric headache. *American Journal of Clinical Hypnosis, 31,* 237–241.

Spanos, N., Brett, P., Menary, E., & Cross, W. (1987). A measure of attitudes toward hypnosis: Relationships with absorption and hypnotic susceptibility. *American Journal of Clinical Hypnosis, 36,* 139–150.

Spiegel, H., & Spiegel, D. (1978). *Trance and treatment: Clinical uses of hypnosis.* New York: Basic Books.

Spinhoven, P. (1987). Hypnosis and behavior therapy: A review. *International Journal of Clinical and Experimental Hypnosis, 35,* 8–31.

Sutcliffe, J., Perry, C., & Sheehan, P. (1970). Relationship of some aspects of imagery and fantasy to hypnotic susceptibility. *Journal of Abnormal Psychology, 76,* 279–287.

Tellegen, A., & Atkinson, G. (1974). Openness to absorbing and self-altering experiences (''absorption''), a trait related to hypnotic susceptibility. *Journal of Abnormal Psychology, 83,* 268–277.

Wadden, A., & Anderton, C. (1982). The clinical uses of hypnosis. *Psychological Bulletin, 91,* 215–243.

Weitzenhoffer, A., & Hilgard, E. (1959). *Stanford Hypnotic Susceptibility Scale, Forms A and B.* Palo Alto, CA: Consulting Psychologists Press.

Weitzenhoffer, A., & Hilgard, E. (1962). *Stanford Hypnotic Susceptibility Scale, Form C.* Palo Alto, CA: Consulting Psychologists Press.

Weitzenhoffer, A., & Hilgard, E. (1967). *Revised Stanford Profile Scales of Hypnotic Susceptibility, Forms I and II*. Palo Alto, CA: Consulting Psychologists Press.

Wilson, S., & Barber, T. (1981). Vivid fantasy and hallucinatory abilities in life histories of excellent hypnotic subjects ("somnabules"): Preliminary report with female subjects. In E. Klinger (Ed.), *Imagery: Concepts, results, and applications* (pp. 133–149). New York: Plenum.

Wilson, S., & Barber, T. (1983). The fantasy-prone personality: Implications for understanding imagery, hypnosis, and parapsychological phenomena. In A. Shiekh (Ed.), *Imagery: Current theory, research, and application* (pp. 340–387). New York: Wiley.

Zeltzer, L., & LeBaron, S. (1984). *The Stanford Hypnotic Clinical Scale for Children—Revised*. Unpublished scale.

3 *Induction and Deepening Techniques with Children*

〓〓

William C. Wester II, Ed.D.

Children are usually great hypnotic subjects and respond to a variety of induction techniques. They come to the hypnotic experience with fewer preconceived notions about hypnosis and with very active imaginations. Preparing the child for hypnosis may depend largely on time. If there is time to prepare the child, as rapport develops, hypnosis typically is enhanced.

PREPARING THE CHILD

Conducting an interview with the child requires professional skill backed by training and experience. The initial interview allows time for a relationship to develop between the child and the therapist. The actual hypnotic process begins before the child ever sees the therapist. A referring colleague, a well-trained staff, a nurse, or a receptionist can set the stage for a receptive child. After the therapist obtains initial data, it is important to talk with the child about hypnosis and the child's expectation of this form of treatment.

Equally important is the preparation of the child's parents. The parents typically have more questions and need to have various myths and misconceptions clarified. It is important to have their support of the process and for them to know exactly what is expected from hypnotic-treatment approach. This author has published a brochure entitled ''Questions and Answers About

---

The induction techniques presented in this chapter are adaptations of the many techniques the author has learned over the years from such excellent teachers as Drs. Judson Reaney, Karen Olness, Gail Gardner, Daniel Kohen, and Franz Baumann.

34

Clinical Hypnosis'' that can be sent to the parents prior to the first session. The brochure contains information on professonal training, misconceptions about hypnosis, and a brief history of the therapeutic use of hypnosis (Wester, 1982).

One should take time to talk with the child's physician or the nursing staff if the child is being seen in the hospital. Good hypnotic work with a child can be undermined by an inappropriate or negative statement from a parent or another professional who should be part of a team in the specific treatment of the child.

There can be other factors to be evaluated by the therapist before utilizing hypnosis. Crasilneck and Hall (1985) identify seven questions to be considered during the initial screening assessment:

1. Why does the patient (child) come for treatment at this time?
2. Who sent the patient (child)?
3. Is the patient (child) sufficiently motivated to give up the symptom?
4. Is the symptom being used to manipulate others?
5. Is the symptom organic or psychogenic?
6. What is the patient's (child's) degree of impulsivity and what is the patient's (child's) level of frustration?
7. What is the patient's (child's) general personality or history?

If the professional does a good job in assessing the child, the hypnotic process and the treatment outcome will be fostered and enhanced.

INDUCTION TECHNIQUES

The choice of an induction technique greatly depends on the personality and needs of the child, the child's preferences, such as sporting events and other interests, and, of course, on what the therapist feels comfortable using for a specific treatment goal. Olness and Gardner (1988) divide induction techniques into visual imagery, auditory imagery, movement imagery, storytelling, ideomotor, progressive relaxation, eye fixation, distraction, and utilization (the use of video- and audiotapes or of the telephone). As can be seen from their list, there are many techniques available. The creative and experienced therapist also can invent a technique to fit the personality and age of the child. Olness and Gardner (1988) recommend specific induction techniques for certain age groups. A tactile technique, such as holding a stuffed animal, may be most appropriate for a 2-year-old. A 4-year-old may respond better to a rag-doll and a 6-year-old to a coin or television technique. Developmentally, a school child (7–11 years of age) may respond best to a favorite-place technique and an adolescent to sports imagery. As therapists gain more experience in working with children, their choice of technique will become somewhat automatic. Part of the fun with this work is being creative. If a good assessment is made, it should be easy to get started with the first induction.

This author has selected three techniques to provide the reader with specific verbalizations. Variations from these scripts are appropriate and can reflect the therapist's personality and experience. A fourth technique, the rag-doll technique, is illustrated in Chapter 7.

Favorite-Place

The therapist proceeds by saying the following:

Just make yourself nice and comfortable in the chair. Now I would like you to put your hands on your lap and to use your eyes to find a spot on one of your hands on which you would like to focus all of your attention. It might be a wrinkle or a fingernail. Now that you have found that spot—that special spot on which you have chosen to focus all of your attention—let yourself really *concentrate on that one spot; let yourself totally concentrate on that spot that was special for you, concentrate on it just as hard as you can. As you do that, you can still be aware of my voice and you can let all of your body become very relaxed and comfortable. Now in a little time—I'm not exactly sure when, but probably soon—your eyes will become so relaxed and comfortable that they will want to close.*

You pick the time that feels just right for you. And when that happens, you can feel even more relaxed and comfortable than you are feeling right now. When that happens, when your eyes close, we can talk about some other very pleasant things that are relaxing and comfortable for you. [Reinforce as needed for eye closure.] That's it—so comfortable and peaceful from the top of your head all the way down to the bottom of your toes. And when you are feeling so relaxed and comfortable, like you feel right now, you might like to imagine that you are in your favorite place in the whole world. Being there right now. Now, that favorite place might be a place you have really been to before, or a place you have only read about, or a place you have dreamed about. But everything about that favorite place is just the way you want it to be. You might be there by yourself or maybe with some very special friend. Of course, you are doing your favorite activities and everything about the day is just the way you would like it to be. I am not sure where your favorite place is—I imagine it might be [information obtained from child in interview]. I know that you know where your favorite place is and that you are enjoying it right now. You can continue to enjoy your favorite place and all of the things you would like to do while we talk about special things you can do when you are relaxed and in your favorite place—things that can help you. [The therapist begins to work on treatment goals with appropriate suggestions and questioning with ideomotor signaling.]

Now you can continue to be in your favorite place for a moment longer. In the next minute or so, it will be time for you to return to the room here with me, feeling refreshed and relaxed and very good about what you have learned and what you can do when [reinforce therapeutic suggestions]. Just let yourself gradually return feeling refreshed and relaxed, ready to open your eyes and to be back here with me. You can go back to your favorite place any time that you want, [child's name].

Welcome back [child's name].

As with most techniques, it is always helpful to process with the child what the child experienced.

Television Imagination

In this technique, the therapist proceeds as follows:

I would like to show you and teach you how you can use your "make believe" ability in areas of your life to help yourself. Would you like to learn how you can help yourself with [child's presenting problem]? [Child responds Yes.] You already have your own imagination. I cannot give you any imagination. I can show you, however, how to use your imagination in a very special way. First, I would like you to get into a very comfortable position. Just put your legs in front of you, with your hands resting comfortably in your lap. You might notice that, in this position, your whole body feels nicely supported, with every part of your body being held up by something. And now, I would like you to close your eyes—that's right—and with your eyes closed, you can enjoy the darkness and the quietness, the peacefulness, and the calmness. You can become more aware of your breathing. Just feel how cool your breath feels as it comes into your body, bringing with each breath energy and oxygen that spread to every corner of your body. With each breath out, you can feel warmth, and your body can just relax all of the muscles in your body. Every time you breathe out, you go deeper and deeper into relaxation and comfort.

As you relax deeper and deeper, I would like you to imagine that a TV screen has appeared before your eyes—a very special TV that would only be found in a very special place. This TV has been made especially for you. Just see the dials on the TV and examine them very carefully and find the ON switch. Just turn on that TV and turn the dial around until you find the program that seems just right for you. It may be a program that you have already seen before, or one that you would only imagine that you would like to see. What is the program that you are seeing right now [child's name]? [Get response from the child and then ask additional questions to increase and enhance image.] You can continue to enjoy that picture for a moment more and then I would like you to turn the dial until you reach a channel where you can see yourself on TV and you find yourself in [wherever the therapist wants the therapeutic environment to be] and you are the star in that program. Have you found that channel? [Child responds.] Good. What are you doing right now in that picture on the TV? [Child responds.] Just continue to watch that program because that is a special TV and you are in control of that TV. [Use therapeutic suggestions related to the presenting problem—stress achievements and positive feelings. Use a posthypnotic suggestion that the child can go back to that special channel whenever the child wishes. The therapist can also ask the child to use "slow motion" suggestions at any time.]

Now turn your dial to any channel you would like to end with that gives you a nice feeling of being you and a nice feeling of being comfortable and peaceful, of being strong and wise, and knowing what is best for yourself and how to find it. You can thank yourself that you have this special TV in your mind and that you can use it any time you wish.

Now it's time for you to turn your set off and to let yourself gradually return to the room here with me, feeling refreshed and relaxed and ready for a nice day—ready to OPEN your eyes NOW. That was very nice [child's name].

Eye Fixation with Imagery

The therapist begins, as usual, by developing rapport with the child.

[Child's name] I would like to teach you something very special that you can learn, and with practice, you can get better and better. The first thing I would like to do is to have you hold this coin [give the child a quarter] up here. [Therapist puts coin between the child's thumb and index finger and moves the arm and hand slightly above eye level.] I would like you to stare at the coin and concentrate all of your attention on some special part of that coin, and as you do, just let yourself get more and more relaxed. As you get more and more relaxed, the coin will get heavier and heavier. As the coin gets heavier and heavier, your arm will also get heavier and heavier. In a moment, the coin will drop from your fingers and your eyes will close and your arm will come back down to rest in your lap. [Wait for response, and

reinforce statements if necessary.] We can now talk about some other pleasant things that can help you to become even more relaxed and comfortable. I would like you to imagine yourself at a wonderful picnic. This is the best picnic you have ever attended—the sky is blue and clear, the clouds are just the way you like them, it's just as cool or as warm a day as you would like it; just let it be the kind of day you would want it to be.

You might want to be at this picnic by yourself or be sharing it with some of your favorite friends and playing some of your favorite games. Somebody at this picnic [child's name] has laid a very special blanket on the ground. I would like you to sit down on that blanket by yourself or with a friend. You find out that this is a very special blanket because you can make that blanket fly. You can make it go as high as you wish or as low, as fast or as slow; you can make it turn left or right, you can do anything you want the blanket to do. You are the pilot and you are in control. You can fly anywhere you wish and see anything you want to see. It is a wonderful feeling to fly along on your blanket, enjoying the day and being in control. Just enjoy what you are doing on this beautiful day, and as you fly along, you might think for a moment [therapeutic suggestions and talk can occur here with the use of ideomotor signals].

[Continue to reinforce that the child is the pilot and in control.] Anytime you want to go to this very special picnic and to fly on your blanket, you can do it—always remembering that you are the pilot and are in control. Every time you practice, it will get easier and easier to [therapeutic goal].

And now, [child's name], I would like you to land your blanket in a place that you like very much—a place back at the picnic where you feel comfortable and very relaxed and safe. When your blanket gently touches the ground, you can open your eyes, feeling refreshed, relaxed, and comfortable. That's right. You did a swell job [child's name]. [Spend a few moments processing the child's experience.]

Techniques For Deepening Hypnosis

In addition to standard induction, it is important to mention something about deepening the hypnotic state. There is some controversy about whether the "depth" of hypnosis has any relationship to the treatment outcome. Erickson (1980) suggested that depth was unimportant while emphasizing that he rarely presented significant suggestions until after 20 minutes of deepening. Based on the author's experience, it does appear that more depth or time is needed to produce certain hypnotic phenomena.

Hammond (1987) describes the following procedures to enhance the depth of the hypnotic state.

1. Fractionation. In this procedure, the patient (child) is alerted and rehypnotized several times.
2. Downward movement. Movement such as walking down a staircase or moving down an escalator is often facilitative.
3. Interspersing patient motivation and needs. "And you are relaxing deeper and deeper because you. . . . "
4. Contingent suggestions. "With every sound of my voice, you can drift deeper and deeper. . . . ," or "With every breath you take, your level of relaxation increases more and more. . . . "
5. Breathing and counting. Counting backwards from 10 to 1 with interspersed suggestions, or focusing on breathing with deepening suggestion, can be included as a deepening technique.

SUMMARY

The induction technique used is only as effective as the receptiveness of the child and the experience of the therapist. Therapists should develop the techniques that work for them. Drawing on the techniques in this chapter may be helpful when individualizing the therapist's approach. By using one's creativity, one can look forward to rewarding times in working with children of various ages.

REFERENCES

Crasilneck, H. B., & Hall, J. A. (1985). *Clinical hypnosis: Principles and application* (2nd ed.). New York: Grune & Stratton.

Erickson, M. H. (1980). In E. L. Rossi (Ed.), *The collected papers of Milton H. Erickson, M.D.*. New York: Irvington.

Hammond, C. (1987). Induction and deepening techniques. In W. C. Wester (Ed.), *Clinical hypnosis: A case management approach*. Cincinnati, OH: BSCI Publications.

Olness, K., & Gardner, G. G. (1988). *Hypnosis and hypnotherapy with children*. Philadelphia: Grune & Stratton.

Wester, W. C. (1982). *Questions and answers about clinical hypnosis*. Columbus, OH: Ohio Psychology Publishing.

4 Special Considerations for Using Hypnosis with Young Children

Leora Kuttner, Ph.D.

There is a surprising dearth of literature on the use of hypnosis with preschool children, and even less published information about hypnosis with infants and toddlers. Despite this, most pediatric clinicians know about children's imaginary playmates, the preschooler's penchant for engaging in fantasy, the active toddler's ability to become "entranced" by a stranger, and the infant's capacity for being soothed by repetitive rhythmic rocking. All of these are hypnotic experiences for younger children, often quite fleeting and different from the adult hypnotic response.

The mode of interacting with the very young child tends to be primarily nonverbal. That may be part of the reason why few clinicians have ventured into this area of research. More recently, there has been a stronger need to address the hypnotic process and therapeutic applications with children under the age of 6 years. In part, this arose because the highest incidence of some childhood illnesses, such as leukemia, occur in the 3 to 5 year age group and, of necessity, clinicians began to explore and develop the powerful tool of hypnosis to address the therapeutic needs of these young and vulnerable children.

In this chapter the theoretical foundations for working with children under 6 years of age are examined and some guidelines for therapeutic intervention are outlined.

FOUNDATIONS

Theoretical Considerations

Hilgard and Morgan (1978) have suggested that the term "hypnosis" cannot be applied to the trance-like states experienced by children under the age of six years. In this seminal paper they recommended that the term "protohypnosis" would more accurately describe the process that occurs when children four to six years of age become involved in an hypnotic experience.

> . . . it is inappropriate to rely upon formal hypnotic procedures. These procedures involve two major elements: (a) the implied difference between voluntary and involuntary action, and (b) the expectation of distraction through self-controlled fantasy. Instead this group is more responsive to a kind of "protohypnosis," in which the distraction has at first been set up in the external situation, that is, the very young child is better able to be distracted by listening to a story or by participating in a verbal game with a friendly adult than by removing himself from the scene through his own fantasy or through reliving an earlier game or experience of his own. Gradually the context of the external situation can be altered in such a way that the child achieves the control. (p. 286)

Hilgard, a pioneer in the use of hypnosis with children, referred to the young child in this "protohypnotic state" as experiencing an "imaginative involvement." In her book *Personality and Hypnosis: A Study of Imaginative Involvement*, Dr. Hilgard (1979) explored through retrospective case studies the association between a child's imaginative involvement and his or her later adult hypnotic talent. She found that the greater the amount of imagination-involvement type of activity the adult had had as a child, the greater was that adult's hypnotic talent. Thus, childhood imaginative involvement seems to be a precursor of adult hypnotic ability.

Hypnosis, as it is experienced and observed in young children, seems to be a somewhat different phenomenon than hypnosis in adults (Hilgard & LeBaron, 1982; Hilgard & Morgan, 1978; Kuttner, 1988; Zeltzer & LeBaron, 1982). Because children under 6 years of age are in the process of gradually developing a sense of what is real and what is not, they can move easily between the states of fantasy and reality. They also demonstrate a flexible tolerance of the demands of these two very different states. For example, a 4-year-old girl becomes a cat called Wendy, crawling on the floor and saying, "Meow!" But when she is called by her real name to come to dinner, she retorts, "Don't call me that!" She wants to maintain the integrity of her fantasy, slipping out of that fantasy to remind her parent and then promptly reentering the fantasy. As in this example, the imaginative involvement or absorbed fantasy state (which is invariably played or acted out) is not readily sustained, partly, because of the child's developing attention span.

It is important to recognize that typical adult behaviors, such as physical relaxation, eye closure, and a visible alteration of state, that usually accompany hypnotic trance, are usually not characteristic of the young child's hypnotic process. Nevertheless, it is striking to observe children as young as 3 years of age who clearly demonstrate the ability to alter sensation, perception, and experience (Gardner, 1977; Kuttner, 1988; Olness, 1975, 1976, 1981; Olness & Gardner, 1988). These children can enter trance wide-eyed and maintain a trance during involved physical activity that is directly related to the trance (Olness & Gardner, 1988; Kuttner, 1988).

IMAGINATIVE INVOLVEMENT

Imaginative involvement is an important concept in the use of hypnosis with young children, drawing attention to the way the child's experience differs from the hypnotic phenomenon in adults. Imaginative involvement suggests that the child is intensely absorbed in a "here-and-now" fantasy experience in which present reality is suspended in the interests of the current imaginative experience. It does not presuppose a dissociative ego state, as can occur in the adult hypnotic state. In these early years, the development of the sense of a defined self is not firm or as stable as in the school-aged child. The term also draws our attention to the imaginative component—a playfulness, a fanciful and fantasyful aspect—that is child centered. From infancy onward, the young child learns most easily and effortlessly about the world through independent or interactive play. It is often only through play that the young child can be engaged in a hypnotic experience and sustained in that trance.

ASSESSMENT

Developmental Considerations

It is fundamental to successful work with children that developmental considerations are always attended to; that is, recognizing that the 2-year-old will be functioning at a very different level than the 3-year-old or 4-year-old. For example, while a 2-year-old child is not capable of "remembering," some 3-year-olds, and most 4-year-olds, can recall significant experiences in the immediate and distant past with some ease.

Despite a few excellent published reports on work with the preschool child (e.g., Olness, 1975, 1976, 1981) and a good review by Gardner (1977), there remain few well-controlled research studies to expand our understanding of the hypnotic process with the young child. The work on hypnotic responsivity (Morgan & Hilgard, 1978/1979) suggests that the preschool child may not be as responsive when compared with the older, school-aged child, and significantly there are no clinical scales to test hypnotic talent that go below 4 years of age. Does this indicate that hypnotic ability then starts at around 4 years of age? This seems unlikely. Gardner (1977) reviews clinical evidence that supports the notion that even in infancy and the toddler years, young children develop reliable ways to soothe and quiet themselves, such as rhythmically rocking. She notes parents who report that playing soothing music, stroking a part of the child's body, or turning on a vacuum cleaner or electric shaver will quiet a fretting infant.

Some authors believe that hypnotic ability is present at birth (Morgan, 1973; Ruch, 1975). My clinical experience suggests that the hypnotic modality (kinesthetic, auditory, visual) may alter as a function of the age of the child—although I can find no research or published literature to confirm it. The younger child (birth to 2 years of age) may be more receptive to repetitive kinesthetic and auditory signals to induce a trance, such as lullabies, where as from 2 years of age onward, visual cues may become more central to trance induction. However, this is merely speculative, and there may also be wide individual differences across children. What is evident, however, is that there is a great deal we do not know about the hypnotic potential of the very young child, and consequently there is a need for research in this intriguing and neglected area.

Individual Considerations

When using hypnotherapy with the young child, it is not only the child's chronological age that needs to be considered. More important, the child's cognitive abilities and emotional development need to be noted, since these may not all correlate with age. For example, a 5-year-old boy recently was referred to me who was cognitively advanced, if not gifted, but who was emotionally inhibited and regressed. He was terrified at being in a hospital ward, and clung to his parents, refusing to allow them to talk directly to the hospital staff. I chose to engage with him via his strength, which was his intellect, and discovered that he was fascinated by dinosaurs. He fluently listed all the dinosaurs, using their Latin nomenclature, and described their characteristics. An imaginative involvement experience using dinosaurs that were worried about the destruction of their universe may have accurately reflected the child's fear of extinction.

The hypnotherapist's task, however, is to take the child's theme and transform it into a therapeutic metaphor to promote change. I therefore presented the dinosaurs as a metaphor of courage and created an imaginative involvement experience so that he was intellectually challenged and his regressed emotional needs could be addressed through suggestions for gradually increased coping. I began by asking him if he wanted to hear an interesting story about how some dinosaurs discovered a new land. He nodded. We were both sitting on his hospital bed.

At first the dinosaurs were frightened; after all, they had never ever been away from their home. They wondered if they would ever find their way back. But there were also so many interesting new forms of life here: new flying creatures, new weird trees, new food. . . . The dinosaurs began to feel slightly stronger inside. It was all so curious and new. They began to explore a little further away from their home base and into this strange new territory, with these bigger trees and new life forms. They began slowly and carefully, because they knew that if they watched, they could learn quickly about this strange place and then would know what was safe and where the dangers were. They then could take care of themselves properly, without having to be nervous and watchful all the time. Now this was particularly true of Tyrannosaurus rex. *He was the bravest of them all, as you well know. Nod your head when you can see him exploring this strange new territory. [He nods his head.] Good. Now, after he had had one sleep, he discovered that there were some very curious and interesting plants that they could eat. Nod your head again when you can see these plants; some will be in bright blue and purple, others may be green and red—you may even see ones that I haven't mentioned. [The child is quiet, absorbed, with his eyes open and fixed on me.] And then he discovered something that made him so happy—a big rock with nobbles on it that he could scratch his back on, because you know it's very hard for a dinosaur to scratch his own back.*

INTERVENTION

Considerations for Induction

Given the young child's blurred boundaries between reality and fantasy and relative ease in entering, leaving, and reentering a trance, I have found it often unnecessary to go through a lengthy induction with children under 6 years of age. It is often sufficient simply to say, "How about if we were to imagine that . . . and you can close your eyes, or if you want to keep them open, that is also okay.''

Olness and Gardner (1988) have an excellent and comprehensive chapter on hypnotic induction techniques for children in their book *Hypnosis and Hypnotherapy with Children*—which remains the definitive text on hypnosis with children. I have found the following to be useful inductions for younger children: mighty oak tree, bouncing ball, television, and a floppy Raggedy Ann doll. Apart from using TV as an induction method, all the others are action-oriented inductions and as such are more appealing to the younger child than are the more internally oriented inductions. Likewise, the therapist must be comfortable with allowing the young child to play out the induction and, in the process, permitting the child to become more absorbed.

Therapeutic Considerations

Given the action-oriented nature of the preschool-aged child, and the distinctiveness of the child's hypnotic process, it is essential that the hypnotherapist adopt a highly flexible hypnotic style, allowing the child to move in and out of trance. With an ongoing sensitivity to the child's moment-by-moment responses, the hypnotic context is then successfully sustained as the child enters, leaves, and reenters the trance. An active absorbing participation then develops between therapist and child such that the therapist paces the child, absorbing his or her attention in an informal child-centered manner.

''Favorite stories'' (Kuttner, 1988) is one of the therapeutic methods that has proved effective in easing the younger child's medically induced pain and distress. In this method, the child's favorite story becomes the hypnotic vehicle to create a pleasant imaginative involvement that will, in turn, lead to a different interpretation of the noxious experience. The favorite story becomes both the mode of induction and the substance of the trance. Hypnotic suggestions and reframing take place within the framework of the story line. Information pertaining to the procedure, if needed or requested, can be interwoven with the story line, as well as direct and indirect suggestions for increased comfort, coping, and reduction of pain.

A controlled study (Kuttner, Bowman & Teasdale, 1988) with 25 children aged 3 to 6 years found that this hypnotic method, at first intervention, was significantly more effective in relieving distress associated with a painful invasive procedure than either behavioral distraction or standard medical practice. Imaginary involvement using a familiar story associated with comfort and security may promote a rapid absorption and narrowing of the child's attention and thus prove effective with the first intervention. This would be a useful method in a pediatric emergency room or in any crisis situation in which trust and rapport need to be quickly established.

With the preschool child, parental dependency is still prevalent and normal. Often in the first few sessions, it is necessary and important to allow the parent to be present in the room since it enhances the young child's feelings of trust and safety. Sometimes, in therapeutically appropriate circumstances, the parent can be included in the hypnotherapeutic experience, as in the following example.

Case Example

Four-year-old Hilary had severe eczema that was marginally responsive to dermatological creams. Her dermatologist referred her, believing that anxiety was playing a large part in maintaining the child's acute state. Hilary presented as a small, quiet and intelligent girl who seemed very sensitive to and aware of her world. She was accompanied by her mother, who appeared concerned, loving, and closely involved with Hilary. It was decided to use an imaginative involvement that could include the mother, since she was primarily responsible for applying the creams four times a day and there was a nonconflictual, loving relationship between the mother and daughter.

Here is a part of the first hypnotherapeutic session:

[Hilary is standing up and her mother and the therapist are kneeling on the carpet near her.]

THERAPIST: So let's take this lovely soft cloud, scoop it up, and put it on the itchy parts so that it makes your skin feel so good, soft, smooth, and very calm [scooping up imaginary armfuls of cloud]. What color is this?

HILARY: [With eyes wide open, staring] It's pink.

THERAPIST: Let's pack it on the parts of your skin that need to feel better. Show me where!

HILARY: [Points to the back of her knees, her hands, and her arms.]

THERAPIST: ["Packs" the pink cloud exactly where Hilary pointed without touching the area directly, but coming within two inches of her arm.] Now this should be beginning to work. How does that feel?

HILARY: Nice.

THERAPIST: Is it on thickly enough?

HILARY: [Quietly nods.]

THERAPIST: You'll notice that the soreness should be easing so that your skin will begin to feel like it used to before you got the eczema. What do you feel now?

HILARY: It's cool.

THERAPIST: That's excellent, Hilary! Your pink cloud is helping your skin heal.

Hilary: [Quietly nods.]

Therapist: Now I wouldn't be surprised that after having the lovely pink cloud, your skin will find it easier than ever before to take the good skin creams in, making the healing last even longer and keeping the redness and soreness away. Would you like Mom to put some pink cloud on?

Hilary: Mum, here! [pointing to her dry red elbows].

Mom: Like this?

Hilary: Yes, and there.

Mom: [Beginning to get into her stride] It's nice and cool like those strawberry yogurt sticks, making you feel good!

Hilary and her mother were instructed to use this hypnotic ritual of packing the pink cloud on Hilary's excoriated skin under her direction, until she felt cool and pleasant, before any medication was applied.

ASSESSMENT OF EFFECTIVENESS

One could argue that Hilary was "playing along" with the therapist's instruction. It is difficult to dispute or to prove otherwise. However, in the clinical situation we have the added advantage of watching for the outcome, and when the outcome is positive—as it was for Hilary, whose eczema became less severe and more responsive to her dermatological creams—we can assume that something else apart from "playing along" had occurred.

Bowers and LeBaron (1986) note that many children find hypnotic suggestions to be as natural as play. That is precisely the challenge for the hypnotherapist who wants to work effectively with the preschool child—the medium becomes play and the therapist's previous notions of relaxation, eye closure, and an internalized process are suspended.

It would appear from clinical examples and the small amount of research to date that the younger child is very capable of responding to the hypnotic process with both direct and indirect suggestions. However, further study, naturalistic observations, and controlled investigations are necessary before we can be more categorical about the younger child's hypnotic talent and the therapist's approach to maximize therapeutic change. At this point, it is clear that the therapist who is playful, creative, spontaneous, and flexible will be rewarded to the full when working hypnotherapeutically with children under 6 years of age.

REFERENCES

Bowers, K. S., & LeBaron, S. L. (1986). Hypnosis and hypnotizability: Implications for clinical intervention. *Hospital Community Psychiatry, 37*, 456–467.

Gardner, G. G. (1977). Hypnosis with infants and preschool children. *American Journal of Clinical Hypnosis, 19*, 158–162.

Hilgard, J. R. (1979). *Personality and hypnosis: A study of imaginative involvement* (2nd ed.). Chicago: University of Chicago Press.

Hilgard, J. R., & LeBaron, S. L. (1982). Relief of anxiety and pain in children and adolescents with cancer: Quantitative measures and clinical observations. *International Journal of Clinical and Experimental Hypnosis, 30*. 417–442.

Hilgard, J. R., & Morgan, A. H. (1978). Treatment of anxiety and pain in childhood cancer through hypnosis. In F. H. Frankel & H. S. Zamansky (Eds.), *Hypnosis at its bicentennial: Selected papers*. New York: Plenum.

Kuttner, L. (1988). Favorite stories: A hypnotic pain-reduction technique for children in acute pain. *American Journal of Clinical Hypnosis, 30*(4), 289–294.

Kuttner, L., Bowman, M., & Teasdale, J. M. (1988). Psychological treatment of distress, pain and anxiety for young children with cancer. *Journal of Developmental and Behavioral Pediatrics, 9*(6), 374–381.

Morgan, A. H. (1973). The heritability of hypnotic susceptibility in twins. *Journal of Abnormal Psychology, 82*, 55–61.

Morgan, A. & Hilgard, J. (1978/1979). The Stanford Hypnotic Clinical Scale for Children. *American Journal of Clinical Hypnosis, 21*, 148–155.

Olness, K. (1975). The use of self-hypnosis in the treatment of childhood nocturnal enuresis: A report on 40 patients. *Clinical Pediatrics, 14*, 273–279.

Olness, K. (1976). Autohypnosis in functional megacolon in children. *American Journal of Clinical Hypnosis, 19*, 28–32.

Olness, K. (1981). Imagery (self-hypnosis) as adjunct therapy in childhood cancer: Clinical experience with 25 patients. *Journal of Pediatric Hematology—Oncology, 3*, 313–321.

Olness, K., & Gardner, G. G. (1988). *Hypnosis and hypnotherapy with children* (2nd ed.). New York: Grune & Stratton.

Ruch, J. C. (1975). Self-hypnosis: The result of heterohypnosis or vice-versa? *International Journal of Clinical and Experimental Hypnosis, 23*, 282–304.

Zeltzer, L., & LeBaron, S. (1982). Hypnotic and non-hypnotic techniques for the reduction of pain and anxiety during painful procedures in children and adolescents with cancer. *Behavioral Pediatrics, 101*(6), 1032–1035.

PART II

PSYCHOLOGICAL APPLICATIONS

5 Hypnosis in Childhood Trauma

Richard P. Kluft, M.D.

Trauma is a broad concept. Theoreticians tend to conceptualize trauma in terms of its impact on the paradigm of psychological functioning to which they subscribe (e.g., Rothstein, 1986), and clinicians are inclined to understand trauma in terms of the situations that they confront in the course of their practice. As a result, the literature of traumatology, although rich and diverse, is often rather uneven and difficult to integrate.

We appreciate that the veteran of intense combat, the victim of a natural disaster, the young woman who has suffered incest, the boy who witnesses a bloody murder, and the young cancer victim who must undergo a series of painful and unsettling diagnostic procedures and therapeutic interventions while confronting the specter of death share the fact that they have "experienced an event that is outside the range of usual experience and would be markedly distressing to almost anyone" (American Psychiatric Association, 1987, p. 250), and that certain generalizations across these groups are possible. Yet we recognize as well that each of these examples differs tremendously from the others in many important dimensions, and that, in some instances, the features held in common may prove to be less impressive or relevant than certain unique characteristics of the particular instances. Interventions that might prove quite potent with the young person afflicted with a malignancy might be of questionable relevance to the veteran of Vietnam combat.

An understanding of the diversity of the field of traumatic stress is essential to an understanding of certain characteristics and limitations of this chapter. Because trauma encompasses so wide a spectrum of human experience, and because so many populations have been studied, so many models explored, and so many interventions attempted, there are many potential combinations of these factors that have not yet become the subject of systematic and rigorous study, and some for which only a small number of anecdotal experiences have been either presented or published. The attempt to address the use of hypnosis in childhood trauma is one of the permutations of these factors for which only a limited and uneven literature exists. Notwithstanding the landmark efforts of Gardner and Olness (1981) to assemble the knowledge available about the uses of hypnosis with children, most of the examples that they cite with regard to childhood trauma were drawn from the populations with which they were most familiar—children traumatized by physical illness and the medical procedures that are necessary for their treatment. The one instance noted of the use of hypnosis in connection with sexual traumatization involved a 17-year-old rape victim, and was quoted from the textbook by Crasilneck and Hall (1975).

This chapter will not repeat the contributions of Gardner and Olness (1981). Instead, it will attempt to discuss the use of hypnosis in the treatment of children who have suffered overwhelming life experiences in the form of child abuse. In so doing, it will consider an area in which little has been published or otherwise reported and must be regarded as a preliminary communication. Unlike better-established applications of hypnosis with children, the state of the art in its use with the victims of child abuse remains largely at the level of anecdotal report. Many major textbooks on hypnosis and psychiatry make no mention of this application. Illustrations will be used to indicate the potential uses of hypnosis in a young man suffering posttraumatic stress disorder (PTSD), in a girl who had been molested, and in a young man who had begun to demonstrate the features of multiple-personality disorder.

FOUNDATIONS

Wellsprings

The use of hypnosis in the treatment of traumatized children appears to have three main wellsprings. The first might be condensed from remarks by Freud (1926/1959) that "the essence of a traumatic situation is an experience of helplessness on the part of the ego in the face of accumulation of excitation, whether of external or internal origin" (p. 81), and by Gardner and Olness (1981) that "the goal in hypnotherapy is always to teach the patient an attitude of hope in the context of mastery" (p. 89). Modern hypnotherapy techniques are very different from the more authoritarian interventions favored in the era during which Freud turned away from hypnosis and developed psychoanalysis. Contemporary hypnotherapists' efforts usually are designed to activate the patient to become more effective in his or her own behalf and to remove the obstacles to such an outcome. This stance, and the efforts that are informed by it, lends itself to the achievement of many of the objectives that are necessary for the recovery from trauma.

The second major source is the long-standing awareness of the usefulness of hypnosis in facilitating the recovery of adult victims of trauma. It has seemed reasonable to attempt to find ways of rendering such techniques accessible to the traumatized youngster. A number of the clinicians known to the author for their use of hypnosis with traumatized children were primarily therapists of adults who, in circumstances in which they found themselves treating such children, adapted their techniques and "learned by the seat of their pants.' Hypnosis has been demonstrated to be effective in childhood multiple-personality disorder (Kluft, 1984, 1985, 1986a), which is understood to be a posttraumatic dissociative psychopathology.

Many have observed that children are less likely to be approached to do the type of abreactive work that plays an important role in the treatment of many traumatized adults; as Williams (1979) has noted, play therapy may accomplish this role more effectively. It is the author's experience that many attempts to do abreactive work with children prove more retraumatizing than therapeutic, but that some children in the late latency and preadolescent age ranges have profited from such techniques. The author resolves this in clinical practice by assessing whether an abreaction is in the process of developing spontaneously and, if it is, by facilitating it quite gently only if the process appears to be "stuck" and causing the patient discomfort. Naturally, this should only be done if one's assessment of the child's ego strengths indicates that it can be safely managed. Otherwise, the process can be diverted, attenuated, or shut down, using techniques developed to control the abreactive processes in patients suffering multiple-personality disorder (Kluft, 1989a).

The third major contributant is drawn from an appreciation of the intimate and intricate interrelationships among trauma, dissociation, and hypnosis. Many of the features of PTSD are clearly dissociative in nature (American Psychiatric Association, 1987; Kluft, Steinberg, & Spitzer, 1988). Trauma is a common antecedent to dissociation (Putnam, 1985), and dissociation is an effective adaptation to the experience of being traumatized or damaged (Spiegel, 1986). These observations are given credence by the discovery that individuals with histories of abuse or childhood punishment later score higher (as a group) than nontraumatized controls on measures of hynotizability (Cooper & London, 1976; Hilgard, 1972; Nash, Lynn, & Givens, 1984; Nowlis, 1969) and dissociation (Sanders, McRoberts, & Tollefson, 1989). Furthermore, patients with multiple-personality disorder, a severe and chronic dissociative disorder, give histories of child abuse in 97–98 percent of recent series (Putnam, Guroff, Silberman, Barban, & Post, 1986; Schultz,

Braun, & Kluft, 1989). It is of interest that Coons and Milstein (1986) were able to document allegations made by 85 percent of a series of such patients.

Hicks (1985) has speculated that traumatization causes a childhood level of hypnotizability to be fixated rather than to become reduced with age. A recent theoretical paper by Bernstein and Putnam (1989) advances the theory that hypnotizability may come from two developmental pathways, one related to absorption and the other to dissociativity. They link the latter to traumatic antecedents. These investigators' ideas are reminiscent of several ideas advanced by Janet a century ago (see Van der Hart & Friedman, 1989).

The sum of these findings suggests that the traumatized individual may well respond with dissociative defenses and symptoms, and that hypnosis, which is highly associated with dissociation phenomenologically and conceptually (Sanders, 1986), may be the method of choice to access and ameliorate many aspects of posttraumatic psychopathology (Spiegel, 1988a, 1988b).

Problems and Controversies

The use of hypnosis in the treatment of many groups of traumatized children is determined mainly on the basis of whether it is likely to be effective and whether it is acceptable to the child and the child's parents. For example, the decision as to whether one might offer comforting hypnotic imagery and pain-reduction strategies to a 7-year-old girl who must face repeated lumbar punctures and/or bone-marrow aspirations is relatively straightforward. There are few alternative strategies that would achieve the same goal. Absent some unusual parental objections or unique circumstances, there is much to be gained and little risk.

In contrast, the case of a 7-year-old girl suffering posttraumatic symptoms after alleging a sexual assault would be much more complex. There are many potential therapeutic approaches, and the use of hypnosis might later be held to have contaminated the credibility of the young woman as a witness. All of the controversies that surround the use of hypnosis in forensic settings would become relevant (Orne, 1979; Tuite, Braun, & Frischholz, 1986). A scenario is conceivable in which the girl might be a genuine incest victim complaining against her abusive father, but her testimony might be judged to be unreliable or confabulated as a result of the use of hypnosis, leading to the acquittal of a guilty defendant and the return of the girl to a traumatic environment. The author has been consulted in a number of such cases, and has yet to find one in which the potential benefits of hypnosis outweighed its potential drawbacks and complications. In general, the use of hypnosis in a situation in which the future testimony of the traumatized child will be essential should be avoided.

It is the author's experience that when a traumatized child interprets hypnosis as an assault or an unwelcome loss of control (i.e., a retraumatization), persistent efforts to use hypnosis are contraindicated. He has found that often a child who originally refuses hypnosis will accept it at a later date, when the child has discovered in the process of therapy that the therapist will not be intrusive or hurtful. Some children will never allow formal hypnosis, but will permit related procedures, especially if they are advanced in a nonthreatening manner. For example, one molested child who refused formal hypnosis and was unable to talk about what had occurred was encouraged to "concentrate real hard" on looking at an animal figure (a dog) that she liked, and then to tell if anything else popped into her mind. Having fixed her gaze, she fell into a trancelike state, wished that the dog had been with her to protect her from "the bad man," and was encouraged, from the perspective of having the dog with her in the present, to continue to talk. This allowed her to begin dealing with the assault. In this case, the forensic issues had already been decided, but the young woman suffered severe residual posttraumatic symptoms.

ASSESSMENT

Consideration of the use of hypnosis in the traumatized child begins with the Hippocratic injunction, *"Primum non nocere"* ("First, do no harm"). As noted above, it is essential to avoid even the remote possibility of contaminating or appearing to contaminate the field with regard to legal issues. Also, it is important to undertake a complete assessment of the child before proceeding. The hypnotherapist, even if he or she is called on to make a brief intervention in the course of an overall therapy conducted by others, should become aware of the diagnostic, dynamic, developmental, familial, medical, and other considerations that affect the child's life space. Hypnosis in the treatment of the traumatized should never be a "shot in the dark."

The author has not attempted to measure hypnotizability in his young subjects prior to proceeding. His reason for not doing so is not related to the cogent observations of Orne (1969), who discussed clinicians' apprehensions about the potential impact of patients' not responding to test items on the patients' favorable expectations about the success of the hypnotic endeavor. Rather, it has been on the basis of his being persuaded that hypnosis is a facilitator of therapy rather than a treatment in and of itself (Frischholz & Spiegel, 1983), and that it often is very difficult to ascertain what proportion of a therapeutic outcome ascribed to hypnotherapy is actually due to the hypnosis per se (Frankel, 1976).

In essence, the author uses hypnosis in traumatized children primarily to enhance mastery, secondarily to alleviate symptoms or interrupt symptomatic behaviors, and thirdly to retrieve information. He has not utilized memory-distortion procedures because he is convinced that despite any short-term gains of increased comfort, they ultimately serve to debase cognition and to increase vulnerability to revictimization (an issue discussed with regard to another patient population in Kluft, 1989b).

Therefore, in his assessment, he is particularly sensitive to the child's ego functions, cognitive and psychodynamic development, and coping styles. He is eager to study the child's experience with authority figures, and the impact that the identity of the traumatizers may have upon the transference. The traumatized youngster may have many characteristics that will influence how hypnosis will be perceived and experienced, and what problems are likely to be encountered. Green (1989) has summarized the sequelae of child abuse, both physical and sexual. Some of the dimensions that should be assessed and their implications for hypnosis considered are (1) cognitive and developmental impairments and central-nervous-system compromise caused by trauma (interventions may have to be simplified); (2) posttraumatic symptoms (which often flare up spontaneously upon the entry into trance); (3) mistrust and pathological object relations (that may influence how the therapist is perceived and whether cooperation is possible—some of these children have little substrate upon which to build a positive transference or expectation of the treatment); (4) primitive defense mechanisms and (5) poor impulse control (which may set the stage for unanticipated regressions); 6) poor self-concept and depression (which may compromise the usually optimistic and upbeat induction techniques often congenial to those who use hypnosis with less injured children); and (7) masochistic, self-destructive, and hypersexual behavior (which makes careful attention to wording and suggestions essential, lest they be amenable to cooption by these pathological tendencies).

The motivation of the potential patient for hypnosis must be assessed, and inaccurate fantasies and fears must be addressed. Family preferences may affect the decision as to whether to use hypnosis. In some instances, families hold strong, irrational beliefs about hypnosis that cannot be dispelled. In others, especially abuse cases, families may resist the use of hypnosis because what has brought the patient to treatment, however repugnant, may be the tip of a rather nasty iceberg. The family fears that hypnosis may cause deeper secrets to be revealed. A certain number of families subscribe to the belief that unpleasant things should be forgotten, and they oppose any therapy that does not endorse this philosophy.

Only after the foregoing factors and the merits of alternative approaches have been considered should a decision be made to use hypnosis. This decision should take place in the process of evolving a strategic plan for the treatment of the traumatized child, and most often will be only one of the modalities brought into play. The scars of trauma do not fade rapidly. The prompt cessation of major symptoms should not be allowed to disguise the patient's need for help. *Example*: A highly symptomatic and dysfunctional young girl who had been raped was referred for hypnosis. It was determined that this referral reflected a magical wish on the part of the family and the referral source to remove the signs and to deny the impact of this devastating event. Indeed, hypnosis relieved most of the patient's acute distress and restored her to a good level of functioning, but longer-term traditional therapy was necessary to deal with her experience and to prevent both chronic maladjustments and a "posttraumatic decline."

INTERVENTION PROCESS

To illustrate the use of hypnosis in the treatment of traumatized children, three case examples will be discussed. A useful framework is the eight Cs model that has been offered by Spiegel (1988a, 1988b). The trauma victim must be helped to Confront what has occurred directly, and to Confess what has been done and been felt. Often this involves helping the patient to distinguish between misplaced and real guilt and shame, because many trauma victims, out of their need to avoid feeling helpless, take responsibility for events and actions that were imposed on them. Active Consolation is necessary. A Condensation of the experience into an image that can focus the event and make it more manageable may be helpful. It is important to bring dissociated memories into Consciousness, in a gradual way that does not overwhelm the patient. Concentration, a characteristic of the hypnotic experience, can help to demarcate the trauma. Through the structuring of experience, the patient is helped to achieve Control of the trauma and the memories of trauma. This allows gradual working through of the painful material in a manageable manner, rather than experiencing one's self at its mercy, vulnerable to being overwhelmed abruptly. Finally, the patient achieves Congruence, the ability to integrate what has occurred into one's conscious awareness of one's self, "so that the traumatic past is not disjunctive and incompatible with the present" (Spiegel, 1988a, p. 916). Naturally, the illustrations will not demonstrate all aspects of this process.

Case Examples

Jonathan—A Boy Who Had Been Brutalized

Jonathan was referred at age 9 for the treatment of severe anxiety, aggressive outbursts against schoolmates, and extreme "jumpiness" around adult males. For instance, while being chastised by a school principal, he misperceived the principal as Hal, his mother's former lover, and quivered in fear. He had developed a pattern of play that involved games of domination and brutalization, causing his friends to abandon him. He could not concentrate in school.

On assessment, Jonathan had virtually every classic sign of PTSD. His history was one of normal development until some behavioral difficulties occurred at the time of his parents' divorce. He had appeared to adjust well until Hal became his mother's live-in lover. Hal brutalized the youngster, beating him for minor misdeeds, humiliating him, and forcing him into abject submission. Things were worse when Hal drank, and Hal became intoxicated several times a week. It was only after Hal beat Jonathan's mother repeatedly that she threw Hal out and filed charges against him. She admitted with great shame that she had not allowed herself to face what had happened to Jonathan.

The decision to use hypnosis was based on Jonathan's severe anxiety and sense of being out of control. It was hoped that he felt some degree of mastery, and that therapy could address the aggressive behaviors that seemed to be his attempt to master (by becoming an active perpetrator) what had been done to him. Probably because his relationship with his father had been good, Jonathan related well to his male therapist, and embraced the idea of hypnosis, which was presented to him as "a special kind of concentration that can be used to solve problems and make your mind stronger."

To enter trance, Jonathan was instructed to do the following.

THERAPIST: Follow my finger so that you just look far up and then still farther, as if you were looking straight up through the top of your head at the sky. Now while you look at the sky, let your eyelids slowly fall like a curtain, and relax. [This is an adaptation for pediatric use of the Spiegel and Spiegel (1978) eye-roll technique.] And as you relax, you'll find that you can concentrate wonderfully well. You get a clear picture in your mind. We'll practice getting clear pictures, and then use concentration to solve some problems. Okay?

JONATHAN: Okay.

THERAPIST: First get a picture of your dog, Brownie. Got it?

JONATHAN: Yeah!

THERAPIST: Great! Now let's see what Brownie will do.

Jonathan describes Brownie doing tricks that he currently cannot do. The therapist understands this to reflect Jonathan's fantasy that the therapy will be empowering. Had the image indicated less powerful motivation, the therapist might have suggested a more congenial scenario, drawing an analogy between spontaneous and suggested hypnotic imagery and spontaneous and therapist-modified stories in Richard Gardner's (1971) mutual storytelling techniques.

THERAPIST: And now let's concentrate on baseball. [selected because Jonathan's fearfulness has generalized to sports, and he is afraid of being hurt by a baseball, etc.] I am going to hit you some grounders. [Jonathan smiles.]

The therapist takes Jonathan from grounders through pop-flies to line-drives, which he knows Jonathan is unwilling to try to catch. With each scenario, he make the following remarks.

THERAPIST: You will be amazed to find that most people don't let themselves concentrate on the ball. They are so worried about things that they forget to watch it straight into the glove. [Jonathan nods.] They let the ball play them, and it can! That little ball can control the best player, if he lets it. And then it's easy to make mistakes or even to get hurt. [Jonathan nods.] Now let's have a pepper game. I am going to hit the ball to you and I won't tell you what I will hit—you just keep your eye on the ball and throw it back. [The therapist avoids imagery of pitching the ball to Jonathan—there is too great a risk that the aggressive aspects of the batter–pitcher confrontation will prove disruptive. He occasionally interjects such comments as: "Good one! Don't lose it in the sun!"] And now that we know you can really concentrate, that you can really keep your eye on the ball, let's see if we can solve some problems. Okay? [Jonathan nods.] Okay, what do you want to work on? [The author finds that such an approach allows therapy to start at a level the patient can tolerate, and often provides valuable information. Usually, however, children say "I don't know," and implicitly or explicitly let the therapist direct the topic.]
JONATHAN: Can I really work on anything?
THERAPIST (sensing something unexpected): Sure.
JONATHAN: Really?
THERAPIST: Really.
JONATHAN: Hal hurt me. [This choice of words is common among the sexually abused and alerts the therapist.]
THERAPIST: Sounds like the kind of hurt that is hard to talk about. [Jonathan nods and begins to cry softly.] But we know you can concentrate even better than you thought, so sooner or later you'll be able to, even if you are sure that you can't right now. Now might not be the right time.

[This is both permissive and directive at once, but phrased in such a way as to indicate that the implicit request is without the potential of loss for either participant.]

JONATHAN: He hurt me bad. [In minutes Jonathan was revealing the details of an anal rape by Hal, and experienced an abreaction. The emergence of this material was totally unforeseen, and probably was facilitated by the partnership that Jonathan and the therapist had forged in the preliminary fantasy "concentration exercises."]

THERAPIST: [After significant abreaction and consolation] So we see that when we concentrate we can face a lot of stuff that really was bad, and put it in perspective.

JONATHAN: What does that mean?

THERAPIST: Well, to see what it really means. Like it doesn't mean that you are weak or bad or queer, but that some jerk was big enough and sick enough to hurt someone he should have taken care of.

Jonathan's behavior improved dramatically between appointments. He was less apprehensive and showed fewer posttraumatic symptoms, but still was aggressive to peers. In the following session, the therapist suggested that Jonathan tell him a story about "a real tough guy, a real bad dude." The story he told clearly emphasized the theme that only by hurting others could Jonathan undo his sense of hurt and powerlessness. In a variation of Gardner's (1971) mutual storytelling technique, the therapist induced trance as above so that Jonathan "could really concentrate on the story that he would hear, and get its true meaning." He also taught him a brief self-hypnotic procedure based on the eye-roll technique of the Spiegels (1978), which he was to use to concentrate better when listening to the tape that the therapist would make of the story he would tell.

The therapist's story was the type told to karate students to teach them not to abuse their skills. The therapist described the tale of a young man who had been badly mistreated and humiliated, and resolved to become a master of karate. This he achieved, and set about mistreating and humiliating others. Finally, and to his horror, as he was attacking a young boy for no good reason, he saw his own face on the boy's face, and realized that he had himself become a monster. He returned to his teachers and learned that the true meaning of strength was to use it to defend the helpless.

Jonathan had little to say about the story, but did listen to the tape regularly. Within a few weeks, he had ceased his bullying and was reported to be breaking up schoolyard scuffles.

These fragments of a treatment illustrate some uses of hypnosis in the treatment of a boy with PTSD resulting from abuse. The focus was on the restoration of mastery and self-control; work on traumata was undertaken as the material emerged. In the course of a year's treatment, Jonathan experienced remission of all symptoms and the resumption of normal development. He was doing well at last contact.

Julie—A Girl Who Felt Dirty

Seven-year-old Julie was the victim of long-term incestuous abuse. When her mother discovered that Julie's father was sexually exploiting the young girl, she left him and arranged for Julie to enter treatment. Julie's psychotherapy resolved some but not all of her posttraumatic symptoms. She continued to have nightmares of her father's forcing intercourse on her, and had developed a compulsion to wash herself dozens of times a day. She always felt she was a dirty little girl, both literally and figuratively. She spent over two hours a day in washing herself, focusing on her genitalia. She fulfilled the criteria of the revised third edition of the *Diagnostic and Statistical Manual of Mental Disorders* for an obsessive-compulsive disorder (American Psychiatric Association, 1987).

A therapist was asked to attempt hypnosis to treat this symptom because it was felt to be clearly posttraumatic in origin. In brief, the therapist decided that the patient's damaged self-image might be responsive to the use of imagery that metaphorically undid her sense of damage, degradation, and humiliation. Some of the theoretical underpinnings of this conceptualization were drawn from recent conceptualizations of the affect of shame (Nathanson, 1987).

Julie entered trance easily through induction by imagery, in this case a variant of the flower-garden technique (Gardner & Olness, 1981). Once Julie could imagine herself in a lovely flower garden, holding a lovely bouquet of all the flowers she could possibly want (a symbolic undoing of "deflowered," a term Julie's mother had used in her presence, but which Julie found confusing), she was told, "And now from right above you in the sky there is a beautiful point of light, like a wonderful star that is so bright that you can see it all day. As you look at it, beautiful rays of light flow down from it, a waterfall of light, a shower of light, that bathes you in its glow. Soon, no matter where you look, all you can see is a field of beautiful light. In just a few seconds, you feel a warm and comfortable sensation that makes you feel so good and clean, so strong and so pure. The light seems to enter you and flow through you, making you feel safe and clean and pure, inside and out. It feels so good to feel old hurts healing, and to know that you can be so very comfortable, and know in every part of your mind and body that you are good, and strong, and at peace." Julie was taught to reinforce this imagery with daily practice sessions.

There is nothing subtle about this intervention. It metaphorically offers Julie the opportunity to receive and accept permission from an authority figure to experience herself as restored and as without blame for her father's incestuous use of her. It allows a suggested somatic sensation to counteract or reframe any ongoing pathological arousal. Implicitly, it suggests that she can master any hypersexual behavior that remains as a sequela to the incest (Green, 1989; Yates, 1982).

The result of this brief intervention was the lasting cessation of the obsessive-compulsive behaviors. She required another year of conventional therapy to work through her incest trauma more thoroughly and to curtail some mild pressures toward hypersexual behavior.

Micky—Who Had To Be Someone Else

Micky presented at the age of 8 with symptoms of amnesia and out-of-character behavior witnessed by others. He had been assumed to be no more than a liar whose denials were particularly convincing. Then it was discovered that on several occasions, when Micky was doing the types of things that he usually disavowed, he had told those who interacted with him that his name was "Billy." A school counselor consulted a therapist known to work with dissociative disorders and had been advised to use a checklist (Fagan & McMahon, 1984) to assess Micky's behavior. Upon demonstrating numerous phenomena suggestive of childhood multiple-personality disorder, Micky was interviewed by the consultant, who quickly encountered "Billy" and other personalities. He documented a history of profound child abuse and notified child-protection agencies.

In the course of therapy, hypnosis was used to access the personalities, work through their histories and concerns, and effect their reconciliation (Kluft, 1985, 1986a). However, the personalities were concerned about their being different ages and sizes. The therapist induced trance and used imagery from the "Star Trek" television series. On the bridge of the starship *Enterprise*, each personality sat in its own special chair, which was designed for travel through time as well as space. Each personality traveled at a different rate, according to its age and readiness to grow. After several such procedures, all experienced themselves as the same age and size. When the personalities were ready to join, another set of "Star Trek" imageries was employed. Under hypnosis, the personalities were guided through a fantasy in which they were brought to the transporter room and beamed down to a planet for separate dangerous missions. In the course of these missions, which the therapist elaborated on extensively and enhanced with suggestions of time distortion, the personalities all discovered that they were, in fact, very much the same. Hence, upon the successful completion of their missions, they could be "beamed up" as one strong boy. Micky enjoyed the experience immensely and showed no signs of separate personalities at a follow-up of several years. The mechanism of the effectiveness of such procedures is unknown.

ASSESSMENT OF EFFECTIVENESS

At this time, the treatment of traumatized children with hypnosis is too new an area to have given rise to controlled studies and the rigorous exploration of outcomes. The literature remains very small and is largely confined to the reporting of successful cases. A minor exception has been Kluft's (1986b) follow-up studies on multiple-personality disorder, which include two childhood cases. Two of his young patients have retained integration and improved function on 11- and eight-year follow-up respectively (Kluft, 1989, unpublished data). However, here also it is impossible to ascertain what role hypnosis played in determining the efficacy of the treatments.

There appear to be too few case reports to allow a "guesstimation" of the efficacy of hypnotherapeutic interventions in childhood trauma, and no hard data to permit a more definitive assessment. Those few reports that do exist indicate the possibility that hypnosis may be of great use in certain cases.

FUTURE TRENDS

As hypnosis grows in acceptance and popularity and is increasingly applied to the treatment of traumatized adults, and as the study of posttraumatic stress in children continues to enter the mainstream of child psychiatry, it appears inevitable that the literature in the treatment of traumatized children with therapies that include hypnosis will grow quite rapidly. It is likely that this growth will, for a time, remain in the form of case studies and reports of open trials of hypnotherapy in work with particular types of childhood trauma. Only when a significant literature of this type has developed and has demonstrated that many have found hypnosis to be useful in such cases will scientific investigators attempt a more systematic type of exploration.

The areas most likely to spearhead the growth of the literature on childhood trauma are the study of the treatment of childhood multiple-personality disorder, which already has a credible foundation, and the use of hypnosis in the treatment of young victims of sexual abuse by therapists who have become convinced of its efficacy in work with the adult victims of such exploitation. Perhaps advances in these areas will prompt those agencies and clinics that serve abused populations to explore the use of hypnosis in their own treatment programs.

REFERENCES

American Psychiatric Association. (1987). *Diagnostic and statistical manual of mental disorders* (3rd ed.—revised). Washington, DC: Author.

Bernstein, E. B., & Putnam, F. W. (1989). Integrating research on dissociation and hypnotizability: Are there two pathways to hypnotizability? *Dissociation, 2,* 32–38.

Coons, P. M., & Milstein, V. (1986). Psychosexual disturbances in multiple personality: Characteristics, etiology, and treatment. *Journal of Clinical Psychiatry, 47,* 101–106.

Cooper, L. M., & London, P. (1976). Children's hypnotic susceptibility, personality and EEG patterns. *International Journal of Clinical and Experimental Hypnosis, 25,* 147–166.

Crasilneck, H.B., & Hall, J.A. (1975). *Clinical hypnosis: Principles and applications.* New York: Grune & Stratton.

Fagan, J., & McMahon, P. P. (1984). Incipient multiple personality in children: Four cases. *Journal of Nervous and Mental Disease, 172,* 26–36.

Frankel, F. H. (1976). *Hypnosis: Trance as a coping mechanism.* New York: Plenum.

Freud, S. (1926/1959). Inhibitions, symptoms, and anxiety. In J. Strachey (Ed.), *Standard edition of the psychological works of Sigmund Freud* (Vol. 20, pp. 77–174). London: Hogarth.

Frischholz, E. J., & Spiegel, D. (1983). Hypnosis is not a therapy. *Bulletin of the British Society for Clinical and Experimental Hypnosis, 6,* 3–8.

Gardner, G. G., & Olness, K. (1981). *Hypnosis and hypnotherapy with children.* New York: Grune & Stratton.

Gardner, R. A. (1971). *Therapeutic communication with children: The mutual storytelling technique.* New York: Science House.

Green, A. H. (1989). Physical and sexual abuse of children. In H. I. Kaplan & B. J. Sadock (Eds.), *Comprehensive textbook of psychiatry/V* (5th ed., Vol. 2, pp. 1962–1970). Baltimore: Williams & Wilkins.

Hicks, R. E. (1985). Discussion: A clinician's perspective. In R. P. Kluft (Ed.), *Childhood antecedents of multiple personality* (pp. 239–258). Washington, DC: American Psychiatric Press.

Hilgard, J. R. (1972). Evidence for a developmental-interactive theory of hypnotic susceptibility. In E. Fromm & R. E. Shor (Eds.), *Hypnosis: Research developments and perspectives* (pp. 787–397). Chicago: Aldine Atherton.

Kluft, R. P. (1984). Multiple personality in childhood. *Psychiatric Clinics of North America 7,* 121–134.

Kluft, R. P. (1985). Hypnotherapy of childhood multiple personality disorder. *American Journal of Clinical Hypnosis, 27,* 201–210.

Kluft, R. P. (1986a). Treating children who have multiple personality disorder. In B. G. Braun (Ed.), *Treatment of multiple personality disorder* (pp. 79–106). Washington, DC: American Psychiatric Press.

Kluft, R. P. (1986b). Personality unification in multiple personality disorder: A follow-up study. In B. G. Graun (Ed.), *Treatment of multiple personality disorder* (pp. 29–60). Washington, DC: American Psychiatric Press.

Kluft, R. P. (1989a). Playing for time: Temporizing techniques in the treatment of multiple personality disorder. *American Journal of Clinical Hypnosis, 32*(2), 90–98.

Kluft, R. P. (1989b). Treating the patient who has been sexually exploited by a prior therapist. *Psychiatric Clinics of North America, 12*, 483–500.

Kluft, R. P., Steinberg, M., & Spitzer, R. L. (1988). DSM–III–R revisions in the dissociative disorders: An exploration of their derivation and rationale. *Dissociation, 1*(1), 39–46.

Nash, M. R., Lynn, S. J., & Givens, D. L. (1984). Adult hypnotic susceptibility, childhood punishment, and child abuse: A brief communication. *International Journal of Clinical and Experimental Hypnosis, 32*, 6–11.

Nathanson, D. L. (Ed.). (1987). *The many faces of shame*. New York: Guilford.

Nowlis, D. P. (1969). The child-rearing antecedents of hypnotic susceptibility and naturally occurring hypnotic-like experiences. *International Journal of Clinical and Experimental Hypnosis, 17*, 109–120.

Orne, M. T. (1969). On the nature of the post-hypnotic suggestion. In L. Chertok (Ed.), *Psychophysiological mechanisms of hypnosis*. Berlin: Springer.

Orne, M. T. (1979). The use and misuse of hypnosis in court. *International Journal of Clinical and Experimental Hypnosis, 27*, 311–341.

Putnam, F. W. (1985). Dissociation as a response to extreme trauma. In R. P. Kluft (Ed.), *Childhood antecedents of multiple personality* (pp. 65–98). Washington, DC: American Psychiatric Press.

Putnam, F. W., Guroff, J. J., Silberman, E. K., Barban, L., & Post, R. M. (1986). The clinical phenomenology of multiple personality disorder. *Journal of Clinical Psychiatry, 47*, 285–293.

Rothstein, A. (Ed.). (1986). *The reconstruction of trauma*. Madison, CT: International Universities Press.

Sanders, S. (Ed.). (1986). Special issue of *American Journal of Hypnosis, 29*, 2.

Sanders, B., McRoberts, G., & Tollefson, C. (1989). Childhood stress and dissociation in a college population. *Dissociation, 2*, 17–23.

Schultz, R., Braun, B. G., & Kluft, R. P. (1989). Multiple personality disorder: Phenomenology of selected variables in comparison to major depression. *Dissociation, 2*, 45–52.

Spiegel, D. (1986). Dissociating damage. *American Journal of Clinical Hypnosis, 29*, 123–131.

Spiegel, D. (1988a). Hypnosis. In J. A. Talbott, R. E. Hales, & S. C. Yudofsky (Eds.), *The American Psychiatric Press textbook of psychiatry* (pp. 907–928). Washington, DC: American Psychiatric Press.

Spiegel, D. (1988b). Dissociation and hypnosis in posttraumatic stress disorder. *Journal of Traumatic Stress, 1*, 17–33.

Spiegel, H., & Spiegel, D. (1978). *Trance and treatment*. New York: Basic Books.

Tuite, P. A., Braun, B. G., & Frischholz, E. J. (1986). Hypnosis and eyewitness testimony. *Psychiatric Annals, 16*, 91–95.

Van der Hart, O., & Friedman, B. (1989). A reader's guide to Pierre Janet on dissociation: A neglected intellectual heritage. *Dissociation, 2*, 3–16.

Williams, D. T. (1979). Hypnosis as a therapeutic adjunct. In J. D. Noszhpitz (Ed.), *Basic handbook of child psychiatry* (vol. 3). New York: Basic Books.

Yates, A. (1982). Children eroticized by incest. *American Journal of Psychiatry, 139,* 482–485.

6 The Use of Hypnotic Techniques with Sexually Abused Children

Judith W. Rhue, Ph.D.
Steven Jay Lynn, Ph.D.

FOUNDATIONS

Data from a variety of sources present an alarming picture of the scope of childhood sexual abuse. Documented cases of sexual abuse hover around 115,000 per year (Asher, 1988). However, these statistics represent only the tip of the iceberg. Indeed, surveys designed to gauge the magnitude of the problem paint a more ominous picture: 20–30 percent of female children, and 9–12 percent of male children are victims of sexual abuse (Finkelhor, 1984; Herman, 1981; Russell, 1983).

In young sexually abused children, the therapist is likely to encounter sleep disturbances, nightmares, compulsive masturbation, precocious sex play, loss of toilet training, crying with no provocation, staying indoors, and regressed behavior, such as finger sucking or clinging (Brant & Tisza, 1977; Gomes-Schwartz, Horowitz & Sauzier, 1985). In treating school-age sexually abused children, the therapist also may need to treat depression, school failure, truancy, decreased appetite, and running away from home (Justice & Justice, 1979). Additionally, the child must struggle with feelings of helplessness, anxiety, frustration, lowered self-esteem, and, often, anger and disaffiliation.

In this chapter, we will argue that hypnotherapeutic techniques can be used in the assessment of child abuse and in the treatment of its aftereffects. We will focus on the treatment of 4- to 10-year-old sexually abused children. In so doing, we will describe a number of techniques for establishing a therapeutic alliance with the abused child, exploring personal and interpersonal dynamics, and healing the damage to the child's emerging sense of self and security. These techniques may be used as the primary treatment modality or adjunctively with other psychotherapies. The approach reported herein represents a synthesis of the therapeutic interventions we have found to be most effective in our work with 23 children who were victims of sexual abuse.

The fantasy and imagination-based therapeutic procedures we will discuss are "hypnotic" in that they are members of a family of such techniques that have traditionally fallen under this rubric. Our approach encompasses and extends techniques presented by Gardner and Olness (1981), who described how imagery and storytelling techniques could be used to create hypnotic inductions. These procedures are more client-centered and naturalistic than ritualistic, more spontaneous than contrived, and more permissive than authoritative. Nevertheless, many of the techniques can also be used productively following ritualized, or even standardized, hypnotic inductions.

Storytelling, as a hypnotic technique, has been recognized as an effective treatment modality with children in acute pain (Kuttner, 1988) and with children who must endure a variety of difficult medical procedures (Hilgard & LeBaron, 1984). The imaginative involvement engendered by the weaving and retelling of the "story" provides a framework for the discovery and sharing of feelings and life experiences at a level compatible with the child's abilities. The interaction between the therapist and the child combines many of the most desirable aspects of play therapy and art therapy. The techniques we will describe present the therapist with an opportunity to include supportive and comforting suggestions, to use symbolism and metaphor to provide the emotional distance necessary to deal with traumatic experiences, and to explore complex relationship issues of trust, love, anger, and loss.

Rationale for Hypnotherapy with Sexually Abused Children

To our knowledge, this chapter represents the first attempt to delineate a framework for using hypnotic techniques in the treatment of childhood sexual abuse. The value of using hypnotic techniques to treat adult victims of trauma has received only limited attention (MacHovec, 1984). For example, adolescent and adult rape victims have been successfully treated with hypnotherapeutic procedures (Dempster & Balson, 1982; Ebert, 1988) aimed at enhancing feelings of power, control, and personal worth, and reducing symptoms. Although hypnotic techniques have been used to treat adult victims of sexual trauma, the application of these techniques with sexually abused children has been neglected. That hypnotic techniques have not been exploited is unfortunate, inasmuch as such procedures have been successfully implemented with children in controlling pain, treating habit disorders and learning and performance problems, and reducing anticipatory and postchemotherapy illness, as well as in treating a variety of other medical and behavioral problems (Gardner & Olness, 1981).

The available evidence offers promise for the use of fantasy and imagination-based hypnotic techniques in the treatment of sexually abused children. Fantasy, imagination, and play are natural media that the child uses to acquire and practice essential skills and experiences. That children appear to be especially prone to immersing themselves in fantasy and imaginal activities suggests that they should find hypnotic techniques particularly congenial. London, Morgan, and Hilgard (1973) suggest that children's hypnotizability exceeds that of adults because the fantasy play and daydreaming that are so integral to their everyday life are akin to cognitive activities that enliven and abet hypnotic responsiveness. Hypnosis and imaginative play activities often encompass the shared activities of focused concentration and task absorption; temporarily circumscribed, attenuated, and limited reality testing; concrete thought processes; and giving free rein to fantasy to foster a desired imaginal experience. Emotionally, children exhibit an openness to new experience, an intensity of feeling, a desire for mastery, and an aptitude for regressive states that probably contribute to their hypnotizability (O'Grady & Hoffmann, 1984).

Investigations that have relied on adults' reports of their childhood imaginative activities, and research that has examined children's fantasy involvements, have documented a link between a propensity for imaginative involvements in everyday life and hypnotizability (see Rhue & Lynn, 1986). There is reason to believe that at least some sexually abused children are particularly imaginative and responsive to hypnotic procedures. Josephine Hilgard (1979) was the first investigator to discover a connection between high hypnotizability and a history of severe childhood punishment. Wilson and Barber (1983) also found that many of their highly hypnotizable fantasy-prone subjects reported being reared in a harsh environment that, for some subjects, included being subjected to physical punishment and abuse. More recently, we (Lynn & Rhue, 1988) found that fantasizers recollected being physically abused and punished to a greater degree than other subjects did and reported experiencing greater loneliness and isolation as children. In fact, six of the 21 fantasizers we asked about their childhood punishment history reported that they were physically abused as children (e.g., broken bones, bruises, burns), whereas none of the non–fantasy-prone subjects reported a history of abuse.

A number of studies (Nash, Lynn, & Givens, 1984; Nash & Lynn, 1986) have shown that college students who report a history of physical abuse are more hypnotizable than subjects who do not report a history of abuse. Although a recent study (Rhue & Lynn, 1990) failed to find support for the link between abuse and hypnotizability, this investigation did find that adults who reported being either sexually or physically abused during childhood were more fantasy-prone than were nonabused subjects. Thus, extensive fantasy involvements constitute a way of coping with or escaping from a harsh or aversive childhood environment (Hilgard, 1970).

Hilgard (1986) has suggested three reasons why an association exists between a punitive upbringing and hypnotizability. First, subjects raised in such a home environment might be conditioned to respond to authority automatically and without question. Second, they may prevent punishment by learning to play various social roles. And third, they may learn to escape parental punishment by retreating into a comforting world of fantasy and make-believe.

In summary, imagination and fantasy-based hypnotic techniques may be particularly well suited to victims of child abuse. Not only do therapeutic techniques that capitalize on the naturalistic use of imagination as a vehicle to resolve problems and regulate affect have special relevance for the child, but certain abused children appear to be especially inclined to exploit such techniques and to benefit from them.

ASSESSMENT

The negative sequelae of sexual abuse increase in severity with prolonged abuse, the presence of threats of violence, and the emotional or familial closeness of the child's relationship with the abuser (Browne & Finkelhor, 1986). Just what these effects are needs to be carefully assessed, along with the history of abusive treatment. Because the effects of abuse are far from uniform, and the depth and degree of psychic scarring depend on many factors, at minimum, we address the following questions: How willing and able is the child to discuss the abuse and the events surrounding it? To what extent are feelings of self-blame, anger, shame, badness, or of being "damaged" or "broken" present? To what extent is the child's self-esteem and sense of power and control over his or her body affected? Are sexual themes, unusual behaviors, or preoccupations repercussions of abuse? How are the family dynamics and feelings of trust toward the parents affected by the abuse?

Sexually abused children are often threatened by their abusers with disapproval and blame from a parent or parents or physical harm to themselves or others if they disclose the abuse. Such threats are likely to produce anxiety, guilt, and anger that exacerbate existing personality problems. If the abuser is the child's parent, guilt, self-blame, and problems in trusting others are often preeminent themes. The assessment should identify these themes in order to select target behaviors or feelings for modification and to discern transferential implications for the conduct of therapy.

Many children are reluctant to discuss sexual abuse. When abuse is documented, it is important that the therapist gauge the child's level of acceptance and disclosure in relation to the abuse, and to proceed with an appropriately cautious attitude, respectful of the child's needs for privacy, esteem, and control of the relationship. The therapist should make full use of collateral information sources (e.g., social-service agencies, family members) and, if possible, not place the onus solely on the child for disclosing details of the abuse. Indeed, even when abuse has been disclosed, the child may not reveal the full extent of the abuse, minimizing the frequency, duration, and graphic details of abusive instances. In such cases, it is necessary first to establish a therapeutic alliance before tackling more difficult issues, such as feelings of loss, anger, and distorted perceptions of sexuality.

When the abuse is only suspected or alleged, or a child exhibits problems consistent with a history of sexual abuse, the therapist must take a more tentative, cautious, and evaluative approach in order to understand whether sexual abuse has in fact occurred. The focus should be on understanding the child's world without making assumptions about the perpetration of abuse. In such cases, the therapist may use storytelling techniques modified so that abuse and victimization issues are not suggested or implied. We have found it useful to give suggestions for safety and trust, and to build stories around themes of making difficult choices, knowing what and when to tell others, and coping with guilty or embarrassed feelings. Thus, the child is provided with permission to disclose whatever he or she wishes, while attention is focused on relationship building and symptom reduction. Given the possibility of pseudomemory creation (Laurence & Perry, 1983), if compelling evidence of abuse is not forthcoming, the therapist should exercise caution about suggesting or implying its occurrence.

The therapist ought to be concerned with identifying target symptoms for intervention and determining the child's appropriateness and readiness for hypnotic techniques. Hypnotic techniques rely heavily on fantasy-based, imaginative activities. The child's natural imaginative abilities provide a crucible for the healing process. A developmental history can furnish useful data about the child's ability to become involved in imaginative activities. In this regard, information about preferred play activities, degree of fantasy involvement, absorption in fairy tales and stories, and the use of imaginary companions is helpful.

Certain children do not feel comfortable with or are unable to exploit relaxation, guided imagery, and storytelling techniques. For instance, children with an attention-deficit disorder, with or without hyperactivity, tend to be poor candidates for hypnotherapy. They have difficulty maintaining the focused attention and imaginative involvement requisite to imagery-based therapy. Rather, they are more likely to benefit from a play or art therapy in which they can express themselves through physical activity, and can move from activity to activity quickly enough to accommodate their attentional style. Similarly, mentally retarded children, those with neurological disorders, and autistic or severely disturbed children may derive greater benefit from other therapies because of their cognitive deficits, loss of contact with reality, or limited imaginal abilities.

HYPNOTHERAPY WITH SEXUALLY ABUSED CHILDREN

Hypnotherapy proceeds in a stepwise fashion. Building a *safe context* within which feelings about the abuse can be explored is prerequisite to successful hypnotherapy with sexually abused children. Indeed, one of the most important tasks of the therapist is to help the sexually abused child rebuild a trusting relationship with adults. The therapist must be perceived as a trustworthy ally of the child. Because abuse can rend the fragile web of trust with adults, it is vital that the therapist exhibit a flexible, positive, and accepting attitude toward the child. Fortunately, hypnotherapeutic techniques lend themselves to the establishment of a sense of security by permitting the child to proceed at a comfortable, self-controlled pace, and to enter and withdraw from the fantasy environment as needed.

Not infrequently, children disclose the details of abuse gradually over a number of sessions. They often attempt to gauge the therapist's reaction to symbolic or "actual" accounts of abusive events. Implicit or explicit pressures to get the whole story of the abuse "out" are likely to engender resistance. One effective way of encouraging children to talk about themselves and difficult subject matter is to ask the child to recount a favorite story. Fears can be shared and conquered, anger expressed, revenge extracted, sorrow experienced, and loss mourned, if not on a literal, then on a symbolic level. The child can control the imaginal representation of a feared situation associated with abuse that emerges in the story and become desensitized to it by way of repetition. Suggestions for imaginal separation from the situation may be initiated by the child or the therapist if anxiety becomes too great. As the child becomes emotionally secure and can express feelings associated with the abuse with less need for distancing, we give direct suggestions to promote a stronger, unified sense of self and wholeness. Therapeutic work can be conducted with less threat or stress to the child than evoked by reality-based therapies.

The storytelling technique also enhances the therapist's flexibility. For example, the therapist can participate by introducing comforting or protective guardians such as Gandalf, the kindly wizard, E.T., or a 10-foot-high velveteen rabbit to alleviate the child's anxiety if characters in the "story" are hurt, molested, or "bothered." The child may designate the therapist in the role of ally and protector.

In building a safe haven, we encourage the child to describe his or her favorite place, the place where the child is happiest and feels safe, regardless of whether it is an actual place or a fantasized, idealized place. We have encountered a wide range of favorite places: castles with moats, underground "hideouts," treehouses, spaceships, tanks, an underwater cave protected by friendly dolphins, and a large, green metal box on wheels that seemed to resemble a habitable dumpster. We then suggest that the child fill this place with the trappings and/or creatures that he or she likes best. Plump, friendly, stuffed animals abound in these environments, as do family pets, imaginary companions, and occasional articles of self-defense. In working with very anxious children, an imaginary gate may be added so that the child determines who enters and exits.

We give the child full control of all aspects of the story, including whether he or she visits the favorite place alone or is accompanied by us. However, as needed, we intersperse suggestions for relaxation, comfort, and security, as well as such questions as, "How can you feel even better in this place?" Furthermore, we have found it useful to suggest props or devices, such as magic wands, rings, or magic words with special powers, in order to explore the child's wishes ("What three wishes would you like to be granted?") or to create certain effects such as relaxation or amnesia for selected events ("When the magic wand touches you, you will forget everything about . . . , it will seem as if you dreamed it all, only to recall it perfectly when the magic wand touches you again"). Flying horses, magic carpets, and rocket ships, for example, can serve as escape vehicles when needed by a frightened child. And special clothing, such as a suit of armor or a suit with a "disappearing, vanishing button," can create a buffer zone between the child and an overwhelming or oppressive environment.

As this sort of fantasy becomes more familiar and comfortable, the child is encouraged to introduce new stories, from the safety of the favorite place. The therapist begins to tell stories involving children and adults and to have the child suggest various plot endings. Over sessions, the therapist's stories begin to take on a more realistic quality, with issues of trust, fear, hurt, guilt, love, caring, and anger introduced. Nevertheless, the child is encouraged to bring imaginary protectors if he or she feels they are needed. As rapport with the therapist builds, the child is encouraged to relate stories of real-life events that have happened to the child or the child's friends. The child's stories are not questioned; no effort is made to have the child disclose to whom the described events happened. Moreover, interpretation of the meaning of the stories is typically initiated by nondirective questioning or by following the child's insightful remarks.

A second goal of hypnotherapy is the restoration of a sense of personal power and control. In a sexually abusive relationship, the child experiences a loss of power to a dominant, manipulative abuser and a concurrent loss of self-esteem. The child's freedom to control the story and "make it what you want" is emphasized from the outset. The child is also granted power to choose among various stories for the therapist to tell or to choose a story in which the child and therapist alternate in assuming responsibility for the narrative. With practice, working and reworking the feelings and conflicts surrounding the abuse, and the therapist's attention lavished on the child's imaginal creations, the child typically experiences enhanced self-esteem, feelings of mastery, and positive response expectancies about the outcome of therapy that are, not infrequently, mirrored in the stories' contents.

As the child is able to tolerate more direct reference to issues of abuse, the therapist's stories begin to tackle difficult issues, such as the child's right to control who touches his or her body. The child may be asked to suggest stories that would help other abused children know what to do if someone wants to touch them inappropriately or asks the child to touch them inappropriately.

A third goal of hypnotherapy is the reduction of feelings of self-blame, shame, or badness, or of being damaged or broken. For many sexually abused children, a period of two to three years elapses before they disclose the abuse. Abusers often admonish the child not to tell, explaining that the abuse must remain "our secret" (Justice & Justice, 1979). The rationale for this "secret" often takes one of two forms: either the child will get into trouble and be seen as "bad" for allowing sexual intercourse to occur, or the child will get the abuser into trouble instead of protecting his or her parent or friend.

The longer the secret is kept and the sexual contact continues, the greater is the sense of badness. Not infrequently, body-image distortion ensues, with the child seeing himself or herself as damaged and believing that anyone who discovers the secret will apprehend the damage. When the secret is revealed, the child may project guilt onto others, fearing blame by adults for permitting the abuse to continue. In worst-case scenarios, adults actually do blame the child for provoking or tolerating the abuse. In such cases, the child's feelings of guilt and shame are confirmed.

In these circumstances, we recast the child's problem as an irresolute dilemma in which the best possible decision was made. This message is conveyed in story form. The child interacts with imaginary characters who are in situations analogous to those of the abused child, gives them advice, helps them not to blame themselves, and teaches them about what adults should and should not do. The story also challenges the child's perception of badness and uses metaphors to promote insight. Examples include conveying the idea that getting rid of guilt feelings is like getting rid of germs, and that children who have had their tonsils removed require time to recover, just as abused children require time to recover from the effects of abuse. The therapist emphasizes the point that, in each case, the children will eventually feel better.

A fourth therapeutic goal is to promote a sense of wellness and good health. Children who have been sexually abused seem to experience a lowered resistance to stress and a difficulty in coping with frequent or sudden change. They appear to be at risk for developing physical and psychological problems that manifest as vaginal and urinary-tract problems, yeast and ear infections, and a number of psychophysiological illnesses (Adams-Tucker, 1982; Sgroi, 1982; Yates, 1982). Trauma, including that produced by sexual abuse, has been theoretically linked to immune-system suppression, although the evidence is inconclusive (Walker & Bolkotavz, 1988).

The storytelling format can be used to provide suggestions for bodily integrity and good health. Also, we use guided imagery and hyperemperic suggestions (Gibbons, 1979) to teach children how to produce a sense of well-being and relaxation to counteract the effects of stress associated with abuse. Finally, we have found it useful to tell stories about how other children have coped with physical and psychological problems similar to those of the abused child.

A fifth therapeutic goal is to resolve sexual issues. Finkelhor and Browne (1985) use the term "traumatic sexualization" to refer to the process resulting from sexual abuse by which the child's sexuality is molded in a developmentally inappropriate and dysfunctional pattern. Sexually abused children are confronted with adult sexual behaviors prematurely. Those who experience physical pain as a result of the sexual abuse may develop an association between fear and sex. In such cases, the child may require the therapist's help to separate physical affection, and later sexuality, from pain.

However, in most cases of sexual abuse, the child has experienced minimal physical pain; instead, sexual behaviors have frequently been paired with positive physical sensations, statements of affection and love, and a peculiar specialness because the child learns that sexual activities earn extra attention and material goods. The therapist may be faced with a child who has acquired an inappropriate repertoire of sexual behavior, is confused about his or her sexual self-concept, and imputes unusual emotional associations to sexual activities. Storytelling may be employed to help the child learn appropriate ways of earning material rewards via nonsexual means. Initially, fantasy/cartoon characters may be used in scenarios in which the characters strive to gain rewards, such as a new spaceship or a glowing purple turtle. Gradually, the therapist develops more realistic stories of children whose experiences are analogous to those of the abused child. Suggestion and repetition are used to bond positive emotions to age-appropriate methods of coping. Ultimately, sexuality is recast as a gift, not a commodity.

THE CASE OF LEAH

Leah, age 8, was sexually abused by a male baby-sitter weekly over a period of about one year. Abuse consisted of fondling, oral sex, and masturbation. The baby-sitter had repeatedly told Leah that she must keep their "secret," and that her mother would be angry at her if she told. Leah revealed the situation to her mother when the baby-sitter attempted to have intercourse with her. At the time she began in therapy, Leah was irritable and withdrawn, had nightmares, and cried over seemingly minor issues. Charges had been filed against the baby-sitter and Leah had testified before a grand jury at his indictment, an event that proved extremely stressful for her, and she was likely to have to testify again at his trial, which was scheduled to begin in about three months.

Session 2

THERAPIST: Hello, Leah, it's good to see you. How are you today?

LEAH: [Silence]

THERAPIST: I understand that you've had a pretty tough time lately. It must have been difficult to tell your mother about your baby-sitter's behavior.

LEAH: I hate him and I never want to see him again.

THERAPIST: Sounds like you're pretty angry with him and you sure have a right to be. I want to help you feel better. Your mom says that you've not been having much fun lately.

LEAH: I'm afraid that he's going to come to my house and do something to me. He's mad cause I told. Last night I thought I saw him looking in my bedroom window. It was real dark, but I heard something.

THERAPIST: Your mom tells me that he is in jail, but it sounds like you're still pretty worried.

LEAH: I don't want to talk about it no more [crying].

THERAPIST: I can understand that it's hard to talk about. So, instead let's talk about what we're going to do with the rest of our time today and each time we meet. OK?

LEAH: Yeah, I guess so. [Still crying, little interest.]

THERAPIST: I'm going to tell you a story.

LEAH: A story, that's all? I don't have to tell you what he did? [Looks surprised, crying ceases.]

THERAPIST: All you have to do is to listen very closely. You don't need to say anything if you don't want to. Do you have a good imagination?

LEAH: I guess so.

THERAPIST: Do you like fairy tales or stories about animals or cartoons?

LEAH: My mom used to read me stories, but she doesn't any more. I guess I'm too old.

THERAPIST: Well, I like to tell stories and I'm a lot older than you.

LEAH: Yeah, you are.

THERAPIST: OK, get comfortable because I'm going to tell you a story about my favorite place. Next time we meet, you can tell me about your favorite place. It can be real or imaginary and you can make it anything you like. But now I'm going to tell you about a magic cottage. You can shut your eyes to see it better or leave them open.

LEAH: [Eyes open, watching therapist intently] I want them open.

THERAPIST: Good, you can use them to help me see the cottage clearly. Add anything you see in case I miss something. First, we have to go through the gate to enter the magic path. Here, let's both hold out our hands, palms up, so we can find the big key to the gate. Can you see it in your hand?

LEAH: Yeah, it's heavy.

THERAPIST: Do you want to use it to unlock the gate?

LEAH: Yeah [giggles]. This is funny.

THERAPIST: Thanks for opening the gate. Let's walk down the path. Do you want to hold my hand?

LEAH: No, I'll just walk beside you.

THERAPIST: Well, we'll walk along here by the tall trees. I really like looking at the flowers. Let's stop and smell them. They're so pretty. Which one are you smelling?

LEAH: A yellow one.

THERAPIST: Yes, that one's lovely. Do you want to pick it?

LEAH: [Nods yes.]

THERAPIST: Go ahead. You can bring it with you to the cottage. It isn't very far, just ahead in the clearing. It's built of wood and looks a bit like a gingerbread cottage.

LEAH: Well, just as long as there are no witches.

THERAPIST: No, we can make it just what we want and allow only friends to visit it.

Leah quickly became involved in the therapy process. During visits to the enchanted cottage, which she adopted almost from the outset as her own, her affect was bright, and she arranged and rearranged toys, school supplies, and kitchen appliances. During the fourth session, she began to talk about her room at home and then spontaneously spoke of the baby-sitter and how he would take a nap with her in her room. She responded to several questions from the therapist (she had previously been extremely reluctant to discuss the abuse at all), and then returned to "her" room in the enchanted cottage. During the next several sessions, she progressively disclosed feelings toward the abuser and his requests of her. Just before the 14th session, Leah and her mother were informed by the court that the trial was beginning and that Leah's testimony would be needed within the next week. Her anxiety was visible from the time she arrived for the session.

Session 14

LEAH: [Clutching her stuffed dog] I don't want to walk. You [therapist] carry me to the cottage.

THERAPIST: It seems like you need some support today. Well, suppose we take a magic-carpet ride to the cottage. What kind of rug would you like to ride on?

LEAH: A red fluffy one.

THERAPIST: You may feel so relaxed that you decide to close your eyes during the carpet ride or you can leave them open. Sometimes you can see the carpet better with them closed.

LEAH: [Closing eyes and then opening them again] How will we know when we get to the cottage if our eyes are closed? We might miss it.

THERAPIST: Rex, your stuffed dog, can ride in the front and keep his eyes open. Sometimes things that seem hard can be solved easily when we work together.

LEAH: OK, let's go. [When she arrived at the cottage, Leah busied herself "cooking a meal."]

LEAH: Here, you stupid old judge, I'll throw the pot at you.

THERAPIST: Is this the judge who will be at the trial?

LEAH: Yeah, and that stupid Mr. X [the defendant's attorney]. I hate him. He said I made it all up [at the grand jury hearing]. And Y [the abuser] is going to be looking at me. I'll hit them all with the pans in my kitchen.

THERAPIST: Let's plan how to make going to court better.

LEAH: Yeah, but all those people will be looking at me, and I don't like to say what he did.

THERAPIST: Well, perhaps we need to provide you with a magic suit so that those words and questions can't hurt you. That way, you will be able to listen to them and answer whatever they ask, but you'll know that the questions and looks can't really get to you.

LEAH: I know what I want—a suit of armor. I saw a guy wearing one on TV last night.

THERAPIST: OK, an imaginary suit of armor for you. You can put on these pieces as I hand them to you. First, here are the pieces for your feet. You can just put them over your shoes. Now, a long piece over each leg. See, they're not too heavy, but they make you feel really secure. OK, here's one for your back and one for your front. Good. Do you want a helmet with a faceplate?

LEAH: Yeah, one that opens and closes, in case I want a soft drink [giggles].

THERAPIST: Now, run your hand over the suit and tell me what it feels like.

LEAH: It's smooth and shiny. I like it.

THERAPIST: Can any words get through it, do you think? If so, we can make it stronger.

LEAH: No, I like it just the way it is. I can see my reflection in it [holding arms up in front of her]. I look pretty tough, don't you think so?

THERAPIST: Tough, without a doubt. You can wear it during court and no one else will see it. But it will protect you and you will be able to feel safe and relaxed and think carefully about your answers.

LEAH: Yeah, and that judge will be real impressed, won't he?

Leah testified without becoming unduly upset. She later modified the armor suit so that it was all in one piece and required only being zipped up in the front. She felt it was easier if she didn't always need help putting it on. Over the next six months of therapy, the therapist worked with her to improve her self-image. She felt that others could tell that she had been "touched," and she was extremely fearful that the other girls in her Brownie troop would find out and that no one would like her. The therapist also taught Leah techniques for saying "No" and asserting herself if anyone else should try to touch her inappropriately. This was done by asking Leah's advice and, sometimes, having her talk directly to imaginary children with problems who visited her in the cottage and had fears or problems that she could help to resolve. During this time, her school grades improved and her behavior at home returned to what her mother described as "the old Leah." At the 38th session, termination was discussed, although Leah was given choices as to whether to continue seeing the therapist every two or three weeks. During this period, Leah locked the cottage and gave the therapist the key, "just in case." After seeing Leah less and less frequently over the next four months, the therapist asked Leah how she would like to spend their final session. She decided on a party with cake and ice cream.

ASSESSMENT OF OUTCOME

Assessment is an ongoing process. Indeed, the child's behavior and response to hypnotic procedures should be carefully monitored over the course of treatment. The use of hypnotic techniques must be tailored to each child's unique needs. The therapist needs to exhibit considerable flexibility and sensitivity to the child's responses so that suggestions given and the story narrative's tone, affect, imagery, and pacing facilitate imaginative involvement.

An ongoing assessment should evaluate the child's progress vis-à-vis treatment goals and monitor the degree to which relevant target behaviors and issues have been resolved. Rather than rigidly compacting therapy into a set time frame or number of sessions, an ongoing evaluation of the child's degree of distress, needs, and strengths dictates the investment and time spent in each step of therapy. Indeed, prolonged or more intensive therapy is likely to be required in cases involving severe abuse. In making decisions about terminating therapy, the therapist needs to evaluate the child's symptom picture, level of overall coping, and social and emotional development. We believe that the establishment of "insight" into complex emotional issues is unnecessary and unworkable for many children. Keeping children in therapy for many years risks making the abuse a never-ending issue that defies resolution. When the therapist feels that the child is functioning at a developmentally appropriate level, and when the child no longer exhibits symptoms that hamper his or her functioning, it is appropriate to terminate therapy.

CONCLUDING COMMENTS

Although we have had good success with the treatment we have described, we have not conducted a systematic investigation of its efficacy. In the absence of a controlled investigation, it is premature to suggest that our approach is superior to any number of other therapeutic interventions for treating the sexually abused child. At present, the boundary conditions of imagery-based therapies and the limits of their applicability are relatively amorphous and undefined. Moreover, storytelling, guided imagery, and direct suggestion cannot be applied profitably in the absence of a theory-driven understanding of the child's conflicts and the behavioral and dynamic meaning of the abuse-related symptoms. Nevertheless, it is our hope that the hypnotherapeutic procedures we have delineated will provide the sensitive clinician with a valuable inroad into the experiential world of the abused child and with a vehicle for intervening in the troubled child's behalf.

REFERENCES

Adams-Tucker, C. (1982). Proximate effects of sexual abuse in childhood: A report on 28 children. *American Journal of Psychiatry, 139*, 1252–1256.

Asher, S. J. (1988). The effects of childhood sexual abuse: A review of the issues and evidence. In L. E. A. Walker (Ed.), *Handbook on sexual abuse of children*. New York: Springer.

Brandt, R., & Tisza, V. (1977). The sexually misused child. *American Journal of Orthopsychiatry, 44*, 80–87.

Browne, A. & Finkelhor, D. (1986). Impact of child sexual abuse: A review of the research. *Psychological Bulletin, 99*, 1, 66–77.

Dempster, C. R., & Balson, P. M. (1982). Hypnotherapy of the victim experience. Presented at Ninth International Congress of Hypnosis and Psychosomatic Medicine, Glasgow, Scotland.

Ebert, B. W. (1988). Hypnosis and rape victims. *American Journal of Clinical Hypnosis, 31*, 50–56.

Finkelhor, D. (1984). *Child sexual abuse: New theory and research*. New York: Free Press.

Finkelhor, D. & Browne, A. (1985). The traumatic impact of child sexual abuse: A conceptualization. *American Journal of Orthopsychiatry, 55*, 530–541.

Gardner, G., & Olness, K. (1981). *Hypnosis and hypnotherapy with children*. New York: Grune & Stratton.

Gibbons, D. E. (1979). *Applied hypnosis and hyperemperia*. New York: Plenum.

Gomes-Schwartz, B., Horowitz, J. M., & Sauzier, M. (1985). Severity of emotional distress among sexually abused preschool, school-age, and adolescent children. *Hospital and Community Psychiatry, 36*, 503–508.

Herman, J. (1981). *Father-daughter incest*. Cambridge, MA: Harvard University Press.

Hilgard, J. R. (1970). *Personality and hypnosis, a study of imaginative involvement*. Chicago: University of Chicago Press.

Hilgard, J. R. (1979). *Personality and hypnosis, a study of imaginative involvement* (2nd ed.). Chicago: University of Chicago Press.

Hilgard, J. R., & LeBaron, S. (1984). *Hypnotherapy of pain in children with cancer*. Los Altos, CA: Kaufman.

Hilgard, E. R. (1986). *Divided consciousness: Multiple controls in human thought and actions*. New York: Wiley.

Justice, B., & Justice, R. (1979). *The broken taboo: Sex in the family*. New York: Human Sciences Press.

Kuttner, L. (1988). Favorite stories: A hypnotic pain-reduction technique for children in acute pain. *American Journal of Clinical Hypnosis, 30*, 289–295.

Laurence, J. R., & Perry, C. W. (1983). Hypnotically created memories among highly hypnotizable subjects. *Science, 222*, 523–524.

London, P., Morgan, A. H., & Hilgard, E. R. (1973). Age differences in susceptibility to hypnosis. *International Journal of Clinical and Experimental Hypnosis, 21*, 78–85.

Lynn, S. J., & Rhue, J. W. (1988). Fantasy proneness: Hypnosis, developmental antecedents, and psychopathology. *American Psychologist, 43*, 35–44.

MacHovec, F. J. (1984). The use of brief hypnosis for posttraumatic stress disorders. *Emotional First Aid, 1*, 14–22.

Nash, M. R., Lynn, S. J., & Givens, D. L. (1984). Adult hypnotic susceptibility, childhood punishment and child abuse: A brief communication. *International Journal of Clinical and Experimental Hypnosis, 32*, 1, 6–11.

Nash, M. J., & Lynn, S. J. (1986). Child abuse and hypnotic ability. *Journal–Imagination, Cognition, and Personality, 5*, 211–217.

O'Grady, D. J., & Hoffmann, C. (1984). Hypnosis with children and adolescents in the medical setting. In W. Wester & A. Smith (Eds.), *Clinical hypnosis: A multidisciplinary approach*. Philadelphia: Lippincott.

Rhue, J. W., & Lynn, S. J. (1986). Fantasy proneness and psychopathology. *Journal of Personality and Social Psychology, 53*, 327–336.

Rhue, J. W., & Lynn, S. J. (1990). *Child abuse, imagination, and hypnotizability*. Manuscript submitted for publication.

Russell, D. (1983). The incidence and prevalence of intrafamilial and extrafamiliar sexual abuse of female children. *Child Abuse and Neglect, 7*, 133–146.

Sgroi, S. M. (1982). A conceptual framwork for child sexual abuse. In S. M. Sgroi (Ed.), *Handbook of clinical intervention in child sexual abuse*. Lexington, MA: Lexington Books.

Walker, L. E. A., & Bolkovatz, M. A. (1988). Play therapy with children who have experienced sexual assault. In L. E. A. Walker (Ed.), *Handbook on Sexual Abuse of Children*. New York: Springer.

Wilson, S. C., & Barber, T. X. (1983). The fantasy-prone personality: Implications for understanding imagery, hypnosis, and parapsychological phenomena. In A. A. Sheikh (Ed.), *Imagery: Current theory, research, and application* (pp. 340–390). New York: Wiley.

Yates, A. (1982). Children eroticized by incest. *American Journal of Psychiatry, 139*, 482–485.

7 Habits

William C. Wester II, Ed.D.

The treatment of habit disorders in children can be fun and rewarding. It can be fun because most children are excellent hypnotic subjects who can get excited about induction techniques, behavioral charts, and rewards. It can be rewarding because the success rate is high.

How do we define a habit? A habit is "a constant, often unconscious, inclination to perform an act, acquired through its frequent repetition" (*American Heritage Dictionary*, 1985).

Just like a child's old "blankie," an undesired habit may be difficult to discard. In the child, hypnosis can be used to treat such conditions as intractable coughing, tongue thrusting, bruxism, hairpulling, sleepwalking, speech problems, tics, thumb sucking, stammering, stuttering, encopresis, nail biting, enuresis, overeating, substance abuse, self-stimulatory behaviors such as rocking and head banging, and other undesirable habits.

Although emotional issues may perpetuate or initiate some habits, many may never have been associated with significant psychological factors. Other habits that once may have served an important function may have outlived their usefulness, only to "inhabit" the child. This later phenomenon may also be called "empty habit."

The therapist must determine whether the habit serves an important function before proceeding with hypnosis as the treatment of choice. Other pre-treatment questions to be considered would include: Is the child personally motivated to change the habit behavior? Are there certain developmental issues to be considered as in thumb sucking or enuresis? Is the child receiving significant secondary gain for exhibiting this habit? If there is a major psychodynamic issue present, should other psychotherapies alone, or perhaps coupled with hypnosis, be used? Judicious and effective utilization of hypnosis therefore requires thoughtful and careful inquiry.

Three strategies are frequently recommended when treating habits with hypnotherapy. First, the therapist should be familiar with the various ways to use a symptom as described by Minuchin (1974). These include (1) focusing on the symptom, (2) exaggerating the symptom, (3) deemphasizing the symptom, (4) shifting to another symptom, and (5) relabeling the symptom.

Second, the therapist can use a direct (suggestion) technique to remove the symptom. Though symptom substitution is frequently talked about in clinical practice, it is rarely encountered (Conn, 1961; Gardner & Olness, 1981). This strategy would suggest that the child no longer needs the habit, accepts the suggestions, and allows the symptom to be removed.

Third, the therapist can utilize ideomotor signaling. This approach is not an absolute predictor of the child's readiness to eliminate a habit; however, answers with ideomotor signals to questions about the desire to give up the habit can be extremely helpful. The ability to talk about how life would be different without the habit and to imagine the desired outcome while in hypnosis are alternative approaches (Reaney, 1984).

BASIC FOUNDATIONS

Haley (1976) believes that therapeutic directives can bring about successful change. The therapist may tell the child to stop doing something and, if all conditions are good, the habit may stop. However, this approach often increases resistance. The therapist can also tell the child to do something different. This approach is less successful when it consists of just giving good advice and more successful when it directs change in the usual sequence of events. And, finally, one can direct a paradoxical task, such as telling the child to do something the therapist does not want the child to do, because the therapist wants the child to change the behavior by rebelling.

As the definition of habit implies, a habit is "acquired" by frequent "repetition." The definition clearly suggests that a habit is a learned or conditioned response. If one follows a learning and/or behavioral model in the treatment of habit disorders, then other research becomes quite significant. Cautela (1975) uses an operant conditioning framework in which imagery is manipulated to modify behaviors. This process is labeled "covert conditioning." Children are first asked to imagine a particular response and then to imagine receiving various stimuli. There are four basic covert-conditioning techniques. "Covert sensitization" means that the child is asked to imagine a maladaptive response followed by a noxious stimulus (e.g., eating ice cream followed by nausea in the obese child). "Covert positive reinforcement" is the technique whereby imagined adaptive responses are rewarded by imagined pleasant thoughts (e.g., resisting the urge to eat ice cream followed by a very pleasant thought, or what the child perceives as a reward). When the child reports that nothing is reinforcing, then "covert negative reinforcement" might be used. An aversive scene is imagined and is then relieved by a shift to imagining the desired adaptive behavior (e.g., a fearful child imagines being confronted by the fear stimulus and is only relieved by next imagining the adaptive behavior of walking down the street or playing with friends on a beautiful day).

Finally, the behaviors being reinforced by situations or others outside the therapist's control, "covert extinction" may be used. The child imagines performing the undesirable behavior and then imagines no response in the environment (e.g., a child imagines thumb sucking to compete with a younger sibling for attention, and then imagines getting no response or attention from parents).

Additional research will be cited as several of the habit behaviors are further examined.

OBESITY

Unsuccessful results of hypnotherapy with eight obese adolescents were reported by Haber, Nitkin, and Shenker (1979). Aversive response to fattening foods, positive self-esteem, maintenance of an appropriate diet, and increased exercise were suggested. Four patients were not responsive to hypnotic induction. Three of the other four experienced negative effects, including increased anxiety, dissociative behavior, and feelings of depersonalization. Peculiar patient characteristics may have been responsible for the problems. This author has treated many obese children. While many do not reach goal weights, no negative effects have been observed as described by Haber and colleagues (1979).

Kohen, Olness, Colwell, and Heimel (1984) report on a group of 500 children with behavior problems who were treated with hypnotherapy. Of this group, five children who were obese lost weight during periods when they practiced self-hypnosis, and one child maintained significant weight reduction. The specific suggestions used were to visualize looking thinner, buying smaller sizes, enjoying eating the appropriate amount of food for correct weight and health, seeing one's height and weight as compatible on a group chart, and feeling comfortable between meals without eating snacks.

In addition to the suggestions noted above, I incorporate several behavior techniques. My suggestions are developed from the child's stated motivations as elicited during the clinical interview. The child keeps a behavior chart and records an "X" for all "great" days. A child who overeats or eats something inappropriate must mark on the chart what was eaten and at what time. A weight graph is kept and the child is given a list of specific behavioral tasks, such as always eating in the same place when at home, eating more slowly, and waiting 10 minutes if he or she feels like eating something inappropriate. The child brings all of these data along at the next visit. On the second visit, I record the hypnotic session and prescribe that the tape be used at least once every other day. On the third visit, I record the flip side of the tape in order to allow for some variety as the child develops a self-hypnotic model. Sessions are held at three-week intervals, and the child only weighs in once a week.

ENURESIS AND ENCOPRESIS

Although in some cases there is a delay in acquiring the ability to inhibit urination during the night, most children do so early in life. Of those who do not, 65 percent of enuretics treated have shown improvement through hypnotic techniques (Crasilneck & Hall, 1985). In one common technique, the hypnotized child is touched in the bladder area and pressure applied while he or she is told, "When you experience this sensation of pressure in your bladder, your sleep will be immediately interrupted and you will go to the bathroom in a light sleep and urinate." In another technique, the child is not touched, but is told, "When you begin to feel a pressure in your bladder, you will immediately awaken, go to the bathroom, and void."

In a recent study, Edwards and Van Der Spuy (1985) assessed the efficacy of hypnotherapy in the treatment of nocturnal enuresis in boys aged 8–13 years. Treatment consisted of six weekly standardized sessions. Results indicate that hypnotherapy was significantly effective over six months in decreasing nocturnal enuresis, compared with both pretreatment enuresis frequency and no-treatment controls.

Much emphasis has been placed on the psychological concomitants of fecal incontinence (Claydon & Lawson, 1976; Halpern, 1977). The original cause is more often physical than psychological, although there is no doubt that many secondary emotional problems develop in a child with this symptom. The first step should always be a thorough medical evaluation.

It is important for the child to be given some responsibility in the treatment of his or her problem (Fleisher, 1976). The mechanical components are unlikely to be affected by hypnotherapy alone in patients who have had the problem for many years (Olness & Gardner, 1988). Hypnosis can be helpful in eliminating some of the psychological factors surrounding this undesirable habit and gives the child personal responsibility and the opportunity to remain in control of his or her bowels.

Some children who have had long-term soiling will continue to have some residual soiling even though they learn to defecate regularly. This could be due to long-term stretching of the anorectal sphincters.

For a more complete discussion of enuresis and encopresis and the use of hypnosis in the treatment of these problems, the reader is referred to Chapter 16.

NAIL BITING

Although not injurious to one's health, nail biting can be annoying. Often accentuated by anxiety, it usually begins in the grade-school years. Many treatments have already been tried by the time a person turns to hypnosis, including parental nagging and bitter solutions placed on the fingers.

The relaxed state produced by hypnosis may be enough to interrupt an anxiety nail-biting pattern. Children can learn to switch from nail biting to the pleasant images of a favorite place, and posthypnotically will have a heightened awareness of the hand raising toward the mouth. In older adolescent girls, images of long, polished nails help assure the outcome. Overcoming the habit through powers of imagination also gives the child a sense of mastery and control (Reaney, 1984).

Kroger (1977) tells patients to bite one nail on each hand instead of all the nails. From left to right and back again, each of these two nails is bitten tooth by tooth, and the growth of the other nails is praised. Children may be given indirect suggestions such as, "They're all chewed so nice and short. Have you ever chewed on a nice, long nail? They're the best. I wonder which nail will be the first to grow?"

Also useful in overcoming a nail-biting habit is covert conditioning. Sector (1961) reported success in covert sensitization with imagery of revolting scenes each time the child bit his or her nails, reinforcing appropriate nonbiting behavior with pleasant images. Aversive stimuli such as bitter tastes and nausea can be suggested whenever nails are bitten.

In my own practice, I find it useful to take pictures of the child's nails at each visit in order to reinforce success.

THUMB SUCKING

Whereas normal in early childhood, representing a need for oral gratification, when thumb sucking continues into a later age, it can cause shame and social embarrassment (Morban-Laucer, 1961). If thumb sucking persists beyond the first year of school, professional attention is warranted, particularly if it is causing the child notable embarrassment or if it is a source of conflict between parent and child.

The therapist can use both an emotional and an intellectual approach by explaining that prolonged thumb sucking may destroy the curvature of the teeth, requiring future orthodontic correction. After eliciting the child's feelings about his or her appearance, an appeal is made to the child's desire to be more attractive and mature.

An interview under hypnosis, utilizing either age regression to the time when thumb sucking would ordinarily have been given up as an outworn habit or the fantasized theater technique, can ascertain if there is an underlying traumatic or symbolic base for the thumb sucking. Working through them must become a primary goal of treatment if such dynamics are uncovered (Crasilneck & Hall, 1985). The child is told under hypnosis that the thumb will begin to taste bitter, and that this will act as a reminder that he or she no longer wishes to suck the thumb, the bitter taste motivating him or her to remove the habit. Because the symptom has usually become a focus of hostile interaction between the child and parents, any improvement warrants immediate and ample praise. Control of this problem is quite often maintained through self-hypnosis (Crasilneck & Hall, 1985).

SPEECH AND VOICE PROBLEMS

According to Barbara (1959), the theories of stuttering are varied, ranging from psychological to purely neurological and even sociological. Often, simply a careful personal recollection is all that is required for cases in which there is not deep repression. It is not always possible to understand the actual situation out of which the stuttering or stammering arose. Sometimes, a single traumatic situation triggers the stuttering.

It is felt that hypnosis offers some unique aids to the treatment of speech disorders, although there is no question that many stutterers greatly improve with speech therapy and conventional psychotherapy (Crasilneck & Hall, 1985). Hypnosis itself has a calming and tranquilizing effect, and it can minimize anxiety that is sometimes heightened by uncovering information in psychotherapy. Also, under hypnosis, the child is not challenged to give up the speech disorder immediately, but instead is told that he or she will greatly improve. Next, more general suggestions are given for feeling confident and calm when speaking, and a posthypnotic cue may be added that when the patient begins to speak, he or she will feel some of the same relaxation and well-being that were experienced during the hypnotic state. Finally, self-hypnotic techniques are taught to the stutterer to be utilized daily. The outcome of hypnotherapy in stuttering has been reported as moderate to marked improvement (Granone, 1966; Rousey, 1961).

Defects of articulation can also be treated hypnotically. Focusing on imaginative use of fairy tales, folklore, and symbols was Silber's (1973) hypnotherapeutic approach to children with significant problems in articulation. He describes his successful work with a 10-year-old boy seen for 26 sessions over 18 weeks. Two years later, the child continued to speak clearly. "Commitment by cooperation and participation in a creative endeavor of the imagination," said Silber, was the key to success.

Excessive shouting is frequently the major cause of voice problems in children. However, in some cases, vocal nodules or hypertrophy of the vocal bands may be the cause (Laguaite, 1976). She studied 18 children, ages 4–10 years, three of whom did not finish the treatment. Fifteen children were treated with hypnosis, with suggestions focusing on encouraging the child not to yell so much, ego strengthening, and insight-oriented procedures. All but two of the 15 showed either improvement in the appearance of the larynx or the complete disappearance of the nodules.

HAIR PULLING (Trichotillomania)

Pulling hair out of the scalp, eyebrows, or eyelashes can be defined as habitual hair pulling, or trichotillomania. It may also include ingestion of the pulled hair. There may be marked thinning, or only small areas of the scalp may be involved. Like nail biting, hair pulling may be an anxiety symptom or a manifestation of serious emotional conflicts (Reaney, 1984).

Useful in treating hair pulling are covert-conditioning procedures and suggestions for relaxation, in order to decrease anxiety and give the child or adolescent a sense of control. Many interesting hypnotic techniques are directed toward producing a new awareness of discomfort with pulling, as hair-pullers often report experiencing no habit-related pain. Galski (1981) suggested to a 26-year-old severe hair-puller that he would develop a very sensitive scalp, almost as if it had been sunburned. Feeling pain when beginning to pull his hair would elicit a relaxation response and release of the hair. When a 21-year-old showed symptoms of hair pulling, Rowen (1981) regressed the patient to the age of 7 when the symptom began. The therapist suggested that with each succeeding year, the hair pulling would become more painful.

In the children I have seen for hair pulling or "plucking" hairs out of the eyebrows, the most effective direct suggestion seems to be one associated with increasing the child's awareness of the habit. Gardner (1978) suggested increased awareness of hair-pulling behavior to an 8-year-old girl who twisted and pulled out her hair. The child was told that as soon as she lifted her hand for the purpose of pulling her hair, she would recall the phrase, "Stop, please do not hurt" from that part of her that wanted pretty hair. I have found it very effective to take pictures of the improved hair area as a positive reinforcement.

Case Study

A.S., a 7-year-old girl, presented as having an uninhibited neurogenic bladder with an incompetent urethra. Between the ages of 4 and 5, she had been hospitalized three times for cystourethroscopy examinations as a result of her recurring bladder infection. The medical diagnosis was recurrent cystitis with bacteria, but no evidence of chronic cystitis. She was put on medication and seen by her urologist on a monthly basis.

At the time of the initial interview, the child indicated that she had no urinary control and would wet several times per day and evening. The child's mother, age 35, and father, age 37, were both living, and she had one younger brother, age 3½. This child was seen on five different occasions over a four-month period for a total of two hours and 45 minutes. Treatment consisted of hypnotherapy and behavior modification.

Narrative

I would like you to close your eyes for me and just keep your eyes closed as I talk with you. I just want you to get nice and comfortable and let yourself get all relaxed. Just let your breathing become very comfortable and regular—that's right—and begin to let all of your muscles become real floppy and loose and comfortable. If I move your arm in any way, it will be real floppy and real loose. So if I pick it up and let it fall back into your lap, it will be real floppy and loose. So let yourself really relax now even more completely and, as I am talking with you, you can think of something real special. You can think of something real pleasant and nice. You will hear my voice all the time, but you can think of something real nice and special and feel loose and floppy. So if I pick up your arm [therapist lifts both arms to test] you don't even have to think of me—real loose and real floppy. I think this one is more floppy than the other one. Just real floppy—very good; even your foot is just a little floppy. [Therapist lifts a leg by the foot to test it.] Think about that real special place and tell me what you are thinking about. [Child responds: "My two dolls in my room." Therapist repeats what the child says and reinforces.] That's nice. I would like you to think about your favorite toy or game or your favorite TV show and just tell me what that is. [Child responds: "My dolls are my favorite toy."] I just want you to think of your dolls now. You can see them in your mind—those two dolls just sitting on your dresser or desk—just see them there and let yourself relax even more now—relaxed and very floppy, and you can just think about those dolls. It won't even bother you at all if I move your arm. You can just think so much about those dolls that you can be so relaxed and so comfortable. That's right. Just continue to think about those dolls now and how much fun it is to think about them, and then I want you to think about this hand [touch to left hand]. Think about your left hand for a minute and with that left hand I want you to make a fist. That's right. Make it real tight—real tight. That's right. Then relax—very good. And once again, make it real tight and then relax. All the way relaxed now—totally relaxed. Very good.

And in your mind, you can think of the muscles in your bladder. You can think of the muscles in your bladder just like you did with your fist—you can make those muscles tight and you can make those muscles relax—you can make those muscles tight and you can make those muscles relax—just like you did with your fist. Your mind is going to help you now. Your mind is going to help you in several ways so that you don't have the problem with your bladder. You are going to find that you have very good bladder control—that your mind will know when you have to go to the bathroom. And those muscles will remain very tight. There won't be any leakage at all from the bladder. You will remain dry with no leakage from the bladder. Those muscles will be tight. And then when you go to the bathroom, you will be able to let those muscles relax just like you did with your hand, and you will be able to go to the bathroom without any trouble. So all the time during the day and night, except when you feel that you have to go to the bathroom, those muscles will be tight and will keep the bladder fine. When you have to go to the bathroom and you go in the bathroom, then those muscles will relax and you will be able to go to the bathroom easily. [For several days, I also had the child use a watch with a buzzer during the day in order to get a change in the conditioned response.]

As a reminder to your mind, the watch that you have that goes off every hour will be a reminder to your mind that that's the time to go in and go to the bathroom. And you will go in the bathroom and those muscles will relax, and when the muscles relax, you will be able to go to the bathroom. As soon as you are done, then those muscles will be tight again and will close the bladder off so that there will be no leakage until the next time you have to go to the bathroom. And at least for a little while, each time the watch goes off, it will be a reminder to go in and go to the bathroom.

So just let your mind remember once again with your fist how tight you can make those muscles in the bladder [touch hand and nonverbally make the fist] nice and tight and then relaxed. That's right. Your mind will remember now how you are to do that. You will have good bladder control—you will remain dry and you are really going to feel good about that because you know that you can be in control. You have done such a good job with being in control. And you are going to be able to do that now each and every day—feeling really good about that. Just enjoy that relaxation now that you have had. Just enjoy that. Let all the feeling now come back into your body—you are going to feel good—you are going to feel in control—you are going to feel relaxed and good. Just take a couple of moments and then open your eyes. . . . When you do, you will be completely alert—feeling very good.

If you videotape a child's treatment session, take advantage of that by playing the tape for the child. Children love to see themselves on TV, and by viewing the tape, all of your procedures are reinforced.

FUTURE TRENDS

Hypnosis, after almost two centuries of episodic popularity and abandonment, is beginning to be viewed as a standard treatment tool in medicine, psychology, and dentistry. The holistic/eclectic approach is now being taught in medical school and other professional training programs. There will be continued research into new and exciting fields, such as further examining the relationship between hypnosis and the immune system.

It is my opinion that the future will see a greater emphasis on treating some children in small groups. There are many child patient populations that would fit this model, such as those with chronic pain, cancer, or phobias. We need more research to determine if these small groups can be set up in such a way that they will be just as effective as individual treatment. There are many advantages to individualized treatment; however, research is needed on other models now in order to be ready for change. Who knows what will happen as managed-health-care systems continue to make decisions for practitioners as to treatment goals and procedures.

Children are excellent hypnotic subjects when properly motivated to assume some control for their own problem. Thus, we need to continue to examine all of the variables that we see in children in order to provide the highest quality of patient care.

REFERENCES

American Heritage Dictionary (2nd ed.). (1985). Boston: Houghton Mifflin.
Barbara, D. (1959). Stuttering. In S. Arieti (Ed.), *American Handbook of Psychiatry*. New York: Basic Books.

Cautela, J. R. (1975). The use of covert conditioning in hypnotherapy. *International Journal of Clinical Experimental Hypnosis, 23,* 15.

Claydon, G. S., & Lawson, J. (1976). Investigation and management of long-standing chronic constipation in childhood. *Archives of Diseases of Childhood, 51,* 918–923.

Conn, J. H. (1961). Preparing hypnosis in general practice. *Roche Rep, 3,* 3.

Crasilneck, H. B., & Hall, J. A. (1985). *Clinical hypnosis principles and applications.* New York: Grune & Stratton.

Edwards, S. D., & Van Der Spuy, H. I. J. (1985). Hypnotherapy as a treatment for enuresis. *Journal of Child Psychology and Psychiatry, 26*(N1), 161–170.

Fleisher, D. R. (1976). The diagnosis and treatment of disorders of defecation in children. *Pediatric Annals, 5,* 700–722.

Galski, T. J. (1981). The adjunctive use of hypnosis in the treatment of trichotillomania: A case report. *American Journal of Clinical Hypnosis, 23,* 198.

Gardner, G. G. (1978). Hypnotherapy in the management of childhood habit disorders. *Journal of Pediatrics, 92,* 838–840.

Gardner, G. G., & Olness, K. (1981). *Hypnosis and hypnotherapy with children.* New York: Grune & Stratton.

Granone, F. (1966). Hypnotherapy in stuttering. *Minerva Medica (suppl. 3),* 2158–2159.

Haber, C. H., Nitkin, R., & Shenker, L. R. (1979). Adverse reactions to hypnotherapy in obese adolescents: A developmental viewpoint. *Psychiatric Quarterly, 51,* 55–63.

Haley, J. (1976). *Problemsolving therapy: New strategies for effective family therapy.* San Francisco: Jossey-Bass.

Halpern, W. I. (1977). The treatment of encopretic children. *Journal of the American Academy of Child Psychiatry, 16,* 478–499.

Kohen, D., Olness, K., Colwell, S., & Heimel, A. (1984). The use of relaxation-mental imagery (self-hypnosis) in the management of 505 pediatric behavioral encounters. *Developmental and Behavioral Pediatrics, 5,* 21–25.

Kroger, W. S. (1977). *Clinical and experimental hypnosis in medicine, dentistry, and psychology* (2nd ed.). Philadelphia: Lippincott.

Laguaite, J. K. (1976). The use of hypnosis with children with deviant voices. *International Journal of Clinical and Experimental Hypnosis, 24,* 98–104.

Minuchin, S. (1974). *Families and family therapy.* Cambridge, MA: Harvard University Press.

Morban-Laucer, F. A. (1961). Sucking habits in the child and their origins in psychological traumas. *American Journal of Clinical Hypnosis, 4,* 128.

Olness, K., & Gardner, G. G. (1988). *Hypnosis and hypnotherapy with children* (2nd ed.). Philadelphia: Grune & Stratton.

Reaney, J. B. (1984). Hypnosis in the treatment of habit disorders. In W. Wester & A. Smith (Eds.), *Clinical hypnosis: A multidisciplinary approach.* Philadelphia: Lippincott.

Rowen, R. (1981). Hypnotic age regression in the treatment of self-destructive habit: Trichotillomania. *American Journal of Clinical Hypnosis, 23,* 195.

Rousey, C. L. (1961). Hypnosis in speech pathology and audiology. *Journal of Speech and Hearing Disorders, 26,* 258–267.

Sector, I. (1961). Tongue thrust and nailbiting simultaneously treated during hypnosis: A case report. *American Journal of Clinical Hypnosis, 4,* 51.

Silber, S. (1973). Fairy tales and symbols in hypnotherapy of children with certain speech disorders. *International Journal of Clinical and Experimental Hypnosis, 21,* 272–283.

Wester, W. C. (1987). *Clinical hypnosis: A case mangement approach.* Cincinnati, OH: BSCI Publications.

Wester, W. C., & Smith, A. H. (1984). *Clinical hypnosis: A multidisciplinary approach.* Philadelphia: Lippincott.

8 Tics

Martin H. Young, Ph.D.

Tics have been the subject of scientific inquiry since 1825 (Itard) with multiple motor tics accompanied by explosive utterances first being described as a syndrome by Gilles de la Tourette in 1885. Tics are the primary feature of three disorders: Tourette's disorder (TD), chronic motor (CMTD) or chronic vocal tic disorder (CVTD), and transient tic disorder (American Psychiatric Association, 1987). Tics vary from specific and easily observable involuntary movements, independent of underlying psychopathology, to a constellation of movements that may constitute a chronic, socially disabling condition that is resistant to a wide variety of treatments (Young & Montano, 1988). As such, tic disorders represent a classical problem suitable for hypnobehavioral intervention and management. However, the application of relaxation, hypnosis, biofeedback, or analogous self-regulatory techniques for complex tic disorders is rarely mentioned in the literature (Tophoff, 1973; Clements, 1972, Friedman, 1980). As an attempt to remedy this lack of information, this chapter has five main purposes: (1) to review the relevant literature on tic disorder and the use of hypnosis in the treatment of tic disorders, with emphasis on the development of techniques that combine hypnosis and behavioral treatment (hypnobehavioral methods); (2) to describe methods of assessing a patient's motivation for treatment, tic characteristics, response to treatment, and imagery potential; (3) to describe a self-management training program for children with tic disorders; (4) to review several case studies utilizing this treatment; and (5) to discuss future directions to further our understanding of hypnosis as a treatment for tic disorders.

OVERVIEW OF TIC DISORDERS AND THEIR TREATMENT

Motor tics vary in their nature, frequency, location, and intensity; however, tics of the face, head, and neck appear to be the most common.

Common vocal tics include coughing, throat clearing, grunting, sniffing, snorting, and barking (American Psychiatric Association, 1987; Abuzzahab & Anderson, 1973, 1974; Shapiro, Shapiro, Bruun, & Sweet, 1978). TD has as its essential features multiple motor and one or more vocal tics appearing either simultaneously or at different times during the course of the illness. CMTD and CVTD have either motor or vocal tics as their main feature, but not both. In a transient tic disorder, single or multiple motor and/or vocal tics may be present, but for no longer than one year, whereas for TD, CMTD, and CVTD, the tics have to be present for more than a year.

TD, CMTD, and CVTD appear to have a similar disease course and onset, but differ in their severity and functional impairment, with TD the most severe. The median age at onset is 7 years old, with most cases beginning before the age of 14. The disease is usually lifelong, though periods of remission lasting weeks to years may occur (Shapiro et al., 1978; Comings & Comings, 1984, 1987). Studies suggest that in CMTD and CVTD, tics last an average of 11 years, with many tics remitting by 15 years of age. For TD, a similar course is noted, with a peak severity between 11 and 15 years of age. Remission in TD is often seen by 21 years of age (Shapiro et al., 1978; Torup, 1962).

The estimated prevalence rate for tic disorders ranges from 5 to 20 percent (Shapiro et al., 1978), and they appear to be three times more common in males than in females (American Psychiatric Association, 1987). Children with tic disorders have a wide range of associated features, including learning disabilities, behavioral disorders (such as attention-deficit hyperactivity disorder), panic attacks, obsessions, compulsions, schizoid behavior, depression, mania, and sleep disorders (Comings & Comings, 1987).

Research evidence suggests that TD, CMTD, or CVTD may be inherited as a simple autosomal dominant disorder (Golden, 1986). Family studies have indicated that these disorders occur in the same pedigrees, and that a patient may move from one diagnostic category to another at any time (Comings & Comings, 1984; Golden, 1986). However, a purely hereditary/biological notion of the etiology of these disorders could not fully account for the great situational variability of tics, effects of stress, or other environmental factors that are noted. A detailed review of the etiological factors in tic disorders, as well as disease characteristics, course, situational/environmental factors, associated features, and incidence, is presented by Barkley (1988).

Tic disorders have been treated by psychotherapy, drug therapy, hypnotherapy, and behavioral therapy. A recent review of the treatment literature (Turpin, 1983) concludes that psychotherapy has proved to be of limited effectiveness in the treatment of people with tics. Although the use of drugs such as haloperidol is well supported by a series of double-blind drug studies in adults (King & Ollendick, 1984), their use with children with TD is less definitive (Golden, 1984) and their side effects more disturbing. In addition, drugs have not been as successful in the treatment of transient tics, CMTD, CMVD, or atypical tic disorders (Wright, Schaeffer, & Solomons, 1979).

Turpin (1983) reviewed the treatment effects of behavior therapy with tic disorders. The most disappointing findings were obtained when massed practice techniques were employed (Yates, 1970). Several studies report well-documented treatment failures or an actual increase in tic rate with massed practice (Feldman & Werry, 1966; Canavan & Powell, 1981). Relaxation training and self-control procedures usually resulted in short-lived improvements (Goldfried & Davison, 1976; Friedman, 1980). Contingency management of tic behaviors has also led to specific effects that proved difficult to generalize outside of the training situation (Varni, Boyd, & Cataldo, 1978; Doleys & Kurtz, 1974; Miller, 1970).

A promising behavioral intervention for simple tics is a package of techniques developed by Azrin and his colleagues (Azrin & Nunn, 1973, 1977; Azrin, Nunn, & Frantz, 1980) employing habit-reversal training that involves teaching the individual to replace the tic behavior with a competing muscle response. This technique is based on the premise that tic behaviors are maintained by response chaining, lack of awareness of their occurrence, and excessive practice and social tolerance of the tics. Treatment takes place in three stages: (1) accurate discrimination and recording of tic movements (awareness training), (2) development and construction of competing muscle movements, and (3) pairing of the tic with the incompatible muscle movements. Habit-reversal treatment has been used in multiple-tic disorders (Finney, Rapoff, Hall, & Christopherson, 1983), however, each tic had to be treated separately.

Habit-reversal training does not have an impact on the uncontrollable subjective "urge" to tic noted by several authors (Bliss, 1980; Bullen & Hemsley, 1983). To address the subjective component, Bullen and Hemsley developed a variant of habit-reversal training called response prevention. Response prevention teaches the individual to prolong the time between the "urge" to tic and the tic behavior.

Hypnotherapy has been employed in a number of single-case studies, with results ranging from complete remission (Lindner & Stevens, 1967; Spithill, 1974; Storms, 1985) to temporary symptom relief (Eisenberg, Acher & Kanner, 1959; Schneck, 1960; Polites, Kruger, & Stevenson, 1965; Fernando, 1967; McKinnon, 1967). Hypnotherapy has also been described as a treatment of tics in a textbook on hypnosis (Gardner & Olness, 1981). Recently, two groups (Kohen & Botts, 1987; Young & Montano, 1988; Zahm, 1987; Young, 1989) have reported on the use of hypnotherapy (relaxation and mental-imagery techniques, or RMI) and hypnobehavioral techniques in successfully treating a series of children and adolescents with TD.

All of the single-case studies described involved adult patients. They also provide little detail on the induction techniques and hypnotic methods used to facilitate tic control. In general, they used hypnosis to obtain an abreaction and the teaching of self-hypnosis.

Gardner and Olness (1981) describe the successful use of hypnotherapy with two children with tic disorders, both of whom experienced a complete remission of their tics. These authors suggest that hypnotherapeutic techniques that are effective with other habit disorders (such as thumb sucking or nail biting) would be helpful in the treatment of children with tics. In addition, they suggest the use of the jettison technique and of imagery that enhances the child's sense of mastery.

In their study, Kohen and Botts (1987) utilized hypnotherapy as an adequate treatment for TD in four latency-aged children. Three of the children were initially on haloperidol and all experienced frequent tics that caused social difficulties. Kohen and Botts describe their induction techniques and hypnotherapy methods in more detail than noted in previous case studies. Treatment consisted of three main components. Initially, the children were taught RMI with emphasis on movement-control metaphors, such as imagining piloting a magic flying blanket or playing an instrument and carefully controlling the movement of one's hands as they create beautiful music. Progressive muscle relaxation was then taught, both as a deepening technique and to focus attention on motor behaviors. Muscle relaxation was taught from the toes upward purposely to focus "last and indirectly" on the tic behaviors. Then the children were given suggestions to imagine an intentional "STOP" sign, as well as additional metaphors to stop their tic movements. The children were taught to utilize their "stop" sign whenever they needed it, such as right *after* a tic appeared or right *before* it happened.

Kohen and Botts (1987) identified three main benefits of RMI as an adjunct in the treatment of TD—a decrease in or elimination of motor tics (relaxation), the fostering of a decrease in vocal tics (self-control), and the enhancement of a sense of self-esteem.

Hypnotherapy was combined with behavioral techniques in two recent studies (Young & Montano, 1988; Young, 1989) on the treatment of TD and associated behavioral problems. Although the literature supports the efficacy of habit-reversal and response-prevention techniques for simple tics as compared with other behavioral methods, clinicians still have the difficult task of determining when such training should be used with a particular patient. A fundamental concept of change is that it occurs more rapidly and effectively when the patient is an integral part of the decision-making process, as has been noted in several articles (Mansdorf, 1986; Wickramasekera, 1974). In a single-case study, Wickramasekera (1974) successfully combined hypnosis with behavior therapy in the treatment of blepharospasm (rapid eye blinking) in a 45-year-old, white, divorced woman. The patient, while in a trance, was requested to choose from one of four treatment methods. Mansdorf (1986) utilized an assertiveness-training program with children with tic disorders prior to using habit-reversal procedures. The technique developed by Young and his associates, called the hypnobehavioral method, allows the patient systematically to self-select which of the two behavioral techniques he or she finds most successful in decreasing his or her tic behaviors.

Self-hypnosis plays multiple roles in the hypnobehavioral method. Theoretically, the role of hypnosis can best be understood within the context of a cognitive interpersonal model that is multiinteractional (Bateson, 1958; Leary, 1957). First, self-hypnosis provides the means by which the child can successfully achieve greater self-awareness, motivation, and concentration, thus helping to maintain a focused interest in treatment. Second, it permits children to self-select habit-reversal or response-prevention techniques to control their tic behaviors in their imagination. Third, it facilitates the reduction of symptoms in imagination. Fourth, it helps the child to modify cognition and perceptions (Meichenbaum, 1976). This allows children to conceptualize their tic behaviors as being within their control and, therefore, subject to change. Fifth, self-hypnosis facilitates the child's sense of self-efficacy (Bandura, 1977). Sixth, it permits the child to reduce symptoms and develop mastery in real life. Therefore, self-hypnosis is felt to decrease overall feelings of stress as well as the targeted tic behaviors.

The hypnobehavioral method will be described in detail later in this chapter. In the next section, issues relevant to assessment are discussed.

ASSESSMENT

Assessing a child's motivation to change a problem (or symptom) is necessary before beginning any treatment program that directly or indirectly affects the child. This issue is relevant to all health-care providers, whether they are physicians, dentists, or mental-health professionals. Olness and Gardner (1978) reviewed this issue in detail, paying particular attention to the pediatric patient and hypnosis. They cautioned health-care professionals to determine whether the symptom the child is presenting (i.e., tics) is "necessary" (of significant secondary gain) for the child and his or her family to function comfortably. If this is so, the child and/or family may not be motivated enough to profit from treatment or might agree to treatment but "sabotage" it in various ways so that it fails. Kohen and Botts (1987) reiterate the need to assess a child's motivation to learn RMI for the treatment of tics. They note that in their experience children who have tics are highly motivated for change.

We have had a similar experience at the University of Massachusetts Medical School. However, we have encountered several children over the past few years who have not wanted to receive treatment despite a tic disorder that interfered with their daily functioning. These chldren appeared to be obtaining a lot of secondary gain from their tic disorder and did not want to change. In addition to the traditional ways of determining a child's motivation for treatment (i.e., asking for the child's perception of the problems, noting the child's participation in the interview, asking about his or her motivation), we have found it helpful to ask child patients over 8 years of age to rate, on a scale from 1 to 10, their motivation to change their symptom *and* their willingness to learn new skills to accomplish this change. The number 1 is said to indicate little to no interest in controlling their tics (or in learning new skills) and 10 is described as indicating the most interest they could imagine in controlling their tics (or in learning new skills). If a child rates himself or herself lower than 6/7 on either scale, the clinician should question, ideally with the child and family, whether treatment, even if appropriate, should begin. We have found this technique very helpful and have noted that children and their families have been very responsive to discussions about whether treatment should be instituted at the present time. One child returned to treatment six months later and benefited greatly (see case 1 below).

A detailed description of each tic behavior is obtained at the time of the initial interview, including when it occurs, which muscle groups are involved, and its frequency, intensity, and duration. This information is requested independently from both the parents and the children. Baseline data are collected by the parents at home after the initial visit. Data collection should be of the same duration (i.e., 10–60 minutes) and frequency (i.e., daily or every other day) throughout treatment in order to determine the treatment's efficacy. We have found that some parents have difficulties with data collection that at first appear to be noncompliance. However, some tics occur at such high frequencies that they may hamper accurate and reliable data collection if parents are asked to record them for too long a time or too often. If this is the case, it is imperative that baseline and ongoing data be collected over shorter intervals (i.e., 10 minutes) or less frequently (i.e., every other day).

Several groups have developed rating scales to be completed by the clinician, parents, teachers, or adolescent patients as an additional source of information about the tic disorder. The Tourette's Syndrome Global Scale (TSGS) was developed by Harcherik, Leckman, Detlor, and Cohen (1984) to be completed by clinicians. It contains sections on motor and vocal tics, as well as on social maladjustment. The sections yield quantitative scores that may be helpful for both initial diagnosis and the assessment of ongoing response to treatment.

Barkley (1988) recently developed the Rating Scale of Tic Disorders, which can be completed by parents, teachers, or adolescents. It has three sections that include questions on motor and vocal tics and places or situations in which they are more problematic, such as home, school, or community settings. Each section yields one or more scores that can be helpful for initial diagnosis, guidance of treatment, and assessment of treatment response.

Before self-hypnosis is taught, we have found it useful to interview the children about activities they find enjoyable and relaxing, and these typically are incorporated into the suggestions for self-hypnosis training. Recently, we have begun to assess children's learning style and imagery potential using a questionnaire developed by Olness (personal communication, 1988). Olness developed the Imagery Evaluation Questionnaire (IEQ) and suggested that it be used to help decide which strategy is best for a particular child. The IEQ asks questions about a child's typical imagery experiences (i.e., imagine smell, taste, sound, temperature, and/or touch), learning style (i.e., visual or auditory), and family traditions. The information obtained from the IEQ may be incorporated into the self-hypnosis training to optimize the child's learning.

INTERVENTION

Hypnobehavioral treatment has three major phases: (1) discrimination training and skill acquisition, (2) skill application and problem resolution, and (3) generalization, symptom mastery, and maintenance.

Discrimination Training and Skill Acquisition

A commonly described characteristic of people who have tics is that they tend to be unaware of the type, frequency, and intensity of their tic behaviors. The first step in phase 1 is to increase the patients' awareness of tiquing and to help them to discriminate the tic from other motor behaviors. This is accomplished in the following manner.

Two methods are used to enhance awareness of tic behaviors. In the first method, the children are asked to identify the tic behaviors they would like to decrease first, and then both parents and children are asked separately to record the frequency of this tic. This recording is to be performed at a time when the tic behaviors are known to occur and can be conveniently noted for a specified time, from 10 minutes to one hour. The second method is designed to help children discriminate the tic behavior from other motor behaviors by observing themselves alone in front of a mirror or face to face with a parent for 15 minutes a day.

Simultaneously, self-hypnosis training is initiated. A naturalistic approach (Gardner & Olness, 1981) utilizing a muscle-relaxation induction technique with visual imagery for deepening the trance state is typically used. Children are interviewed about activities they find enjoyable and relaxing, and these are incorporated into the suggestions for deepening the trance by visual or other types of imagery. Instructions for progressive muscle-relaxation training (Jacobson, 1973) include suggestions that the children let their arms "go floppy like a rag doll." Instructions to deepen the trance state are facilitated by using imagery and asking the children to think of activities they find enjoyable (i.e., fun, pleasant), different sensations associated with these activities, and suggestions of being in control of themselves. For example, "Now that your arms feel floppy, think about something that you've done or would like to do that you really liked and found fun. Imagine yourself being there again . . . the feelings you had . . . the smells, sounds, and the things you saw. Notice how good you feel right now . . . how in control you are of your body, feelings, and thoughts." Children are given an audiotape of their first training session with the therapist and are instructed to listen to the tape for approximately 15 minutes twice a day.

Skill Application and Problem Resolution

The children are requested to identify the subjective urge that precedes their tic behaviors in imagination as part of the instructions in the use of the symptom-prevention technique. Self-hypnosis aids the children by increasing their ability to concentrate and focus on this urge. The therapist and the child, if possible, determine the muscle response that competes with the tic behavior as part of the instructions in the use of the habit-reversal technique. During self-hypnosis, the children are asked to imagine their tic behavior occurring. They are asked to select and apply which of the two procedures is the most successful in decreasing their tiquing. Recently, the use of a rapid induction technique (RIT) has been added to the second phase of treatment (Young, 1989). The child is asked to "relax your body as quickly as you can with your eyes open." At this point in treatment, most children can induce relaxation in five to 30 seconds on their own. They are instructed to practice RIT 10 times a day.

Generalization, Symptom Mastery, and Maintenance

The children are instructed to continue self-hypnosis practice while applying their chosen technique for approximately 15 minutes a day and to practice RIT 10 times a day. During the treatment session, the children are instructed to practice self-hypnosis with their chosen technique to decrease their tiquing behavior. They are requested to use RIT at the first sign of a tic or prior to its occurrence (i.e., at first awareness of the subjective urge to tic). Generalization, outside the treatment session, occurs by instructing the children to use their chosen technique during periods of high-frequency tiquing. Recording of tic behaviors by the children and their parents continues. Symptom mastery is defined as the time when the tic behavior is no longer occurring or when the child reports that he or she has adequate self-control. Parents continue to monitor their children's progress and are instructed to utilize verbal praise and special privileges and/or activities to reward their children for achieving symptom mastery.

Recurrence of tiquing is common among children with TD following initial treatment. Therefore, a relapse-prevention technique (Marlatt & Gordon, 1980, 1985) is employed as a precautionary measure to ensure treatment gains. Relapse prevention consists of discussions with both children and their parents about the probability of tic behaviors recurring. The children are asked to think about how they would respond if relapse occurred and then to imagine during self-hypnosis how to respond successfully. They are then instructed to utilize this approach if and when relapse occurs. Parents are told to expect relapse to occur and to support their child's efforts at self-management.

CASE STUDIES

Two case studies will be presented to illustrate the use of the hypnobehavioral method. The first child was treated with the original method, without RIT. The second was treated with RIT. Both were referred by the same pediatric neurologist at the University of Massachusetts Medical Center.

Case 1: A.F.

A.F. was a boy 9-years and 3 months of age whose abnormal movements were first noted in the first grade. His tics consisted of eye blinking, facial movements, and throat clearing. A.F. was diagnosed with TD. Eye blinking and facial movements took place together and were exacerbated by a separation from his parents who had gone on vacation without him several months before our first visit. A.F. was described by his parents as somewhat uncommunicative and withdrawn. He was not highly motivated for treatment initially, but returned six months after the initial consultation more motivated to control his tics.

A.F. chose to target eye blinking as the tic he wanted to be able to control. He was seen, along with his mother, for four sessions over a four-week period, and was taught the original hypnobehavioral method without RIT.

Baseline data (observed over a six-day period) revealed that the eye-blinking tic was a very-high-frequency behavior, occurring on average 208 times for each 15-minute period observed (range = 58–500). In phase 1, tic behavior decreased to 96 tics per 15 minutes (14 days, range of tic = 26–205). During self-hypnosis (phase 2), A.F. chose the response-prevention technique to control his tics. His sensory cue was a dry, burning sensation in his eyes. Tic behavior decreased to an average of 28 tics per 15 minutes (six days, range of tic = 15–42). During phase 3 of treatment (29 days), tics were further decreased to an average of seven tics per 15 minutes. This level of control was considered to be at the mastery level by A.F. and treatment was terminated.

Phase 2: Narrative

Now that you are as comfortable as you feel you can be, I'd like you to imagine yourself at home at a time when your eye tics happen a lot. As soon as you notice yourself blinking, raise one of your fingers so I know you've noticed it. Good. When you are ready, I'd like you to try, in your imagination, to control or stop your eye blinking, first by trying one of the approaches you've learned, and then by the other way we spoke of. Remember, as soon as you've noticed the dry, burning feeling in your eyes, you should try one, then the other, control method. Remember, one way to control the tics is to relax the muscles of your eyes and face as soon as you feel the burning feeling. Stop relaxing the muscles after the burning feeling goes away. For the other way, as soon as you feel the burning feeling, widen your eyes again and again for five minutes at a time. Take your time trying these ways and let me know which one is best to control or decrease your tics. If you need some help, please let me know. When you've finished trying both ways, let me know which one you think is best.

Commentary

Prior to beginning self-hypnosis, A.F. learned both habit reversal (an exaggerated eye-opening movement) and response prevention (relaxing the muscles around his eyes and face). The narrative begins after A.F. had completed the first phase of self-hypnosis and signaled the therapist that he was ready for the next task. During self-hypnosis, he imagined himself performing his eye-blinking tic at home and was requested to try both tic-control techniques and determine which was more effective in controlling his tics. He found that response prevention was more effective than habit reversal.

Case 2: A.M.

A.M. was a 13½ year-old boy whose abnormal movements began at the age of 7½ after a visit with his father. His parents had been divorced for many years and, as a result, his early life was described as being very chaotic. His tics consisted of eye blinking, shoulder thrusting, mouth opening, and throat clearing. Prior to the initial consultation, his tics had exacerbated after a recent visit with his father. They consisted of head and body shaking so violent that it caused him to fall off a couch. He was also noted to make loud "explosion" noises. A.M. was diagnosed with TD and was started on Klonopin (clonazepam) by the pediatric neurologist to help control his severe tics. This treatment was successful in decreasing his violent spasms. His tics came in clusters, with head and body shaking occurring simultaneously.

A.M. chose to target head shaking as the tic he would like to learn to control. He was seen for eight sessions over a 16-week period, sometimes with his mother present. A.M. was taught the revised hypnobehavioral method with RIT.

Baseline data (observed over an eight-day period) revealed that the head shaking tic occurred an average of 14.9 times per hour (tic range = 0–26). Tic behavior increased during phase 1 (six days) of treatment to 19.8 tics per hour (range = 10–27). Although no apparent change in the frequency of tics was seen during the first two weeks of phase 2 of treatment, A.M. noted, with pride, that his tics were no longer occurring in clusters. At A.M.'s insistence, it was decided to begin to wean him off of Klonopin over the next 30 days. During the last week of phase 2 of treatment (the first week of his weaning off of the Klonopin), a significant decrease in tic behaviors was noted—to an average of 1.7 tics per hour (range = 0–12). During self-hypnosis, A.M. chose the response-prevention technique and was trained to use RIT. In phase 3 of treatment (20 days), while Klonopin was reduced further, tic behaviors were extinguished. Follow-up at six months showed no return of symptoms.

Phase 3: Narrative

Now, I'd like to have you practice your self-control technique in the office to decrease or prevent a head-shaking tic from occurring. As you have done so often in your imagination, I'd like you to relax as quickly as you can as soon as you notice those feelings that come right before a head-shaking tic. Please let me know, with some signal, that you have become as relaxed as you can. . . . Good. Then let me know that you have relaxed the muscles of your head and neck as much as you can . . . Good. Next, let me know when the urge to tic is gone . . . Good. Now return your attention to the room and talk about how you felt when you prevented a tic from happening.

Commentary

In order to assist A.M. to use his self-management technique, he was initially instructed to utilize RIT and the response-prevention technique to decrease or stop his head-shaking tic in the office. At the first sign of an impending tic, A.M. began RIT and then utilized the response-prevention technique (relaxation of the muscles of his head and neck) until his urge to tic had been eliminated. He repeated this several times in the office, demonstrating his ability to control (master) and eliminate his tics. At the end of the session, he was instructed to utilize this approach to control his tics at chosen times at home and school or with his friends.

FUTURE DIRECTIONS

The hypnobehavioral method appears to be an effective psychotherapeutic procedure for the treatment of tic disorders. It utilizes self-hypnosis to allow a child to self-select one of two promising treatment techniques: habit reversal (Azrin & Nunn, 1973) and response prevention (Bliss, 1980; Bullen & Hemsley, 1983). Furthermore, the method represents a brief treatment model that can be easily applied by the clinician and learned by the child.

This method successfully responds to four of six research criticisms outlined by Turpin (1983) in his review of the literature on the treatment of tic disorders. These four criticisms assert (1) the lack of a multiple treatment package, (2) the lack of accurate tic description and tic-disorder classification, (3) the lack of appropriate process measures, and (4) the lack of generalization of treatment effects. Existing studies have not used an experimental design utilizing a contrast group with adequate numbers of subjects to analyze main treatment effects statistically. A future study might compare hypnotic and pharmacological (i.e., haloperidol) management of TD in children. In a similar study, Olness, MacDonald, and Uden (1987) demonstrated that hypnotic intervention is more effective than pharmacological (i.e., propranolol) management of juvenile migraine. Future studies should also utilize standardized methods of describing and counting tics, ensure treatment compliance, and standardize hypnotic treatment.

REFERENCES

Abuzzahab, F. S. & Anderson, F. O. (1973). Gilles de la Tourette syndrome: International registry. *Minnesota Medicine, 56*, 492–496.

Abuzzahab, F. S., & Anderson, F. O. (1974). Gilles de la Tourette's syndrome: Cross cultural analysis and treatment outcome. *Clinical Neurology and Neurosurgery, 1*, 66–74.

American Psychiatric Association (1987). *Diagnostic and statistical manual of mental disorders* (3rd ed.-rev.). Washington, DC: Author.

Azrin, N. H., and Nunn, R. G. (1973). Habit reversal: A method of eliminating nervous habits and tics. *Behavioral Research Therapy, 11*, 619–628.

Azrin, N. H., & Nunn, R. G. (1977). *Habit control: (Stuttering, nail biting, and other nervous habits).* New York: Simon & Schuster.

Azrin, N. H., Nunn, R. G., & Frantz, S. E. (1980). Habit-reversal vs. negative practice treatment of nervous tics. *Behavioral Therapy, 11*, 169–178.

Bandura, A. (1977). Self-efficacy: Toward a unifying theory of behavioral change. *Psychological Review, 84*, 191–215.

Barkley, R. A. (1988). Tic disorder and Gilles de la Tourette syndrome. In E. M. Mash & L. B. Terdal (Eds.). *Behavioral assessment of childhood disorders* (2nd ed.). New York: Guilford.

Bateson, G. (1958). *Naven.* Stanford, CA: Stanford University Press.

Bliss, J. (1980). Sensory experiences of Gilles de la Tourette syndrome. *Archives of General Psychiatry, 37*, 1343–1347.

Bullen, J. G., & Hemsley, D. R. (1983). Sensory experiences as a trigger in Gilles de la Tourette's syndrome. *Journal of Behavioral Therapy and Experimental Psychiatry, 14*, 197—201.

Canavan, A. G. M., & Powell, J. E. (1981). The efficacy of several treatments of Gilles de la Tourette's syndrome as assessed in a single case. Behavioral Research Therapy, 19, 549–556.

Clements, R. O. (1972). Gilles de la Tourette's syndrome—an overview of development and treatment of a case using hypnotherapy, haloperidol, and psychotherapy. *American Journal of Clinical Hypnosis, 14*, 167–172.

Comings, D. E., & Comings, B. G. (1984). Tourette's syndrome and attention deficit disorder with hyperactivity: Are they genetically related? *Journal of the American Academy of Child Psychiatry, 23*, 138–146.

Comings, D. E., & Comings, B. S. (1987). A controlled study of Tourette syndrome. I. Attention deficit disorder, learning disorders and school problems. *American Journal of Human Genetics, 41*, 701–741.

Doleys, D. M. & Kurtz, P. S. (1974). A behavior treatment for the Gilles de la Tourette's syndrome. *Psychological Reports, 35*, 43–48.

Eisenberg, L., Acher, E. A., & Kanner, L. (1959). A clinical study of Gilles de la Tourette's disease (*maladie des tics*) in children. *American Journal of Psychiatry, 115*, 715–726.

Feldman, R. B., & Werry, J. S. (1966) An unsuccessful attempt to treat a tiquer by mass practice. *Behavioral Research Therapy, 4*, 111–117.

Fernando, S. (1967). Gilles de la Tourette's syndrome: A report on four cases and review of published case reports. *British Journal of Psychiatry, 113*, 607–617.

Finney, J. W., Rapoff, M. A., Hall, C. L., & Christopherson, E. R. (1983). Replication and social validation of habit reversal treatment for tics. *Behavior Therapy, 14*, 116–126.

Friedhoff, A. J., & Chase, T. N. (eds.) (1982). *Gilles de la Tourette's syndrome.* New York: Raven Press.

Friedman, S. (1980). Self-control of the treatment of Gilles de la Tourette's syndrome: Case study with 18-month follow-up. *Journal of Consulting and Clinical Psychology, 48*, 400–402.

Gardner, G. G., & Olness, K. (1981). *Hypnosis and hypnotherapy with children.* New York: Grune & Stratton.

Gilles de la Tourette, G. (1885). Etude sur une affection nerveuse caracterisee par de l'incoordination motrice accompagnee d'echolalie et de copralalie. *Archives de Neurologie, 9*, 19–42, 158–200. (See translation in Friedhoff, A. J. & Chase, T. N. 1982, p. 116.)

Golden, G. S. (1986). Tourette syndrome: Recent advances. *Pediatric Neurology, 2*, 189–192.

Goldfried, M. R., & Davison, G. C. (1976). *Clinical behavioral therapy.* New York: Holt.

Harcherik, D. F., Leckman, J. F., Detlor, J., & Cohen, D. J. (1984). A new instrument for clinical studies of Tourette's syndrome. *Journal of the American Academy of Child Psychiatry, 23*, 153–160.

Itard, J. M. G. (1825). Memoire sur quelques fonctions involontaires des appareils de la locomotion, de la prehension, et de la voix. *Archives of General Medicine, 8*, 385–407.

Jacobson, E. (1973). *Teaching and learning. New methods for old arts.* Chicago: National Federation for Progressive Relaxation.

King, A. C., and Ollendick, T. H. (1984). Gilles de la Tourette's disorder: A review. *Journal of Clinical Child Psychology, 13*, 2–9.

Kohen, D. P., & Botts, P. (1987). Relaxation-imagery (self-hypnosis) in Tourette syndrome: Experience with four children. *American Journal of Clinical Hypnosis, 29*, 227–237.

Leary, T. (1957). *Interpersonal diagnosis of personality.* New York: Ronald.

Lindner, H., & Stevens, H. (1967). Hypnotherapy and psychodynamics in the syndrome of Gilles de la Tourette. *International Journal of Clinical and Experimental Hypnosis, 15*, 151–155.

Mansdorf, I. J. (1986). Assertiveness training in the treatment of a child's tic. *Journal of Behavior Therapy in Experimental Psychiatry, 17*, 29–32.

Marlatt, G. A., & Gordon, J. R. (1980). Determinants of relapse: Implication for the maintenance of behavior change. In P. O. Davidson & S. M. Davidson (Eds.), *Behavioral medicine: Changing healthy lifestyles* (pp. 410–452). New York: Brunner/Mazel.

Marlatt, G. A., & Gordon, J. R. (1985). *Relapse prevention.* New York: Guilford.

McKinnon, R. C. (1967). Gilles de la Tourette syndrome: A case showing electroencephalographic changes and response to haloperidol. *Medical Journal of Australia, 2*, 21–22.

Meichenbaum, D. H. (1976). Toward a cognitive theory of self-control. In G. E. Schwartz & D. Shapiro (Eds.), *Consciousness and self-regulation* (Vol. 1). New York: Plenum.

Miller, A. L. (1970). Treatment of a child with Gilles de la Tourette's syndrome using behavior modification techniques. *Journal of Behavior Therapy and Experimental Psychiatry, 1*, 319–321.

Olness, K., & Gardner, G. G. (1978). Some guidelines for uses of hypnotherapy in pediatrics. *Pediatrics, 62*(2), 228–233.

Olness, K., MacDonald, J., & Uden, D. (1987). Prospective study comparing Propranolol, placebo, and hypnosis in management of juvenile migraine. *Pediatrics, 79*(4), 583–597.

Polites, J., Kruger, D., & Stevenson, J. (1965). Sequential treatment of a case of Gilles de la Tourette's syndrome. *British Journal of Medical Psychology, 38*, 43–52.

Schneck, J. M. (1960). Gilles de la Tourette's disease. *American Journal of Psychiatry, 117*, 78–82.

Shapiro, A. K., Shapiro, E., Bruun, R. D., & Sweet, R. D. (1978). *Gilles de la Tourette's syndrome.* New York: Raven.

Spithill, A. (1974). Treatment of a monosymptomatic tic by hypnosis: A case study. *American Journal of Clinical Hypnosis, 17*, 88–93.

Storm, L. (1985). Massed negative practice as a behavioral treatment for Gilles de la Tourette's syndrome. *American Journal of Psychotherapy, 39*(2), 277–281.

Tophoff, M. (1973). Massed practice, relaxation and assertion training in the treatment of Gilles de la Tourette's syndrome. *Journal of Behavior Therapy and Experimental Psychiatry, 4*, 1, 71–73.

Torup, E. (1962). A follow-up study of children with tics. *Acta Paediatrica Scandinavica, 51*, 261–268.

Turpin, G. (1983). The behavioral management of tic disorders. A critical review. *Advances in Behavioral Research and Therapy, 5*, 203–345.

Varni, J. W., Boyd, E. F., & Cataldo, M. F. (1978). Self-monitoring, external reinforcement, and time out procedures in the control of high rate tic behaviors in a hyperactive child. *Journal of Behavior Therapy and Experimental Psychiatry, 9*, 353—358.

Wickramasekera, I. (1974). Hypnosis and the broad-spectrum behavior therapy for blepharospasm: A case study. *International Journal of Clinical and Experimental Hypnosis, 12*, 201–209.

Wright, L., Schaeffer, A. G., & Solomons, G. (1979). *Encyclopedia of pediatric psychology.* Baltimore: University Park Press.

Yates, A. J. (1970). *Behavior therapy.* New York: Wiley.

Young, M. H. (1989). Self-management training in children with tic disorders: Clinical experience with hypnobehavioral treatment. Presented at the 31st Annual Scientific Meeting of the American Society of Clinical Hypnosis, Nashville, TN, March 10, 1989.

Young, M. H. & Montano, R. J. (1988). A new hypnobehavioral method for the treatment of children with Tourette's disorder. *American Journal of Clinical Hypnosis, 31*(2), 97–106.

Zahm, D. N. (1987). Hypnosis in the treatment of Tourette syndrome. In W. C. Wester (Ed.), *Clinical hypnosis: A case management approach*. Cincinnati, OH: BSCI Publications.

9 Hypnosis and Anxiety in Children

Janet R. Schultz, Ph.D.

Conceptualizing anxiety and anxiety disorders in children poses a set of problems unique in psychodiagnostic endeavors. First, there is no universally accepted definition of anxiety. Gordon Paul (1969) wrote about the problems inherent in the reification of anxiety and the overly flexible use of the word clinically. Central to most views of anxiety, however, is apprehension about a person's own well-being or that of someone (and, at times, something) significant to that person. This threat can be one's physical, emotional, social, or spiritual well-being and in turn has impact measurable on at least three levels: cognitive-experiential (relies on self-report), behavioral (relies on observation), and physiological (relies on such measures as heart rate or galvanic skin response) (cf. Clarke & Jackson, 1983). To compound the problem, the three levels do not necessarily change in tandem or show the same intensity of arousal (cf. Hodgson & Rachman, 1974).

Another definitional problem is the lack of a clear, uniform distinction between fear and anxiety. In the revised third edition of the *Diagnostic and Statistical Manual of Mental Disorders* (DSM-III-R) (American Psychiatric Association, 1987), the terms are used almost indistinguishably, but fear is used as a subset of anxiety, often reflecting primarily the subjective experience. Some theorists (cf. Clarke & Jackson, 1983) distinguish between the two on the basis of the presence or absence of objective danger signs.

Second, anxiety is a common, even mundane, experience in the lives of adults and children alike. Unlike most other psychic phenomena that are central to psychiatric diagnoses, anxiety is often an appropriate response to events. It can be a desirable response; one task of parenthood is to teach

113

children fear of realistically dangerous objects or events (e.g., "Hot!"). Anxiety is known to result in positive effects under certain circumstances. For example, anxiety can serve a readying or facilitating function, as when people are "psyched up" for a challenge.

Third, in children, anxiety is not only a common, but a statistically normal occurrence. MacFarlane, Allen, and Honzik (1954) found mild to moderate fears in 90 percent of their sample of children under 12. Many children hold several fears at a time (LaPouse & Monk, 1959), with girls reporting (if not experiencing) more fears than boys (Ollendick, 1979).

Fourth, not only is anxiety common in children, but its emergence follows a predictable developmental path. Infants from birth display the Moro reflex, a form of startle response that usually follows either loud noises or a loss of sense of support. Bowlby (1975) found an almost universal emergence of fear of separation before the first birthday. Ilg and Ames (1955) provided a list of the most common fears for various points in the first 10 years of life, based on work of the Gesell Institute. Sensory-based fears (for example, sights or sounds) and separation predominate until the age of 3. After 3 years of age, fears of the dark, the unusual, physical injury, and animals increase in frequency. Social fears (such as fears of school, social rejection, or failure) are associated with school age. Agras, Sylvester, and Oliveau (1969) found that fears of doctors, injections, darkness, and strangers declined sharply in adolescence and early adult life, while fears of animals, heights, enclosed spaces, and social situations faded later.

Since fears and anxiety are an integral part of the human experience, it becomes difficult to establish when they become a diagnosable concern. This picture becomes even foggier when the secondary role anxiety plays in other psychological disorders is recognized. The DSM-III-R lists anxiety as an associated feature of personality disorders, substance abuse, depression, and most forms of what traditionally have been considered the neuroses.

Anxiety can be a problem of degree. Anxiety disorders are often defined as responses that are "out of proportion" to the actual threat at hand. A secondary aspect can be the manner in which anxiety is expressed. A third parameter is the frequency with which the feared object is encountered. For example, a snake phobia in an urban child may render part of an occasional trip to the zoo uncomfortable whereas the same fear might render a rural child housebound. For most clinicians, degree of impairment of a person's life is the critical test for deciding when treatment is indicated.

Distinguishing anxiety, fears, and phobias is particularly difficult in the pediatric population because children do not necessarily share the same information or conceptual base as adults. As Clarke and Jackson (1983) pointed out, in adults, fears are distinguished from phobias by consensus of the presence or absence of realistic danger. Children, in contrast, often understand the phobic situation to be dangerous or believe that it is hazardous on the basis of immature logic. This is in strong contrast to adult phobics who acknowledge freely, for example, that their tension and fear in response to a picture of a snake are totally without basis in reality. The concept of panic disorder as a diagnostic entity has been relatively infrequently applied to children. Empirical studies are rare, as well. The paucity of data relates to the prevalence pattern of panic disorder; children may experience panic but panic disorder emerges most frequently after adolescence (DSM-III-R).

As might be anticipated from these conceptual and definitional difficulties, the literature on pediatric fears and phobias is less than ideal. As recently as 1974, Miller, Barrett, and Hampe entitled their review "Phobias of Childhood in a Prescientific Era." Not much has changed in the 15 years or so that have elapsed. Yet in the face of the lack of clarity, anxiety disorders in children have been a focus of treatment for several clinically important reasons: First, childhood fears and phobias are quite visible, often significantly disrupting a child's life. The resulting discomfort can be intense and the child's sphere of life activities severely circumscribed. Second, childhood fears and phobias often markedly, but indirectly, disrupt the lives of adults significant in a child's life. Parents often limit their own activities or plan ahead to help the child avoid the feared situations. The adults themselves experience considerable anticipatory discomfort when the child's feared situation cannot be avoided, as in the case of injections or school.

Third, there is a growing awareness that some fears and phobias in children, even of mild or moderate severity, persist and may increase dramatically in intensity. Agras and colleagues (1969) identified phobias as having a particularly prolonged and disabling course. Gittelman and Klein (1984) found separation anxiety to be an important factor in the development of agoraphobia with panic. Studies vary somewhat, but 18–50 percent of adult agoraphobics reported histories of separation anxiety in childhood (Breier, Charney, and Heninger, 1986). Clarke and Jackson (1983) pointed out that when a child who is considered "school phobic" grows up so that school is no longer required, the same pattern of behaviors earns the person the label of agoraphobic.

Fourth, anxiety has also been implicated in the etiology and/or maintenance of certain pediatric psychophysiological disorders, such as asthma, headaches, hives, tics, ulcers, sleep disorders, irritable bowel syndrome, and enuresis. It has also been suggested that substance abuse in some adolescents is an attempt to reduce anxiety.

ANXIETY DISORDERS IN CHILDREN

There are basically six, not entirely independent, anxiety disorders that have been described in children. The first of these, separation anxiety, has as an essential feature excessive anxiety concerning separation from those to whom the child is attached. The reaction must be beyond that which is expected for someone at the child's developmental level. Symptoms include distress to the point of panic. In many respects, this disorder is the childhood equivalent of agoraphobia since the latter does not generally develop until a person is in early adulthood, but both keep a person close to home.

Avoidant disorder of childhood or adolescence is characterized by an excessive shrinking from contact with unfamiliar people, despite good relationships with familiar figures. These children generally appear socially withdrawn, timid, and lacking in self-confidence. Most of them have another anxiety disorder, especially overanxious disorder.

Overanxious disorder has as a central feature excessive or unrealistic anxiety or worry, and it is similar to the diagnosis of generalized anxiety disorder, usually found in adults. Children with overanxious disorder complain of frequent physical concomitants of anxiety. Sleep-onset difficulty is common and the child often appears nervous much of the time. Because of his or her fears, the child may spend much time inquiring about discomforts or dangers of various situations. Reassurance is needed about events and/or the child's competence and the view others hold of his or her performance. Habit disorders are common with this diagnosis.

Social phobias reflect performance anxiety and fear of embarrassment or humiliation. Anticipatory anxiety is common if a feared situation is unavoidable. Exposure to the phobic stimulus results in an immediate anxiety response, often with physiological symptoms.

Simple phobias (sometimes known as ''specific phobias'') are marked by persistent fear of a circumscribed object or situation. Fear of embarrassment, if present, is secondary. These phobias are what most people think of when phobia is mentioned: fear of animals, heights, closed spaces, needles, and so on.

Posttraumatic stress disorder (PTSD) develops after a psychologically distressing event that is outside the range of typical human experiences. While there is some disagreement about the role developmental level plays in the formation of the disorder, there is growing consensus that children can experience PTSD. Flashbacks to the traumatic event, constriction of affect, and diminished interest in significant activities are generally noted. Children also report tension-related physical symptoms and a sense of a foreshortened future. Phobic avoidance of situations similar to the original trauma may significantly curtail activities and interfere with interpersonal relationships.

HYPNOSIS AND ANXIETY

While there is a considerable body of literature describing the use of hypnosis with anxiety, there has been little attempt to differentiate among the various disorders. The discussion here will follow the more symptom-specific orientation of the hypnosis literature that can be applied to any of the anxiety disorders.

Hypnosis has been used both primarily and adjunctively to treat anxiety disorders in children, with one of the earliest published accounts being Mason's 1897 treatment of a child who was too frightened to cooperate with medical treatment. Since then, numerous case reports, and far fewer empirical studies, have provided evidence of the efficacy of hypnosis for treating anxiety in children.

Anxiety in Psychophysiological Disorders

The nonspecific anxiety (sometimes known as free-floating anxiety) associated with psychophysiological disorders and overanxious disorders has been addressed directly in hypnosis, usually with suggestions for relaxation, comfort, and confidence. Most studies of hypnotherapy of the psychophysiological disorders do not separate the effects of reduction of anxiety from the direct suggestion for symptom removal or prevention. Almost universally, however, anxiety reduction is considered a major component of successful interventions. Many disorders have been treated in this way but the most prominent is asthma. Ambrose (1968) described asthma as "the illness par excellence to treat with hypnosis and suggestion" (p. 4).

Significant improvement in the frequency of asthma attacks after hypnotic suggestion (either auto- or hetero-) of general relaxation and easy breathing has been reported (Diego, 1961; Aronoff, Aronoff, & Peck, 1975; Collison, 1975; Barbour, 1980). Kohen, Olness, Colwell, and Heimel (1984) reported that 90 percent of their 40 pediatric asthmatic patients had reduced school absences, fewer emergency-room visits, and fewer appointments with physicians following the use of relaxation/mental imagery.

While there are other reports of hypnotherapeutic treatment of asthma, they do not focus on the anxiety component. As Creer, Renne, and Chai (1982) suggest, relaxation is probably most useful to asthmatics when used as part of systematic desensitization where the maladaptive anxiety or fear responses secondary to asthma are targeted for intervention rather than alteration of lung function. This essentially recasts hypnotic intervention with asthma as treatment for the anxiety related to the asthma.

Among other examples of psychophysiological disorders where anxiety reduction has been a significant factor in successful hypnotherapeutic treatment are hives (Gardner & Olness, 1981; Kohen et al., 1984), intractable itching (Mirvish, 1978; Olness, 1977), and headaches (Gardner & Olness, 1981; Kohen et al., 1984).

Anxiety-Related Sleep Problems

Another symptom common to the anxiety disorders is sleep disruption. Jacobs (1962) reported treating the fear of the dark in a 6-year-old who could not fall asleep without her mother being present. This symptom represents one manifestation of separation anxiety. Despite multiple stressors that appear to have contributed to her fears, suggestions of her parents' love for her and their intent to keep her safe, along with suggestions that she would be happier, braver, and stronger "like Mighty Mouse," resolved her sleep fears. In a later article, Jacobs (1964) presented the case of an 8-year-old who was afraid to fall asleep after her grandmother's death. At the funeral, she had been told by an adult friend of the family that "death was nothing to worry about; it was just like going to sleep." Subsequently, she became afraid to sleep because she might die. Her mother carried out an effective treatment at home using bedtime reassurances and suggestions for restful sleep. In addition, her nightly bedtime prayer was changed so as not to include "if I die before I wake."

Personalized fairy tales were developed by Levine (1980) to help a sexually molested 8-year-old and a precocious 3-year-old overcome the anxiety that interfered with their falling asleep. Levine tailored stories to the preferences, interests, and needs of each of the girls. The fantasy characters demonstrated alternative ways to respond to the child's situation. In a similar vein, Tilton (1984) used images of superheros as part of his hypnotic treatment of several children, including a 5-year-old boy who was afraid of both the dark and falling asleep.

For some children, nightmares reach such a frequency and intensity that the children become afraid to go to sleep. Gardner (1978) reported successfully reducing recurrent nightmares in children by using the following method. If there is a known precipitating event, the child is encouraged to recall that event in hypnosis. Then the child is helped to feel more able to deal with the situation effectively. Whether or not the precipitant can be identified, the child is first given suggestions of safety and then suggestions to redream the nightmare under hypnosis. On this occasion, however, the child is to alter the dream so that he or she becomes the master of the situation rather than the frightened victim. Suggestions are made that the child can do the same when actually sleeping. Gardner reported that one or two sessions of hypnotherapy usually sufficed in this kind of treatment; the child's sense of control and mastery are central to this approach. Similarly, Taboada (1975) used suggestions of mastery and pleasure in the anxiety-provoking situation, delivered in hypnosis, to end the 15-night series of terrors in a 7-year-old.

Koe (1989) treated a teenager who had had night terrors virtually nightly for more than half of his life. He had had a thorough sleep evaluation and, after other treatments such as tranquilizers and psychotherapy had been ineffective, the boy was referred for hypnotherapy. Koe induced a terror in hypnotherapy and thus came to recognize the importance of external sounds as triggers. Posthypnotic suggestion for decreased awareness of sounds and sensations while sleeping resulted in a dramatic decrease in, and soon after the cessation of, the night terrors.

Anxiety Related to Medical Intervention

Anxiety is also associated with the diagnosis and treatment of medical conditions. One of the most common of the anxiety-provoking medical stimuli is needles. Hypnosis has been an effective anxiety reducer for all varieties of needle concerns. While the incidence of needle phobia is not known in the pediatric population, Agras and associates (1969) found the prevalence of reported injection phobia to be 140 in 1,000 for 20-year-olds, and there is anecdotal evidence that the incidence for children is considerably higher. Olness and Gardner (1978) treated a 7-year-old needle-phobic boy who required repeated intravenous infusions of plasma by teaching him self-hypnosis for relaxation and the "switch-off" technique. Less than three weeks of treatment time was required. Dash (1981) used three hypnotherapy sessions to treat a severe needle phobia in a 5-year-old cardiac patient in need of intravenous antibiotics. The successful effects of this treatment lasted at least until a two-year follow-up. Gardner and Olness (1981) described treating a 17-year-old with meningitis for his hysterical response to repeated intravenous starts. Imagery, in vivo desensitization, and hypnosis were combined successfully with lasting effect. Generalization to injections occurred without further treatment.

Hilgard and LeBaron (1984) used suggestions for turning the smell of an alcohol pad into "pleasant perfume" and putting a hand "to sleep" to eliminate needle fear in a 7-year-old cancer patient who required numerous "finger sticks." They also reported reducing anxiety about injections, spinal taps, and bone-marrow aspirations. Hodel, Gemunder, O'Grady, Steffen, and Lampkin (1982) found that hypnotic interventions reduced self-report and behavioral signs of anxiety in pediatric oncology patients undergoing bone-marrow aspirations. Several writers have emphasized the anticipatory nature of the phobic reaction to needles, labeling anxiety as the primary determinant of the child's responses rather than actual pain or other aspects of the experience (cf. Clarke & Jackson, 1983; Zeltzer & LeBaron, 1982).

Kohen (1980) used hypnosis to deal with the anxiety of first pelvic examinations for teenage girls. The intervention was designed not only to reduce anxiety, but also to work preventively to reduce the probability of anxiety at future examinations by fostering a sense of competency and mastery. Education about the procedure, the use of imagery of pleasant activities, suggestions of relaxation and comfort, and posthypnotic suggestions to relax even more easily and quickly for future pelvic examinations made up the program.

The unexpected nature of a trip to the emergency room and the traumatic or intense character of the injury or illness that precipitates the visit combine to make these situations unusually anxiety provoking. Kohen (1986) found hypnosis to be helpful in reducing the pain and anxiety of pediatric emergency-room visits, and he outlined what he felt were significant features of the work: an increase in personal control over frightening and unknown circumstances, the communication of reassuring calm, rapid relaxation, and direct intervention in discomfort. Overall, the task was seen to be to create expectancies to allow the development of desirable responses in a situation where children and families already show heightened states of focused alertness, high suggestibility, and intense listening.

Anxiety with regard to illness-related events does not always end when children are discharged from the hospital. Jacobs (1964) presented a case history of a 9-year-old boy who was afraid to go to sleep following a tonsillectomy and adenoidectomy. The boy claimed he smelled the anesthetic whenever he fell asleep. Education about the reason for his surgery was coupled with suggestions in hypnosis (1) reinforcing his security in the love of his parents; (2) reassuring him that he was getting bigger and better every day; (3) providing imagery of riding in a sailboat, smelling the fresh sea breezes; and (4) going into deep, relaxing sleep. Three hypnotherapy sessions were all that were required to return sleep to normal within 10 days.

Dental Phobia

Procedures closely related to anxiety-provoking medical interventions are those of dentists. While anecdotal accounts suggest higher rates, estimates of the percentage of children anxious enough to present dental-management problems range from 6 percent (Weinstein, 1980) to 16 percent (Sticker & Howitt, 1965). Anxiety can interfere with keeping dental appointments, cooperating during sessions (Ayers, 1982), and the retrospective view of pain experienced (Klepac, McDonald, Hauge, & Dowling, 1980).

The dental literature addresses both prevention of anxiety and its treatment. For example, Shaw (1975); Erickson, Hershman, and Secter (1961); and Bernick (1972) all emphasize the importance of helping children perceive dental experiences in a positive light, even before treatment begins. Recommendations to limit anxiety in pediatric dental patients have included allowing children to experiment with dental instruments, helping parents to foster positive expectations, and having dental personnel choose words and explanations carefully so as to set expectations of comfort, mastery, and even pleasure.

The treatment literature, however, does not separate the effects of relaxation, desensitization, and analgesia through hypnosis. Clinically, the distinction is not crucial, but there is no evidence that all the treatment components are necessary or that they might work independently.

Kroll (1962) treated a 5-year-old girl with serious cardiac problems (a poor candidate for general anesthetic), who was frightened and violently resistant to attempts to work on her teeth. Hypnotic techniques were used to gain cooperation for a series of important but painless procedures (e.g., x-rays). Once trust was built, hypnosis was combined with a local anesthetic and the work was completed safely.

Smith (1965) described using a light trance and pleasurable memories to decrease anxiety and thus increase cooperation with anesthesia for tooth extraction. Bernick (1972) used glove anesthesia with a 13-year-old boy who feared dental work, especially injections. Crasilneck and Hall (1975) reported the successful use of hypnosis to reduce pain and anxiety in a 10-year-old boy who refused to go to the dentist. Both abreaction of previous dental trauma and posthypnotic suggestions for relaxation and well-being during dental work were used.

Hilgard and Hilgard (1975) described the use of a combination of hypnosis and chemical anesthetic to carry out dental procedures on a 14-year-old dental phobic who became agitated in the absence of painful stimuli. She was calmed by hypnosis, but in order to maintain calmness in the face of painful treatment, both hypnosis and local anesthetic were necessary. Interestingly, neither method was effective alone. Neiburger (1978) found children were more cooperative and less anxious during dental prophylaxis when given a suggestion that they would experience a tickling feeling and perhaps want to laugh during the procedures. He referred to these as "sensory confusion" suggestions. Thompson (1963) used hypnosis to help a 12-year-old girl dental phobic to "let go" of her fears from previous experiences. Imagery of her teeth, with and without treatment, was also used. The combination allowed successful dental treatment.

School Phobia

School phobia is a relatively frequent presenting complaint in children. It is more often reported in girls, unlike most juvenile psychological problems.

The incidence of school phobia is believed to be about 17 in 1,000 (Kennedy, 1965) and 2–8 percent of referrals in child-guidance clinics are for this problem (Kahn & Nursten, 1962). The name, however, is more reflective of the uniformity of symptoms than of the similarity of etiology. For some children, the problem is a fear of events associated with school itself (e.g., harsh teacher, teasing, motion sickness on the school bus, or being bullied on the playground). More often, however, this symptom reflects separation anxiety; that is, a fear of leaving major attachment figures (Kennedy, 1965).

Lazarus and Abramovitz (1962) reported the successful treatment of an 8-year-old girl with school phobia in four sessions. Although "emotive imagery" was not termed hypnosis by its investigators, this technique has characteristics that make it difficult to distinguish it from trance induction. Essentially, because progressive muscle-relaxation training was often difficult to use with children, Lazarus and Abramovitz developed the technique to be anxiety inhibiting in the process of desensitizing children. First, the child's superheroes and favorite characters were identified. Then the child was asked to close his or her eyes and imagine a sequence of events close to his or her everyday life, but within which would be woven a story regarding this heroic alter ego. This would be done in such a way as to arouse the affective reactions that are seen as incompatible with anxiety. Once accomplished, events of the systematic desensitization hierarchy are gradually introduced into the story context.

Crasilneck and Hall (1975) and Lawlor (1976) reported their successful treatment of school phobia in young children. Hypnosis was used to determine the underlying concerns, which were then resolved by waking-state discussion and/or environmental manipulation. Crasilneck and Hall favor the use of hypnosis in school phobia because the rapid symptom relief reduces the likelihood of secondary gain.

Performance Anxiety

Certainly, one aspect of school refusal for some children is their discomfort with the continuous performance and public evaluation demanded in the majority of classrooms. Most of the literature deals with these problems in college-aged adults; however, Krippner (1966) studied the use of hypnosis with both older students and those in elementary and high school. Klauber (1984) recommended the use of hypnosis for children afraid to make errors. He also recommended both strong support from teachers and direct suggestions for participation and assertiveness for shy children who are afraid to speak in class. Klauber also reported using hypnosis to determine the dynamics of test anxiety. Waking-state discussion and family sessions were used to address the underlying issues.

Animal Fears

Another common fear in children that can take on life-disturbing proportions is a fear of animals. For example, Gardner and Olness (1984) described a 5-year-old boy who refused to go outside because he might meet a dog. Lazarus and Abramovitz (1962) used their "emotive imagery" technique to treat a 14-year-old child with a dog phobia of three years' duration. The boy's fear was so intense that he took two buses to school rather than possibly face dogs on the otherwise short walk. Imagery of his driving a beautiful Alfa Romeo was paired with gradually escalating images of dogs within the context of car stories. He became comfortable with the idea and the reality of dogs. A 12-month follow-up indicated no sign of his previous phobia.

Crasilneck and Hall (1975) used hypnosis to understand the dynamics of animal phobias and then to treat them. A grade-school girl feared cats because of their accidental association with masturbatory guilt. The precipitant was uncovered using age regression. Treatment consisted of having her, in hypnosis, view the event as if occurring on a stage, more objectively using her now older ego ("theater technique").

Miscellaneous Fears

Fear of the dark is a common concern in normal children that can reach phobic proportions. As in the case described by Jacobs (1962) and cited above, this fear may delay sleep onset, but it does not inherently do so. While hypnotherapy has not been routinely applied to typical fear of darkness, it has been used to treat intense and incapacitating fears. Lazarus and Abramovitz (1962) used their emotive-imagery technique to treat a bright 10-year-old boy who was ridiculed by his older brother because of his excessive fear of the dark. This fear also imposed severe restrictions on his social activities and those of his parents, especially in the evenings. Images of going on crime-fighting missions accompanied, at gradually increasing distances, by "Superman" and "Captain Silver" were used. Three of these desensitization sessions essentially resolved his fear. His general adjustment and school achievement also improved.

A variety of less frequently expressed fears in children have been treated using hypnosis. Kohen and associates (1984) reported treating teenagers with compulsive attention to insignificant or nonexistent physical changes that they termed "cancerphobia." Olness (1986) described desensitizing in hypnosis an 11-year-old with a fear of flying in airplanes that developed after he had flown during a thunderstorm four years earlier. This author has used hypnotic suggestions for relaxation, comfort, and coping as part of the treatment of a bright, verbal 5-year-old who was phobic of sirens. Last, but certainly not least, Gardner described in several articles the use of hypnosis to provide a sense of mastery and calm for a dying child (e.g., Gardner, 1976).

Posttraumatic Stress Disorder

Treatment of PTSD is an area that is relatively new, especially in children. Some of the symptoms of PTSD have been treated with hypnosis, including the distress that is evoked upon exposure to objects associated with the traumatic event, distressing dreams, depression, and free-floating anxiety. Hypnosis has long been used to facilitate abreaction after trauma. For example, Crasilneck and Hall (1975) described using hypnosis to help a 17-year-old girl recall and abreact her rape experience. With the growing evidence that sexual abuse often leads to a childhood form of PTSD (Wolfe, Gentile, & Wolfe, 1989) and the relatively large number of children who are abused, there appears to be a need for a more specialized approach for hypnosis to address PTSD in children. Chapters 5 and 6 present important formulations for this area.

ASSESSMENT

The assessment of children presenting with anxiety and/or phobias demands several steps. First, the general functioning level of the child should be evaluated. Ideally, areas to be covered include intellectual, academic, social, and emotional functioning. The purpose of this evaluation is fourfold:

1. To rule out more pressing psychological problems that either may make hypnosis an undesirable approach or need to be addressed prior to the presenting complaint (Gardner & Olness, 1984).
2. To determine stressors and problem areas in the child's life that might contribute to anxiety and that could later disinhibit the treated phobia (Clarke & Jackson, 1983; Bowlby, 1975).
3. To understand the impact the presenting problem has on the child and the child's family members.
4. To establish what the child's strengths and weaknesses are for therapeutic use.

Once it has been established that the anxiety disorder is the primary problem, that problem itself needs to be evaluated further. While, for research purposes, anxiety is usually assessed on three levels—self-report, overt behavior, and physiological changes—in clinical practice with children, rarely are all three evaluated. Usually, parent report and self-report of the impact, frequency, severity, and duration of the fear, as well as the behavioral indicators and limitations it imposes, are necessary, however. The primary goal is to establish that the symptom, in fact, represents a situation outside the norm of developmental fears and that intervention appears appropriate. The various theoretical aspects of assessing anxiety are outside the scope of this chapter.

Hilgard and LeBaron (1982) pointed out that in evaluating a child over the age of 10, the therapist needs to put more weight on self-report relative to parent observations because the child has an increased capacity to control his or her behavior despite internal distress. Other features to be assessed include secondary gain for anxiety symptoms and the motivation for change held by both parents and child.

At this point, some clinicians might embark on a measure of hypnotic responsivity, although by some estimates few therapists engage in this practice (Cohen, 1989). The process of assessment can be useful even if it is not standard clinical practice. Using the Stanford Hypnosis Clinical Scale for Children (SHCSS) of Morgan and Hilgard (1979) or the Children's Hypnotic Susceptibility Scale (CHSS) of London (1963) obtains information as to the child's hypnotic strengths while giving the patient a sample of the hypnotic process without the potential pressure of using it for symptom removal.

On the other hand, since hypnotic responsivity peaks in childhood (London & Cooper, 1969) and because phobic patients (at least adults) appear particularly responsive, such assessment may provide relatively little new information beyond the base rates. Frankel and Orne (1976) found a significant difference between hypnotic susceptibility of adult phobics and that of smokers seeking treatment for their habit. Not one phobic was nonresponsive, in contrast to almost a third of the smokers. Foenander, Burrows, Gerschmann, and Horne (1980) found hypnotic responsivity to be greater in adult phobics than in the normal population. These findings have not been extended to children, however.

Clinicians often try to assess the dynamics or etiology of the child's fear or phobia. If hypnosis has been decided on as theoretically useful and practically feasible, then this assessment phase is generally accomplished in hypnosis. Age regression is often used to determine underlying aspects of the anxiety (cf. Schneck, 1966). At other times, regression may occur spontaneously (Stampfl & Lewis, 1967). Clarke and Jackson (1983) suggest that once the basic fear has been clarified, further detail can be obtained by asking such questions as: "What could make this situation more anxiety provoking?" or "If you couldn't escape the situation, how could you make it better?"

Ideomotor signaling can be useful to determine if there are other fears present that need to be addressed. Such signals can also be used to assess motivation through responses to such questions as: "Is it okay if you are not frightened next time . . . ?" If a negative response ensues, further evaluation of the significance of the symptoms is necessary. This includes expectations of events that would transpire in the absence of the fear, secondary gain accrued, and the role of the symptom for the patient's family system.

THE INTERVENTION PROCESS

Because the literature regarding hypnotherapy of anxiety disorders often blurs diagnosis and treatment or anxiety reduction and analgesia, there is little evidence that a particular aspect of treatment is essential. However, one or more of the following basic processes occurred in the cited treatments of childhood anxiety and phobia.

1. *Relaxation.* Achieved by direct suggestion, deep breathing, progressive muscle relaxation, or other induction techniques, this state could be seen as inhibiting anxiety by its incompatibility with tension.
2. *Hypnoanalysis.* Technique is used for identifying dynamics of anxiety and/or as an opportunity to view a precipitating event with older, wiser eyes.
3. *Improvement of coping strategies or "ego strengthening."* Usually in response to a direct suggestion, the patient perceives himself or herself as stronger, smarter, braver, and so on.
4. *Changing attributions of situations.* The meanings of events are altered by theater technique, hypnoanalysis, negative effects, or suggestions for sensory confusion.
5. *Exposure to feared stimuli in a safe setting.* Behavior therapists, cognitive-behavior therapists, Gestalt therapists, Sigmund Freud, and children's grandmothers tend to have one construct in common: when it comes to fears and phobias, talking is not enough. As Clarke and Jackson (1983) succinctly stated, "Exposure is *the* treatment for phobic anxiety" (p. 201) (emphasis in original). Whether through the adventures of story characters, the careful use of hierarchically arranged images, or entrance into a situation under the protective influence of a superhero, hypnotic techniques and suggestions expose the patient to the feared stimuli in a relaxed state and in safety. Posthypnotic suggestions may also be used to expedite in vivo exposure without rapid escape or overwhelming anxiety.

6. *Increasing a feeling of self-efficacy and control.* Providing tools for controlling the feared response to the feared object, situation, or thought may be central to therapeutic interventions. Bandura (1977) proposed this notion originally in the context of analyzing change in the treatment of fear and avoidance. Self-efficacy refers to a person's expectations that he or she can successfully behave in ways that lead to a desired outcome. Self-efficacy and perceived control may be particularly powerful for children who have diminished real control and influence relative to adults.

It should also be noted that in many of the case reports of hypnotic treatment of anxiety and phobias, nonhypnotic interventions also were used. In the cases involving children, almost all of these out-of-trance activities served to alter the physical, emotional, or social environment. Parents were advised as to management skills, divorced fathers were asked to cease threats of sending a child to live with his or her mother, medical personnel were taught to foster positive expectations, and so on. As in almost any therapeutic work with children, parents and other powerful adults need to be included.

The Presentation of Hypnosis

Anxiety is a powerful emotion that can be subjectively overwhelming. Because of its impact on therapeutic processes, special preparation is useful and technical proficiency is particularly important.

It is well known that people have a variety of misconceptions about hypnosis. Parents may have had experiences with stage or parlor-trick hypnosis while their children may have unrealistic views of the procedure, sometimes based on what they have learned from such experts in the field as D. Duck. Anxious children, and their often-anxious parents, may require additional preparation time. Not only should common myths be dispelled, but discussion should cover fears that may extend to the hypnotherapeutic relationship. For example, some children with performance anxiety may be particularly concerned with failure or that they will disappoint their therapist or parents. Children with separation anxiety may or may not tolerate their parents waiting outside during sessions. Children with fears of the dark or sleep need to have procedures altered and/or time taken to discuss implications for suggestions of eye closure. The loss of control anticipated in hypnosis can be particularly anxiety-provoking for those with social anxieties or panic disorder. Since the child patients generally know they are in treatment for their fears, it is often useful to reassure them that there will be no surprise exposure to feared stimuli and that the therapist cannot and will not force them to face a fear before they can handle the situation.

Hypnotherapists vary as to their approach to parents. In addition to the usual caveats for child therapists about parents, it is critical that the therapist know, and take into account, the role of the anxiety in the parent–child relationship. A thorough assessment, providing a framework that can be built upon in ongoing hypnotherapy, helps with treatment planning. For example, overprotective parents accustomed to helping the child avoid feared stimuli may need to experience hypnosis first, and then observe the child in a trance. Ultimately, though, helping the child to enter treatment sessions alone and to take responsibility for home practice may be as therapeutic as the hypnotic interventions themselves. Similarly, assisting the parents in supporting the child's progress requires knowledge of, and often changes in, secondary gain, the parents' expectations, and the parents' own comfort level with the feared object. Gardner and Olness (1981) described changing treatment strategies entirely once it was learned that the real fear was the mother's and the presenting complaint of the 5-year-old's "extreme fear" represented obedience rather than phobia.

RESEARCH DIRECTIONS

While there is no empirical evidence that anxious children cannot benefit from the same induction and deepening techniques as other children, there have been some clinically developed recommendations. For example, Clarke and Jackson (1983) stated that the process by which one becomes phobic is similar to that of hypnosis, perhaps through increased suggestibility. Spiegel (1974) wrote about the highly susceptible person being open to both positive and negative field forces. There is a need to determine whether the relationship between hypnotizability and phobias holds for children. The relatively high rates of fears and phobias in children co-occur with a relatively high level of responsivity for children as a group. If it turns out that the highly responsive children tend to be more anxious, some further important questions will arise: Do all highly responsive children develop more fears? If so, what is the mechanism of fear acquisition? If not, why not? What are protective factors in temperament or environment? How are phobic children of low responsivity different from phobic children of high responsivity? The influence of cognitive development during childhood on responsiveness and the timing of phobia onset is also important.

A second area of theoretical interest is directly related to the first: What are the physiological changes that occur in hypnosis for anxiety control? Are these changes primary or secondary to, or simultaneous with, the cognitive-affective changes? This area has implications for psychophysiological disorders affected by anxiety.

From a more clinical perspective, several areas seem promising. The first is a component analysis of treatment packages for anxiety disorders in children. The literature is clear that many different kinds of approaches can be taken within hypnotherapy. Hypnosis also generally is only one of several techniques used with childhood fears and phobias; usually, parents are involved, environmental manipulations take place, and often much basic education of the child about the feared objects is accomplished. Knowing the relative weights that should be assigned to the components under specific circumstances would improve the efficiency and power of treatment interventions.

Two specific areas within the anxiety disorders are particularly lacking in development relative to others for children. The utility of hypnotherapy for panic disorders and PTSD in children has not been established, despite theoretical reasons to anticipate its effectiveness.

REFERENCES

Agras, W. S., Sylvester, D., & Oliveau, D. C. (1969). The epidemiology of common fears and phobias. *Comprehensive Psychiatry, 10,* 151–156.

Ambrose, G. (1968) Hypnosis in the treatment of children. *American Journal of Clinical Hypnosis, 11,* 1–5.

American Psychiatric Association (1987). *The diagnostic and statistical manual* (3rd ed., rev.). Washington, DC: Author.

Aronoff, G. M., Aronoff, S., & Peck, L. W. (1975). Hypnotherapy in the treatment of bronchial asthma. *Annals of Allergy, 34,* 356–362.

Ayers, W. A. (1982). *Behavioral factors influencing dental treatment.* Chicago: Bureau of Economic and Behavioral Research, American Dental Association.

Bandura, A. (1977). Self-efficacy: Toward a unifying theory of behavioral change. *Psychological Review, 84,* 191–215.

Barbour, J. (1980). Medigrams: Self-hypnosis and asthma. *American Family Physician, 21,* 173.

Bernick, S. M. (1972). Relaxation, suggestion, and hypnosis in dentistry. *Pediatric Dentistry, 11,* 72.

Bowlby, J. (1975). *Attachment and loss* (Vol. 2). Middlesex, England: Penguin Books.

Breier, A., Charney, D. S., & Heninger, G. R. (1986). Agoraphobia with panic attacks. *Archives of General Psychiatry, 43,* 1029–1037.

Clarke, J. C., & Jackson, J. A. (1983). *Hypnosis and behavior therapy.* New York: Springer.

Cohen, S. B. (1989). Clinical uses of measures of hypnotizability. *American Journal of Clinical Hypnosis, 32,* 4–9.

Collison, D. R. (1975). Which asthmatic patients should be treated by hypnotherapy? *Medical Journal of Australia, 1,* 776–781.

Crasilneck, H. B., & Hall, J. A. (1975). *Clinical hypnosis: Principles and applications.* New York: Grune & Stratton.

Creer, T. L. (1980). Self management behavioral strategies for asthmatics. *Behavioral Medicine, 7,* 14–24.

Creer, T. L., Renne, C. M., & Chai, M. (1982). The application of behavioral techniques to asthma. In D. C. Russo & J. W. Varni (Eds.), *Behavioral pediatrics: Research and practice*. New York: Plenum.

Dash, J. (1981). Rapid hypno-behavioral treatment of a needle phobia in a five-year-old cardiac patient. *Journal of Pediatric Psychology, 6,* 37–42.

Diego, R. V. (1961). Hypnosis in the treatment of the asthmatic child. *Bulletin of the Tulane Medical Society, 20,* 307–313.

Erickson, M., Hershman, S., & Secter, I. (1961). *The practical application of medical and dental hypnosis*. Chicago: Seminars on Hypnosis Publishing.

Foenander, G., Burrows, G. D., Gerschmann, J., & Horne, D. J. (1980). Phobic behavior and hypnotic susceptibility. *Australian Journal of Clinical and Experimental Hypnosis, 8,* 41–46.

Frankel, F. H., & Orne, M. T. (1976). Hypnotizability and phobic behavior. *Archives of General Psychiatry, 33,* 1259–1261.

Gardner, G. G. (1974). Hypnosis with children. *International Journal of Clinical and Experimental Hypnosis, 22,* 20–38.

Gardner, G. G. (1976). Childhood death and human dignity: Hypnosis for David. *International Journal of Clinical and Experimental Hypnosis, 24,* 122–139.

Gardner, G. G. (1978). The use of hypnotherapy in a pediatric setting. In E. Gellert (Ed.), *Psychosocial aspects of pediatric care*. New York: Grune & Stratton.

Gardner, G. G., & Hinton, R. M. (1980). Hypnosis with children. In Burrows & Dennerstein (Eds.), *Handbook of hypnosis and psychosomatic medicine*. Amsterdam: Elsevier/North Holland Biomedical Press.

Gardner, G. G., & Olness, K. (1981). *Hypnosis and hypnotherapy with children*. New York: Grune & Stratton.

Gittelman, R., & Klein, D. F. (1984). Relationship between separation anxiety and panic and agoraphobic disorders. *Psychopathology, 179,* 56–68.

Hilgard, E., & Hilgard, J. (1975). *Hypnosis in the relief of pain*. Los Altos, CA: Kaufmann.

Hilgard, J., & LeBaron, S. (1982). Relief of anxiety and pain in children and adolescents with cancer: Quantitative measures and clinical observations. *International Journal of Clinical and Experimental Hypnosis, 30,* 417–442.

Hilgard, J., & LeBaron, S. (1984). *Hypnotherapy of pain in children with cancer*. Los Altos, CA: Kaufmann.

Hodel, T, Gemunder, C., O'Grady, D. J., Steffen, J. J., & Lampkin, B. (1982). Hypnosis for leukemic children for coping with medical procedural distress. Presented at the American Psychological Association Annual Meeting, Washington, DC.

Hodgson, R., & Rachman, S. (1974). Desynchrony in measures of fear. *Behavior Research and Therapy, 12,* 319–326.

Ilg, F. L., & Ames, L. B. (1955). *Child behavior*. New York: Harper.

Jacobs, L. (1962). Hypnosis in clinical pediatrics. *New York State Journal of Medicine, 62,* 3781–3786.

Jacobs, L. (1964). Sleep problems of children: Treatment by hypnosis. *New York State Journal of Medicine, 64,* 629–634.

Kahn, J. H., & Nursten, J. P. (1962). School refusal: A comprehensive view of school phobias and other failures of school attendance. *American Journal of Orthopsychiatry, 32*, 707–718.

Kennedy, W. A. (1965). School phobia: Rapid treatment of 50 cases. *Journal of Abnormal Psychology, 70*, 285—289.

Klauber, R. W. (1984). Hypnosis in education and school psychology. In W. Wester & A. Smith (Eds.), *Clinical hypnosis: A multidisciplinary approach*. Philadelphia: Lippincott.

Klepac, R. K., McDonald, M., Hauge, G., & Dowling, J. (1980). Reactions to pain among subjects high and low in dental fear. *Journal of Behavioral Medicine, 3*, 373–384.

Kluft, R. P. (1991). Hypnosis in childhood trauma. In W. C. Wester & D. J. O'Grady (Eds.), *Clinical hypnosis with children*. New York: Brunner/Mazel.

Koe, G. G. (1989). Hypnotic treatment of sleep terror disorder: A case report. *American Journal of Clinical Hypnosis, 32*, 36–40.

Kohen, D. P. (1980). Relaxation–mental imagery (hypnosis) and pelvic examinations in adolescents. *Journal of Behavior and Development Pediatrics, 1*, 180–186.

Kohen, D. P. (1986). Applications of relaxation/mental imagery (self-hypnosis) in pediatric emergencies. *International Journal of Clinical and Experimental Hypnosis, 34*, 283–294.

Kohen, D. P., Olness, K. N., Colwell, S., & Heimel, A. (1984). The use of relaxation–mental imagery (self-hypnosis) in the management of 505 pediatric behavioral encounters. *Developmental and Behavioral Pediatrics, 5*, 21–25.

Krippner, S. (1966). The use of hypnosis with elementary and secondary school children in a summer reading clinic. *American Journal of Clinical Hypnosis, 8*, 261–269.

Kroll, T. (1962). Hypnosis for the poor risk dental patient. *American Journal of Clinical Hypnosis, 5*, 142–144.

LaPouse, R., & Monk, N. (1959). Fears and worries in a representative sample of children. *American Journal of Orthopsychiatry, 29*, 803–818.

Lawlor, E. D. (1976). Hypnotic intervention with "school phobic" children. *International Journal of Clinical and Experimental Hypnosis, 24*, 74–86.

Lazarus, A. A., & Abromovitz, A. (1962). The use of "emotive imagery" in the treatment of children's phobias. *Journal of Mental Science, 108*, 191–195.

Levine, E. (1980). Indirect suggestions through personalized fairy tales for treatment of childhood insomnia. *American Journal of Clinical Hypnosis, 23*, 57–63.

London, P. (1963). *Children's hypnotic susceptibility scale*. Palo Alto, CA: Consulting Psychologists Press.

London, P., & Cooper, L. (1969). Norms of hypnotic responsiveness in children. *Developmental Psychology, 1*, 113–124.

MacFarlane, J. W., Allen, L., & Honzik, M. P. (1954). *A developmental study of the behavior problems of normal children between 21 months and 14 years*. Berkeley, CA: University of California Press.

Mason, R. D. (1987). Educational uses of hypnotism: A reply to Professor Lightner Witner's editorial. *Pediatrics, 3*, 97–105.

Miller, L. C., Barrett, C. L., & Hampe, E. (1974). Phobias of childhood in a prescientific era. In A. Davids (Ed.), *Child personality and psychopathology: Current topics*. New York: Wiley.

Mirvish, I. (1978). Hypnotherapy for the child with chronic eczema: A case report. *South African Medical Journal, 54*, 410–412.

Morgan, A., & Hilgard, J. (1979). The Stanford Hypnotic Clinical Scale for Children. *American Journal of Clinical Hypnosis, 21*, 134–147.

Neiburger, E. J. (1978). Child response to suggestion: Study of age, sex, time, and income levels during dental care. *Journal of Dentistry for Children, 47*, 396–402.

Ollendick, T. H. (1979). Fear reduction techniques with children. In M. Hersen, R. M. Eisler, & P. M. Miller (Eds.), *Progress in behavior modification* (Vol. 8). New York: Academic.

Olness, K. (1977). In-service hypnosis education in a children's hospital. *American Journal of Clinical Hypnosis, 20*, 80–83.

Olness, K. (1981). Imagery (self-hypnosis) as adjunct therapy in childhood cancer: Clinical experience with 25 patients. *American Journal of Pediatric Hematology/Oncology, 3*, 313–321.

Olness, K. (1986). Hypnotherapy in children. *Postgraduate Medicine, 79*, 95–105.

Olness, K., & Gardner, G. G. (1978). Some guidelines for uses of hypnotherapy in pediatrics. *Pediatrics, 62*, 228–233.

Paul, G. L. (1969). Outcome of systematic desensitization. II. Controlled investigations of individual treatment variations and current status. In C. N. Franks (Ed.), *Behavior therapy: Appraisal and status*. New York: McGraw-Hill.

Rhue, J., & Lynn S. (1991). The use of hypnotic techniques with sexually abused children. In W. C. Wester & D. J. O'Grady (Eds.), *Clinical hypnosis with children*. New York: Brunner/Mazel.

Schneck, J. M. (1966). Hypnoanalytic elucidation of a childhood germ phobia. *International Journal of Clinical and Experimental Hypnosis, 14*, 305–307.

Shaw, O. (1975). Dental anxiety in children. *British Dental Journal, 139*, 134–139.

Smith, S. R. (1965). The uses and limitations of hypnosis in children's dentistry. *British Dental Journal, 119*, 499–501.

Spiegel, H. (1974). The grade 5 syndrome: The highly hypnotizable person. *International Journal of Clinical and Experimental Hypnosis, 22*, 303–319.

Stampfl, T. G., & Lewis, D. J. (1967). Essentials of implosive therapy: A learning theory-based psychodynamics behavioral therapy. *Journal of Abnormal Psychology, 72*, 496–503.

Sticker, G., & Howitt, J. W. (1965). Physiological recording during simulated dental appointments. *New York State Dental Journal, 3*, 204.

Taboada, E. L. (1975). Night terrors in a child treated with hypnosis. *American Journal of Clinical Hypnosis, 17*, 270–271.

Thompson, R. G. (1963). A rationale for suggestion in dentistry. *American Journal of Clinical Hypnosis, 5*, 181–186.

Tifton, P. (1984). The hypnotic hero: A technique for hypnosis with children. *International Journal of Clinical and Experimental Hypnosis, 32*, 4, 366–375.

Weinstein, P. (1980). Identifying patterns of behavior during treatment of children. In B. Ingersoll & W. McKutcheon (Eds.), *Proceedings of the second national conference on behavioral dentistry.* Morgantown, WV: University of West Virginia Press.

Wolfe, V., Gentile, C., & Wolfe, D. (1989). The impact of sexual abuse on children: A PTSD formulation. *Behavior Therapy, 20,* 215–228.

Zeltzer, L., & LeBaron, S. (1982). Hypnosis and nonhypnotic techniques for reduction of pain and anxiety during painful procedures in children and adolescents with cancer. *Journal of Pediatrics, 101,* 1032–1035.

10 Hypnotherapy of Childhood Somatoform Disorders

Gary Elkins, Ph.D.

Perhaps more than any other health professionals, those who practice hypnosis and psychosomatic medicine with children are confronted with the emotional and psychological aspects of disease etiology and symptom presentation. In medical practice, children are generally brought by their parents and the focus is usually on a physical symptom or a complex of symptoms. The doctor must have considerable expertise in the physiology of disease. However, expertise in the physiology alone is not enough. The child's presentation of symptoms may be affected by psychological factors as well. In clinical practice, the dynamics of the child's family, stressful events in the child's life, and school or environmental concerns may be of primary importance in understanding the cause of symptoms and in planning treatment. The practitioner of hypnotherapy for childhood psychosomatic disorders should be especially cognizant of these influences. A short case history, taken from the early work of Anton Mesmer (often regarded as the father of hypnosis), illustrates this point.

Among patients treated by Mesmer (Tinterow, 1970) was a teenage girl whose complaints included poor sight, depression, rage, and episodes of delirium and seizures. Mesmer began to treat the girl using his technique of "therapeutic passes" and "mesmerism." The therapy was successful; the girl's sight was restored, and she was reported to be symptom-free. The father then stopped treatment prematurely as the girl's disability pension was to be terminated. The presenting symptoms returned. Mesmer again was asked to treat the patient, and once again her symptoms were removed.

However, after the girl returned home, she relapsed again. Mesmer specu-lated that parental influences were of primary importance and that the girl may have been urged to generate symptoms.

WHAT IS PSYCHOSOMATIC?

In the third edition of the *Diagnostic and Statistical Manual of Mental Disorders* (DSM-III) (American Psychiatric Association, 1987) the essential feature of somatoform disorders is defined as:

physical symptoms suggesting physical disorder (hence somatoform) for which there are no demonstrable organic findings or known physio-logic mechanisms, and for which there is positive evidence or strong presumption that the symptoms are linked to psychological facts or conflicts. (p. 255)

Also, a separate category is reserved for a diagnosis referred to as "psy-chological factors affecting physical condition." This diagnosis is rather broadly defined to include numerous symptoms. The DSM-III states:

This category can apply to any physical condition to which psychologi-cal facts are judged to be contributory. It can be used to describe disorders that in the past have been referred to as either "psychoso-matic" or "psychophysiological."

Common examples of physical conditions for which this category may be appropriate include, but are not limited to, obesity, tension, headaches, migraine headaches, angina pectoris, painful menstruation, sacroliac pain, neurodermatitis, acne, rheumatoid arthritis, asthma, tachycardia, gastric ul-cer, duodenal ulcer, cardiospasm, nausea and vomiting, ulcerative colitis, and frequency of micturition (p. 333).

These definitions exemplify the complexity of the interrelationship be-tween *psyche* and *soma*. While there is general agreement that the two interact, it is also clear that there is no simple or direct relationship between the body and mind. There is, in fact, a diversity of opinions about the etiology of "psychosomatic" symptoms.

Patients suffering from physical symptoms without clear organic etiology are often believed to have difficulty in expressing their emotions. This psy-chodynamic formulation proposes that repression or suppression of threaten-ing emotions leads to physical symptoms. The patient tends to "hold emo-tions inward" so that the emotion is transformed into a physical expression

(Alexander, 1950). This view relates specific personality characteristics, interpersonal conflicts, and emotions to specific psychosomatic symptoms. For example, a patient who states that a conflict in the family "makes me sick" may develop abdominal pain and nausea. Hypnotherapy may be directed toward uncovering and resolving the underlying emotional conflict.

An alternative view is that of social learning theory. This formulation emphasizes the effects of modeling and social reinforcement. The child may learn a "sick role" that is then reinforced through attention and social support. An adult or another child with physical complaints serves as a model that the child unconsciously learns to imitate. Modeling is demonstrated in the child who has difficulty in school and whose parent has chronic headaches. The child's complaint of headache (learned from the parent) may bring about an exemption from school (avoidance learning) and increased attention and nurturing from family, peers, teachers, and physicians (social reinforcement).

A third conceptualization may be referred to as a "stress-coping model" of psychosomatic disorders. The individual attempts to cope with a stressful situation but feels overwhelmed when existing coping mechanisms are inadequate. Therapeutic approaches such as stress management, self-control relaxation, and self-hypnosis are used to teach the patient specific skills to enhance a greater sense of control and self-efficacy.

These diverging views have recently been integrated around the general concept that an understanding of psychosomatic symptoms requires a knowledge of biological processes as well as social-psychological facts. A biopsychosocial model has been proposed (Van Egeren & Fahrega, 1976) that attempts to integrate the physical, psychodynamic, and social aspects into a holistic approach to diagnosis and treatment. A combination of diverse approaches such as behavioral therapy, family counseling, hypnosis, and pharmacotherapy is utilized concurrently. One needs to be flexible and approach the child and family by taking into consideration the particular dynamics, beliefs, and needs of the individual (Diamond, Havens, & Jones, 1978), using all or only some of the available approaches. Let us turn our attention to some specific psychosomatic disorders in children.

LITERATURE REVIEW

Any attempt to review all possible psychosomatic symptoms in children would probably fall short of its goal. The range is so great that some investigations have suggested that virtually all physical disorders are at least partly psychosomatic. This review, therefore, will be limited to a few of the more investigated and clinically common problems.

Abdominal Pain

The symptom of recurrent abdominal pain is perhaps the most common complaint in childhood. It is somewhat more common in girls than boys. In any particular child, both organic and psychologic causes must be considered (Schaefer, Millman, & Levine, 1979).

However, estimates are that only 8 percent of children with this complaint are found later to have an identifiable organic etiology (Apley, 1975). More often, emotion is found to be expressed as "my stomach hurts." The complaint may become chronic as secondary gain factors enter the picture.

Gardner and Olness (1981) reported a case of a 15-year-old girl referred for psychogenic abdominal pain of six months' duration. Numerous laboratory and diagnostic tests had been carried out, all of which were normal. The patient had lost weight and previous treatments had been unsuccessful. The parents were divorced. The girl was in the custody of the mother and visited the father, who had remarried, on weekends. The patient was taught self-hypnosis, with minimal improvement. When she returned, hypnosis was used with the suggestion that she age regress to an event that she had enjoyed and a time when she felt more in control. She was also asked to become aware of things that were troublesome to her. She reported subjective improvement in symptoms. A week later, she moved into the home of her father. She continued to use hypnosis and continued follow-up appointments for review of hypnotherapy for two years. All symptoms stopped and she had no recurrence of abdominal pain.

The present author treated a 9-year-old girl, Susan, who was referred by her pediatrician because of abdominal pain of four months' duration. Medical evaluation had been unremarkable. Interestingly, her complaints had been minimal during the summer vacation and on weekends. Susan was an only child, and in spite of having missed two weeks of school, maintained excellent grades. There were no major family conflicts; however, much of the parents' interaction with Susan revolved around their concern for her physical health. The mother had a history of tension headaches. During the initial interview, the mother spontaneously mentioned that the patient greatly "pressured" herself about grades and, in fact, cried when she received a B in one subject when all of her other grades were As. A diagnosis of psychogenic abdominal pain was made. Susan was seen and taught self-hypnosis. The imagery of playing with "Pete's Magic Dragon" (an image that the patient particularly enjoyed) was combined with suggestions for relaxation, self-control, and mastery. In addition, the parents were asked to stop discussing the patient's symptoms, to return her to school, and simply to support her use of self-hypnosis. It was emphasized that the responsibility was the patient's. the patient was able greatly to reduce her discomfort during the first hypnotherapy session in the author's office. On five subsequent visits, psychotherapy and suggestions during hypnosis focused on her becoming less perfectionistic and increasing her self-acceptance. The patient's complaints stopped after one month, and there was no symptom substitution during a one-and-a-half-year follow-up period.

An interesting case was reported by Williams and Singh (1976). The patient was an 11-year-old boy hospitalized for chronic abdominal pain, apparently of functional origin. During the hypnotherapy session, the child was given the following suggestions: (1) "Cooped-up feelings can cause tension." (2) "Tension can cause physical pain." (3) "By relaxing, I can reduce tension and eliminate pain." He was also taught self-hypnosis. At a 20-month follow-up, he had had only one episode of abdominal pain.

Psychogenic Seizures

It is a difficult undertaking to distinguish among purely neurogenic seizures, seizures of a hysterical or psychogenic etiology, and a combination of these factors. The physical presentations are similar and may be indistinguishable through observation alone. As far as possible, it is important first to establish the degree to which organic factors are involved. Hypnosis may be useful in diagnosis. A case example follows.

Kevin, a 10-year-old boy, was admitted to the physical-medicine unit because of uncontrolled seizures. He had missed seven weeks of school owing to almost daily seizures. The patient had been diagnosed as having a seizure disorder five years earlier and was placed on a regimen of Dilantin—initially with good results. However, his seizures began to recur two years prior to the hospital admission after the death of a younger brother who had fallen from the back of a moving truck in which both he and the patient had been riding. The patient was observed by the nursing staff to be very clinging and he would have seizures (up to 14 per day) when his requests for attention were not immediately met. Psychogenic seizures were suspected; his seizures consisted of trembling movements in his arms and legs.

The present author was consulted to assist with further diagnosis and treatment. Kevin proved to be an excellent subject and quickly responded to hypnotic suggestions. During the hypnotherapy session, the author suggested that he could begin to have a seizure when he was touched on the forehead. The patient responded to this suggestion and then was able to terminate the seizure when requested. In addition, a posthypnotic suggestion was given that when his pediatrician later touched his forehead, seizure activity would again result. The next day during electroencephalographic (EEG) recording, the sequence of hypnotic induction and suggestion was repeated. The EEG tracings were normal throughout the "seizure." During later sessions, the patient was taught self-hypnosis with suggestions for control of his seizures. Kevin was an avid science-fiction fan. The imagery used was of his being in a spaceship with the mission of shooting down enemy "rockets." Suggestions were given that each "rocket represents a part of a seizure" and "as you shoot down each rocket, the seizure becomes less and less as you relax more and more." The patient began to practice self-hypnosis on a daily basis. Over the next three weeks, his seizures eventually stopped. The family entered counseling to deal with the grief over the loss of the younger brother. At a three-year follow-up, the patient's seizures had remained under control.

Gardner (1973) described her treatment of an 8-year-old girl with familial epilepsy. The seizure episodes consisted clinically of brief eye-fluttering spells, which were relatively well controlled when she entered kindergarten. However, in the spring of that year, she began to have increased seizures that were associated with increased irritability and hyperactivity. Two years later, she manifested almost constant "eye fluttering" and could not function at home or at school.

In the hospital, it was observed that the spells greatly diminished when she felt she was not being observed or was engaged in a solitary activity such as watching television. The patient was taught self-hypnosis with suggestions for increased control and relaxation: "If you really want to be very relaxed, you can imagine balloons tied to your wrist, and you can let the balloons pull your hand up little by little. You can let your hand feel so light that it floats up higher and higher until it touches your face and flops again down in your lap" (p. 168). The patient was also given suggestions for ego strengthening (Hartland, 1971), daily practice of relaxation, and the ability to keep her eyes open. The patient was seen for a total of 18 hypnotherapy and play therapy sessions over a three-month period. The seizure frequency markedly decreased; she reentered school with marked improvement and was continuing to make progress both at home and school 10 months after treatment had begun.

Williams, Spiegel, and Mostofsky (1978) briefly described a case of an 8-year-old boy who was initially diagnosed as having psychomotor epilepsy of one month's duration. His seizures were not controlled on 90 mg of phenobarbital per day or 150 mg of phenytoin sodium per day. A careful review of the previous EEG revealed that it had been "overread." Psychiatric evaluation indicated that the seizures were of a psychogenic nature. A combination of hypnosis and family therapy was instituted with favorable results. Follow-up 10 months later found him to be seizure-free without using any anticonvulsant medication.

Conversion Disorder

Most children with conversion symptoms are seen in medical rather than psychiatric settings. Symptoms of hysteria may include a wide range of sensory and motor functions, such as pain (Williams, 1979), blindness (Theodor & Mandelcorn, 1973), paralysis (Crasilneck & Hall, 1985), mass psychogenic illness (Elkins, Gamino, & Rynearson, 1988), coughing (Elkins & Carter, 1986), and weakness (Gardner & Olness, 1981). A survey of conversion reactions in pediatric departments of two large hospitals by Rae (1977) found that half of the children complained of headaches and/or abdominal pain.

Maloney (1980) conducted a review of 105 cases of conversion reaction in children seen at a large medical center. The onset of conversion symptoms was almost uniformly (97 percent) related to some stress in the family. For example, Maloney described a 13-year-old boy who developed intractable sneezing the day after his father entered the hospital for a back operation. Also, the majority of patients (58 percent) were found to have unresolved grief reactions. Bressler (1965) notes that the conversion symptoms may represent an identification with a deceased friend or relative. For example, a child developed headaches after his father died of a brain tumor. Also of interest, Maloney found with surprising consistency that depression and family conflicts were manifest in the families of children with conversion disorders. Fully 85 percent of the families had one parent who was clinically depressed and 77 percent of the families showed an inability to discuss feelings and had communication problems.

The prognosis for treatment of conversion disorders is generally positive, but becomes less favorable when the condition becomes chronic or treatment is delayed. Thus, the focus should be on early intervention. The diagnosis of conversion reaction depends on first ruling out an organic etiology of the patient's symptoms. For example, seen by the author, a 14-year-old girl with arm paralysis and numbness had symptoms that followed no known anatomical or neurological pathways. Psychological evaluation and psychometric testing indicated a conversion reaction.

Olness and Gardner (1978) reported an 8-year-old boy with progressive pain and weakness in the extremities of two weeks' duration; he could not walk or use his hands. Neurological examination revealed conflict between the boy and parents around independence–dependence issuess. Hypnosis was used to resolve the physical symptoms. Two sessions of hypnotherapy focused on the use of imagery "to recall previous good health and transfer these feelings to the present." He regained full use of his arms and legs and the hypersensitivity to pain resolved. He had been followed in outpatient psychotherapy with no resolution of symptoms. Hypnosis allowed the timely resolution of symptoms and avoided the possible complication of prolonged secondary gain.

Williams and Singh (1976) described their hypnotherapy approach with Maria, an 8-year-old Puerto Rican girl, admitted to the hospital with a progression of visual difficulties of a three-week duration. Her complaints were of such impaired visual acuity and peripheral vision that she was unable to function in school. Neurological, ophthalmological, and psychiatric evaluations all pointed to a conversion reaction. A number of important stressful events included: (1) two months earlier, a female cousin of Maria's had an accidental enucleation of her right eye; (2) one month earlier, a new infant was born in Maria's household; (3) three weeks prior to admission, Maria saw a television program portraying an episode of hysterical blindness; (4) two weeks prior to admission, Maria's class was changed; and (5) one week earlier, a man on the street pulled Maria's hair and then ran off.

A hypnotic exercise was developed and used concurrently with supportive explanation and family sessions. The hypnotic exercise, first with Maria alone and then in a joint session with Maria and her mother, involved Maria's repeating out loud the following statements while in a trance state:

1. "When people are very scared and upset, they may stop being able to see."
2. "By relaxing [with this exercise], I can overcome my scared and upset feelings."
3. "As soon as I am able to see better, I can go home and do all the things I like to do."

After the second session, Maria was discharged with only a mild subjective report of "blurriness." When she was seen 10 days later, her symptoms had completely resolved. At a 17-month follow-up, there was no recurrence of visual or behavioral problems.

Elkins and Carter (1986) described the use of hypnotherapy in the treatment of childhood psychogenic coughing. The patient, Larry, was 11 years, 10 months old. He had a chronic cough of such severity that it resulted in his missing about one month of school. The patient's symptoms began with a sore throat and mild cough. He was tested by his pediatrician, which resulted in a positive strep screen, and he was treated with penicillin. However, his cough became worse. He was seen 14 days later complaining of severe episodes of coughing that lasted up to five hours at a time. He was taking Phenergan with Codeine, which did not alleviate the cough. Tossin cough syrup was then tried, but the cough continued to worsen. On one occasion, his parents brought him to the emergency room, where he received an injection of morphine that stopped the cough, but for only a few hours.

The coughing, described by the father as a very distracting "loud barking," was of such severity that Larry was unable to attend school. The symptoms had continued for seven weeks before referral for hypnotherapy. Prior to referral, all medical and laboratory tests were found to be normal.

The patient was an only child and a good student in school. He stated that he wanted to return to school, but expressed some reluctance to return until he "was well." The use of hypnosis was discussed with both the child and parents, and they were interested and supportive of "anything that would help."

During the initial visit, it was learned that the patient enjoyed movies and especially liked the movie "Star Wars." This provided the basis for a "science-fiction imagery" (Elkins & Carter, 1981) technique. Larry was asked to take a deep breath and close his eyes. He was led, via mental imagery, on an imaging journey into space with "Luke Skywalker," where he met a friendly "Dr. Zargon" who provided a "wonderful medicine" to "cure his cough." At this point, the therapist lightly touched the patient around his neck with suggestions for relaxation, and "as the medicine is applied, your cough becomes less and less." The imagery resulted in immediate symptomatic relief as the coughing stopped. The patient was instructed in the daily practice of hypnosis using a tape recording. He was then returned to school full-time. The parents were asked to award him a special prize after he was able to attend school for a full week and to give daily praise for school attendance. The symptoms gradually stopped over the next seven days. At a seven-month follow-up, he had no symptoms or cough, was involved in school and extracurricular activities, and showed no symptom substitution. It was hypothesized that excessive parental attention and school avoidance had been contributing to the patient's intractable cough.

Sarles (1975) cited a case of a 16-year-old girl who was totally paralyzed from her neck down. Diagnostic studies failed to find any evidence of organic disease. Psychiatric evaluation revealed that her symptoms began after she was severely criticized for kissing a boy and was warned that every step she took would be watched. The patient was involved in eight weeks of treatment, which included family counseling and hypnosis that focused on age regression to uncover the dynamics and conflicts relative to her paralysis. Although no follow-up was reported, the patient made a complete recovery during the course of therapy.

The studies reviewed thus far reveal that a variety of hypnotherapeutic methods are employed with positive results. There are some common features among the differing approaches. What follows is a description of the author's approach to assessment and the planning of hypnotherapeutic interventions, which will be illustrated in a more detailed case study.

DIAGNOSIS AND HYPNOTHERAPY WITH
CHILDHOOD SOMATOFORM DISORDER

Assessment

When children develop symptoms of a psychosomatic nature, the first avenue of professional contact is within a medical milieu. Generally, children are first evaluated by their pediatrician and appropriate neurological and laboratory studies are carried out. As far as possible, organic causes of symptoms should be ruled out before the institution of psychological intervention and treatment. For example, the child with headaches first should receive a thorough and complete medical evaluation. The diagnosis of somatization or conversion disorder cannot be made on the basis of psychological testing or a psychiatric interview alone.

The second step is a thorough psychological assessment. This may include intellectual and personality test batteries as indicated by the clinician's judgment. In the initial consultation, the therapist seeks to understand and make sense of both the origins of the patient's symptoms and the factors that contribute to its maintenance. Included is an assessment of (1) stress factors, (2) modeling effects, (3) family dynamics, (4) reinforcement and secondary gain factors, (5) the child's own motivation and interests, and (6) hypnotizability.

In the consultation with the child and family, the therapist looks at any stress in the child's environment or major changes that have occurred. Green, Walker, Hickson, and Thompson (1985) found that patients with recurrent pain without organic etiology reported significantly higher life stress than comparison patients with organic findings. Negative events most commonly experienced in their study included failing grades, arguments between parents, family illness, peer conflicts, death in the family, sibling rivalry, arguments with parents, and losing a friend.

Family dynamics are also explored. The clinician may inquire as to whether anyone else in the family has a similar problem. It is useful to determine whether anyone else serves as a model for the child's symptoms and behavior, and also to ask or observe how the parents and siblings respond to the patient. Does the symptom result in reinforcement? For example, when the child complains of headaches, is he or she cuddled and given ice cream? Also, what do the parents believe about the problem? Are they resentful of psychological referral? Are they angry? What have they heard from their pediatrician? And, importantly, what are the parents' and child's beliefs and attitudes toward hypnosis? During this interview, I explore the child's interests, likes and dislikes, and development level in order to formulate an appropriate hypnotic induction.

Family Conference

A conference is held with the parents and child, and may include the referring physician as well. Usually, I see the parents first. During this meeting, I try to establish some level of rapport. Without a minimal degree of parental support, the most skillful hypnotic intentions are likely to fail. Our goal at this meeting is to (1) give the diagnosis and (2) formulate and agree upon a treatment plan. Apley (1977) refers to the commonly held "triple fallacy," which states that (1) physical symptoms must have (2) physical causes, which must have (3) physical treatments. The child and parents no longer can cling to a purely physical model of cause and treatment. I try first to encourage the family to express understanding, and I then try to present the diagnosis in a way that fits the child and parents' model of the world and that is acceptable and nonoffensive to them. The family is helped to understand the contribution of psychological factors, and the use of hypnosis is openly discussed and a treatment plan outlined.

Behavioral Management/Family Counseling

In addition to hypnotherapy, the treatment model I employ also includes what is commonly thought of as behavior therapy. If the child has been receiving rewards and attention for symptomatic behavior, then the parents are asked to ignore the behavior and instead to reinforce appropriate coping. For example, once the child has been able to attend a full week of school, the parents may be asked to give a special reward. If it is found, for example, that the child's behavior is really symptomatic of an underlying marital problem such as alcoholism, or if the parent is excessively dependent on the child, then marriage and/or family therapy is also recommended.

Hypnotherapy

Hypnosis is presented to the child as *a skill to be learned and mastered*. The emphasis is on enhancing the child's sense of self-control. This "teaching model" of hypnosis gives the child greater control over and responsibility for symptoms. A nonauthoritarian approach is usually taken that avoids forcing and instead gives the child the opportunity to learn hypnosis. The actual induction is individualized to suit the child's level of development, interests, fantasy, and likes. The child is seen for hypnotherapy, which may include altering symptoms, uncovering psychodynamics, and teaching self-hypnosis.

The initial hypnotic induction allows the emergence of some general idea of the child's responsiveness to hypnosis as a treatment. Hypnosis is a potent intervention and the possibility of rapid change and self-control is communicated to the child and parents. It is suggested during the preinduction talk that significant change may occur after the first hypnotherapy session.

Clinically, I do not use any of the standardized hypnotic susceptibility scales. However, it is often useful to demonstrate some "tests" of hypnotic responsiveness such as arm levitation or glove analgesia. This helps to increase the child's confidence and conviction in his or her ability to exert control. In order to demonstrate the child's degree of control, the child may be asked to produce symptoms (i.e., "the abdominal pain begins now") and then to reduce the symptoms (i.e., "as you now relax, the pain grows less and less") during the hypnotic induction and hypnotherapy.

In virtually all instances, I teach the child self-hypnosis. Usually, this also means making an audiotape recording of a session and giving it to the child for home practice. It is the child's responsibility to remember to practice hypnosis. The parents are usually asked to avoid reminding the child or otherwise trying to "take over" the child's responsibility (Olness, 1976). Rather, the parental role is to avoid attention to symptoms and to provide a supportive environment for the child's mastery of hypnosis.

The process of hypnotic induction and hypnotherapy is demonstrated in this case example of a child with chronic tension headaches. The accompanying narrative illustrates the type of induction, use of personal imagery, deepening, direct suggestion for symptomatic control, and self-hypnosis emphasizing the child's sense of mastery.

Case Example

Larry was a 14-year-old boy admitted to the hospital because of persistent and severe headaches. He had made numerous visits to the emergency department and pediatric clinic because of the headaches. Neurological and medical studies had been carried out, including an EEG, computed tomographic scan, and a spinal tap, which were entirely normal. He was on Tylenol with Codeine and Periactin. He had missed eight weeks of school prior to the consultation and was on a homebound program.

The headaches were bilateral and associated with neck tightness and shoulder stiffness. The parents denied any significant stress or conflict at home or school. He had maintained good grades and verbalized that he enjoyed school. In his discussion of medical problems, he was very conversant. For example, he stated during the initial visit, "I have the classic symptoms of allergy," and "My migraine headaches are in the usual localized areas." It was noted that the mother also had chronic headaches. In fact, the mother did not attend that session because she was at home "in bed with a sick headache.'' It was supposed that there was a component of identification with the mother with regard to headache symptoms and that school avoidance had become a secondary problem.

The parents did accept a partial psychological explanation of the headaches. In fact, they told me that after receiving the diagnosis of psychogenic headaches and the recommendation at the family conference that he return to school, the following events took place that evening at home.

"Larry became very upset at this, angry, and his headache started getting worse,'' they said. The parents reacted by trying to get him to calm down, having him sit in a whirlpool, and so on. But, in their words, he "worked himself up into a headache.'' By this they meant he became very nervous and was "trying to hyperventilate.'' They eventually got him to calm down by giving him a great deal of attention, reassurance, and compassion; administering Tylenol and Valium; and calling the family doctor. Larry had not returned to school.

The patient was then seen for hypnotherapy. The goal of the session was to gain symptomatic control of his headache and to instruct him in the use of hypnosis for self-control. The following is a transcript of that session. Further, it was emphasized to the parents that Larry should return to school and that they should avoid reinforcing symptoms by paying special attention to him or allowing absence from school.

Hypnotherapy with Larry

First take in all the air you can hold in your lungs. Hold, and as you exhale, now let your eyelids come down, closing.   Induction
That's right. All the way down. Very good. Exhale. Relax. Deeper and deeper. Relax. Each time you feel pressure on your right shoulder, Larry, that will be a cue to go into an even deeper state of hypnosis. Drifting deeper and deeper. Just like you were drifting down, just kind of drifting down,   Deepening
like you were in an elevator.

You are on the 10th floor in an elevator and every floor that you passed, going deeper and deeper in a deeper state of hypnosis as you do with each breath you exhale. More relaxed. Ten . . . nine . . . eight. Head, neck, and shoulders relax.   Relaxation
Shoulders slumping. Arms beginning to feel heavy. Eight—breathing each time you exhale, relaxing more. Seven. Elevator going down past the floors. Seven. Six. Five. Halfway there. Twice as relaxed. Four. That wave of relaxation spreading down to your legs. Feet beginning to feel heavy. Four.

Three. Two. All the way down now to one. Any tension that remains can be released now.

Now, Larry, a part of your mind can begin to drift. Just letting your mind drift to another place and that might be to go fishing. A part of your mind is able to relax you and let go of tension. While you go on a fishing trip now and see that happen. There you are at the river. Notice whether or not it's a warm day. And whether or not the water is cool; certainly it is cooler than the air around you so that you cannot only breathe the air, but feel it on your face and skin. Perhaps even a slight breeze, Larry, that blows through and that breeze can be so relaxing so that the muscles of your forehead just begin to relax. That's right. Doing very well. So that as you're there you may want to watch what's happened with the fishing and get ready to enjoy catching some fish. As you cast, the line goes out into the water and you get a bite and catch the first fish. You set the hook and begin to reel it in, bringing the fish in. And if it's all right with you, Larry, each time you cast out, as you reel in, the headache becomes less and less, less and less. Any discomfort becoming less and less and you are able to relax even more.

And so I'll know where you are, whenever you're aware of any sense of headache I'd like for you to raise one finger on your right hand or your thumb, whichever is right for you. That's right. Any amount of headache that you can feel now. Just raising that finger, or perhaps you've already gotten rid of the headache, and if that's occurred, I'd like for you to raise your thumb. Very good. Very good. That's right, just let that thumb come back down and just continue each time you cast out and you reel in, the headache becoming less and less. Feeling the tension go out of your shoulders. The muscles of your neck relax. Breathing slowly and more comfortably. Drifting all the way down, deeper and deeper, relaxed.

Just as relaxed as you need to be, just as relaxed as you want to be. Feeling of spreading comfort, and as you are fishing there, finding that it's warm enough, that your throat may feel a little dry, thirsty, and finding that you may find yourself going back to the shore. There is some cool water there, delicious, cold, clear, fresh water and it's hot today and feeling the warmth of the sunshine on the top of your head so that by the time you get there, you just want to sit down

Dissociation

Self-control

Multisensory Experience

Mental Imagery

Associating Symptom Control with Personal Imagery Symptom Control

Suggestion Relaxation

Personalized Mental Imagery

Multisensory Imagery

under a shade tree. And as you're there under the tree, drinking that cool water and enjoying it, and how relaxing and comfortable it is, how cold water can taste and how refreshing cold water can be. While you are sitting under that tree and the shade, watch the water of the river flow past. Maybe seeing the fish down at the bank that you've caught. Feeling more and more relaxed so as you're there, just resting under a tree and watching the river flow by.

Relaxation

Larry, any time in the future that you begin, just begin, to have a headache, you now have a way of controlling it by thinking the word "relax" and creating a feeling of relaxation across your forehead, neck, and shoulders. Learning more and more so then, as you practice self-hypnosis, becoming better and better at it. You can become so deeply relaxed whenever you want by practicing self-hypnosis. Alerting now as I count from three to one. Relaxed, three, becoming consciously alert. Two, more alert. One, alert, relaxed, and feeling good and normal in every way.

Emphasizing Maste and Self-Control

Alerting

REFERENCES

Alexander, F. (1950). *Psychosomatic medicine*. New York: Norton.

American Psychiatric Association (1987). *Diagnostic and statistical manual of mental disorders* (3rd ed., rev.). Washington, DC: Author.

Apley, J. (1975). *The child with abdominal pain* (2nd ed.). Oxford: Blackwell Scientific.

Bressler, B. (1965). Ulcerative colitis as an anniversary symptom. *Psychoanalytic Review, 43*, 381-383.

Crasilneck, H. D., & Hall, J. A. (1985). *Clinical hypnosis: Principle and application* (2nd ed.). New York: Grune & Stratton.

Diamond, R. E., Havens, R. A., & Jones, A. C. (1978). A conceptual framework for the practice of prescription eclecticism in psychotherapy. *American Psychologist, 33*, 239-248.

Elkins, G. R., & Carter, B. D. (1986). Hypnotherapy in the treatment of childhood psychogenic coughing: A case report. *American Journal of Clinical Hypnosis, 29*, 59-63.

Elkins, G. R., Gamino, L. A., & Rynearson, R. R. (1988). Mass psychogenic illness, trance states and suggestion. *American Journal of Clinical Hypnosis, 30*, 267-275.

Gardner, G. G. (1973). Use of hypnosis for psychogenic epilepsy in a child. *American Journal of Clinical Hypnosis, 15*, 166-169.

Gardner, G. G., & Olness, K. (1981). *Hypnosis and hypnotherapy with children*. New York: Grune & Stratton.

Green, J. W., Walker, L. S., Hickson, G., & Thompson, J. (1985). Stressful life events and somatic complaints in adolescents. *Pediatrics, 75,* 19-22.

Hartland, J. (1971). Further observations on the use of "ego strengthening" techniques. *American Journal of Clinical Hypnosis, 14,* 1-8.

Maloney, M. J. (1980). Diagnosing hysterical conversion reactions in children. *Journal of Pediatrics, 97,* 1016-1020.

Olness, K. (1976). Autohypnosis in functional megacolor in children. *American Journal of Clinical Hypnosis, 19,* 28-32.

Olness, K., & Gardner, G. G. (1978). Some guidelines for use of hypnotherapy in pediatrics. *Pediatrics, 62,* 28-32.

Rae, W. A. (1977). Childhood conversion reactions: A review of incidence in pediatric settings. *Journal of Clinical Child Psychology, 6,* 69-72.

Sarles, R. M. (1975). The use of hypnosis with hospitalized children. *Journal of Clinical Child Psychology, 4,* 36-38.

Schaefer, C. E., Millman, H. L., & Levine, G. E. (1979). *Therapies for psychosomatic disorders in children.* San Francisco: Jossey-Bass.

Theodor, L. H., & Mandelcorn, M. S. (1973). Hysterical blindness: A case report and study using a modern psychophysical technique. *Journal of Abnormal Psychology, 82,* 552-553.

Tinterow, M. M. (1970). *Foundations of hypnosis: From Mesmer to Freud.* Springfield, IL: Charles C. Thomas.

Van Egeren, L., & Fahrega, H. (1976). Behavioral science and medical education: A biobehavioral perspective. *Social Science and Medicine, 10,* 535-539.

Williams, D. T. (1979). Hypnosis as a therapeutic adjunct. In J. D. Noshpitz (Ed.), *Basic handbook of child psychiatry* (Vol. 3). New York: Basic Books.

Williams, D. T., & Singh, M. (1976). Hypnosis as a facilitating therapeutic adjunct in child psychiatry. *Journal of the American Academy of Child Psychiatry, 15,* 326-342.

Williams, D. T., Spiegel, H., & Mostolsky, D. I. (1978). Neurogenic and hysterical seizures in children and adolescents: Differential diagnosis and therapeutic considerations. *American Journal of Psychiatry, 135,* 82-86.

11 Hypnosis in the Treatment of Behavior Disorders

Charles G. Guyer II, Ed.D.

For many years, the term emotional disturbance has been utilized to describe such varied conditions as schizophrenia, autism, depression, anxiety, phobias, psychosomatic illness, and any untold number of anomalies. This term and the problems it represents grew largely out of the fields of psychology and medicine, but there is a lack of consensus across professions as to what it means. Seriously emotionally disturbed is the term that is used in Public Law 94-142 (which is the law that guarantees all children a right to an equal education regardless of handicap), and is also that most frequently found in research articles to describe deviant behavior in children (Wood, 1979). Most states use emotionally handicapped or a similar term as a way of describing children to be placed in special classes when deviate behaviors are exhibited (Mack, 1980).

DEFINITION OF BEHAVIOR DISORDERED

The term behavior disordered is in common use today by educators, psychologists, and physicians, as it is considered less stigmatizing, suggests less severe problems, and is more practical than the term emotionally disturbed. It is more practical because it describes the problem as an observable behavior rather than as an intrapsychic disorder. The term behavior disorder grew out of the behavioral model and has been accepted by teachers more readily than the medically based term emotionally disturbed. Educators feel more comfortable with tangible behaviors than with disturbed emotions, which they are unable to describe, and many now use the term emotionally disturbed to refer to more seriously impaired children. However, the terms behavior disordered and emotionally disturbed are still often interchanged, which leads to confusion in communications among educators, psychologists, and physicians.

In this chapter, a behavior disorder will be defined as a behavior that violates societal expectations in a specific setting. It is important to note that this definition places the power to identify a child with a behavioral problem in the hands of those who hold authority over the child. Thus, a number of factors influence the decision as to which child is labeled behavior disordered, including (1) the authority figures' tolerance for various behaviors, (2) the setting in which the behavior takes place, (3) the persistence of the behavior over time, and (4) the training and background of the authority figure observing the behavior.

Tolerance

Everyone has preferences for certain types of behavior and dislikes other types of behavior, and so parents too, differ drastically in their opinion of what is acceptable. Some parents, for example, allow their children to move around in church and to whisper during the sermon; others demand that the child sit erect, with both feet on the floor, and remain silent. According to Helton and Oakland (1977), teachers prefer to teach children who are passive and conforming, and Coleman and Gilliam (1983) found unfavorable teacher attitudes toward aggressive students. These studies, however, do note that the tolerance levels of individual teachers vary greatly. One teacher may not react to a child's being away from his or her desk, another may chastise the child, and still another may encourage such independent behavior.

Setting

The tolerance of an authority figure for a certain behavior will vary with the setting where the behavior occurs. The authority figure makes a judgment concerning the appropriateness of the behavior given a specific setting (e.g., noisy behavior is expected on the playground, but not during math class).

Persistence

An authority figure may accept an occasional deviance from the expected behavioral norms (e.g., talking in math class), but this behavior may become identified as a problem if it persists over time.

Professional Training

When a child has come to the attention of a professional person because of negative behavior, that professional must make an assessment as to whether the behavior is indeed deviant. Every professional operates according to a system of beliefs that have become ingrained as a result of the person's training and personal history. Thus, an educator, a psychologist, or a physician will make an assessment of a given child's behavior based, to some degree, on the assessor's experiential past. Hobbs (1975) notes that the same child "may be viewed as mentally ill by a physician, as emotionally disturbed by a psychologist, and as a behavior disordered child by a special educator" (p. 57).

It is generally agreed that children and adolescents who carry the label "behavior disordered" are characterized by aggressive, impulsive behavior that infringes on the basic rights of others. This type of behavior is generally viewed as being in violation of accepted social norms. And because social norms are often laws, the judicial system may become involved with the child, which often leads to some type of incarceration. Though many juvenile centers employ psychologists, physicians, and special educators, the general approach to such a child is the same as that frequently applied to a criminal. And in recent years, behavior-modification techniques have grown in popularity in correctional settings.

In spite of the difficulties encountered in defining the term behavior disorder, there is a growing trend toward utilizing this term in practice and research.

HYPNOTIC INTERVENTION

Although hypnotherapy is often the last resort in treating a behavior-disordered child, there is an emerging body of literature concerning this topic. Most empirical research focuses on the utilization of relaxation training and reciprocal inhibition with children and adolescents (Guyer & Guyer, 1984). These methods have been implemented successfully in the treatment of adolescent "acting out behavior" (Corter, Whiteside, & Haizlip, 1986), hyperactivity (Raymer & Poppen, 1985; Denkowski & Denkowski, 1984), trichotillomania (DeLuca & Holborn, 1984), and learning problems (Richter, 1984), and in the treatment of antisocial behavior in children (Kazdin, 1987). The literature is dominated by case studies in which hypnosis was specifically used to treat behavior disorders.

There are many reasons for behavior disorders in preadolescent children. The problem is sometimes attributed to tension discharge. Tension may be created by family problems, inconsistent parenting, or school adjustment. Aggressive behavior may emanate from feelings of rejection and often is used as an attention-getting device. A behavior disorder frequently represents inadequate and maladaptive defenses against anxiety, tension, and a poor self-concept. The goal of therapy, then, is to aid the child in creating mechanisms to cope with these feelings in a more functional manner. The value of hypnotherapy in this task was emphasized by Williams (1979), who stated: "Hypnosis can accelerate and augment the impact of psychotherapeutic intervention . . . the increased therapeutic leverage afforded by hypnosis can often facilitate both the conversion of insight into action and the more rapid relief of disabling symptoms" (p. 108). Baker (1983) feels that hypnosis can enhance the speed of psychotherapeutic intervention in achieving specific goals. Ambrose (1968) successfully implemented hypnotherapy to reduce tension and offer positive posthypnotic suggestions. Along with the hypnotherapy, a parental reeducation program was undertaken.

Williams and Singh (1976) describe the case of a 10-year-old boy who presented with a three-year history of temper tantrums. He had been diagnosed with minimal brain dysfunction and tension-discharge disorder with depressive features. The boy had not responded to previous interventions, which consisted of chemotherapy, behavior-modification therapy, and talking therapy. However, his tantrum behavior decreased with only three hypnotherapy sessions. The hypnotherapy was utilized in conjunction with medication, special placement, family therapy, and autogenic training.

Bauman (1970) built a case for considering drug abuse in adolescence a behavioral problem. He reported that the incidence of marijuana use in junior high school was as high as 30–40 percent, and that by the college level its use had reached 80 percent. Bauman utilized visual-imagery induction techniques to eliminate drug abuse in adolescents. He described a technique in which he used revivification of an earlier "good trip" for a happy drug experience. He then had the patient develop this hypnotically hallucinated drug experience into one which, in the patient's opinion, was more intense and profitable than the original experience. The positives of the self-induced experience were emphasized to the adolescent (i.e., it is not against the law, it is free, it is totally under the adolescent's control). This technique, Bauman found, was not successful with marijuana users, probably owing to a lack of motivation to change as most of them did not believe that marijuana was harmful to their health. Bauman did find that his approach worked with users of LSD and of amphetamines, as these users' understanding that their drugs of choice were dangerous gave them sufficient motivation to change.

Kohen, Olness, Colwell, and Heimel (1984) reviewed the outcomes of hypnotherapeutic interventions for 505 children and adolescents seen for an array of problems, ranging from enuresis to chronic pain and including behavior disorders. They reported that 51 percent of the children seen by them achieved complete remission of their problems (some of which were intrinsically chronic), 32 percent achieved significant improvement, and 9 percent showed initial or some improvement; 7 percent exhibited no change or improvement.

Lawlor (1976) suggests that hypnosis can be effective with school-phobic children. She describes the case of a 5-year-old boy, the eldest in a sibship of three. The child had developed normally until he became old enough to enter school. He then became fearful and began having tantrums each morning before going to school. Lawlor induced hypnosis by eye fixation on a beam of light from a penlight. Under hypnosis, the child revealed a fear of sibling rivalry and a fearfulness that his mother would die while he was away at school. It turned out that his grandmother, to whom he was very close, had died shortly before he began school. In Lawlor's approach, hypnosis was utilized as an uncovering technique. Once the difficulties were identified, a behavioral program was established that included the parents and school personnel. The child responded positively and was able to enter school without difficulty the following year.

Petty (1976) prefers to work entirely with the parents, and describes in great detail his use of hypnosis to desensitize parents to tantrum behavior in their children. He presents a case study of a 35-year-old mother whose 4-year-old daughter was referred to Petty for overactivity, belligerence, rebelliousness, and explosive behavior. The tantrums occurred when the child "did not get her way." The parent was instructed to extinguish this behavior by ignoring the tantrum. A contingency contract was set up under which the mother made the child's afternoon snack contingent on 30 minutes of tantrum-free behavior prior to the snack. The mother was also instructed to leave the room when her daughter threw a tantrum. However, the mother was unable to follow through on these instructions to ignore the tantrum behavior, and so Petty instigated a reciprocal inhibition paradigm. He utilized arm-levitation induction for relaxation through hypnosis. Under hypnosis, the mother was instructed to visualize her daughter's last tantrum behavior and to see herself as not disturbed by this behavior. The woman was then told to visualize a future tantrum of her daughter and to see herself feeling no anxiety while ignoring the tantrum. The behavior-modification techniques of extinction and contingency contracting were continued for three months, after which the mother reported that the daughter's tantrum behavior had improved dramatically.

Protinsky (1983) blended formal hypnotic induction and strategic family therapy to eliminate unwanted behaviors in three children. He described three cases (an 11-year-old girl, a 13-year-old boy, and a 14-year-old boy) in which he successfully utilized this approach. Protinsky interpeted the dysfunctional behavior of the child in each case to be protective of the parents in some manner. He viewed the child as parenting the parent and utilized hypnosis to bring insight to each family member that this role reversal was actually present. He then employed strategic family-therapy interventions to prevent a repetition of these protective sequences and to solidify the appropriate role of each family member in the family hierarchy.

ASSESSING THE CHILD FOR HYPNOTIC INTERVENTION

It is generally accepted by researchers and clinicians that children, as a group, are more responsive to hypnosis than adults. West and Deckert (1965) point out that there are few complications with the proper use of hypnosis, which they define to mean that the intervention is made by a fully trained professional who is skilled at hypnotic work.

Some hypnotherapists feel that persons with problems that shorten their attention span and ability to concentrate cannot be hypnotized (Ambrose, 1968; Gardner, 1974). If this assertion were indeed a fact, it would not be possible to use hypnosis in treating children with behavior disorders as they often exhibit a short attention span and poor concentration.

In recent years, many hypnotherapists have published on the topic of the hypnotic ability of schizophrenic, psychotic, and mentally retarded people, all of whom are noted for their short attention span and lack of concentration. Joan Murray-Jobsis is one of the most recent prolific writers in the use of hypnosis with psychotic patients (Murray-Jobsis, 1988; Scagnelli-Jobsis, 1982; Scagnelli, 1980). Baker (1983) supports the implementation of hypnosis with psychotic patients and presents a paradigm for its use. Haberman (1986) builds a case for the use of hypnotherapy with schizophrenic patients. Werbel, Mulhern, and Dubi (1983) and Owens (1980) have utilized hypnosis successfully with mentally retarded patients.

My own experience has been that behavior-disordered children can and do enter hypnosis easily. Sarles (1975) feels that the most common reason for the failure of hypnosis with children is the inability of the therapist to adapt to the cognitive, emotional, and experiential levels of the child. It is my experience that children with behavior disorders fall under the same assessment criteria for hypnosis as do other children. Gardner and Olness (1981) suggest that there is a curvilinear relationship between age and hypnotic responsivity, with a peak in middle childhood. There is a general feeling among child hypnotherapists that children under 4 years of age cannot be hypnotized. I have not found this to be the case in my own clinical work. This notion is true only if one adheres to the more traditional techniques of challenging and reinforcement. The use of permissive techniques has proved successful for many hypnotherapists with young children under the age of 4. Solovey and Milechnin (1955) found that with children indirect suggestion was more effective than direct authoritative methods in removing symptoms. There does appear to be a decrease in hypnotizability when a person reaches adolescence, however (London, 1962). Cooper (1966) found no sex differences in children's ability to be hypnotized. Sarles (1975) feels that children are perfect subjects for hypnosis owing to their lack of rigidity, ready access to fantasy, and excellent imaginations. Most children readily enter a trusting and accepting relationship with adults.

There are three important questions to be evaluated by the hypnotherapist before utilizing hypnosis with children who have been labeled as having a behavior disorder.

1. What led the parents to bring the child to treatment at this time?
2. How is the symptom benefiting the child?
3. Is the therapist comfortable with the use of hypnosis in this particular case?

Why Now?

What led the parents to bring the child to treatment at this time? It is important to know whether it is the parents or some other authority figure who is unhappy with the child's behavior. In other words, who defined the problem as a behavior disorder? What are the reasons for bringing the child to treatment now? Why not yesterday? Why not tomorrow? Frequently, the parents select a therapist who uses hypnosis because they feel that they "have tried everything else." Hypnosis is the last resort. The parents may expect magical results, or they may feel that there is no hope—but they must give it one last try. They may feel that hypnosis is not credible, but the school or physician strongly suggested that the child see a therapist who specifically employs hypnosis. The parents' reason for seeking a hypnotherapist will have a major effect on the hypnotherapeutic approach implemented by the professional. It will also dictate whether hypnosis is utilized individually or in combination with other methods.

How Is the Symptom Benefiting the Patient?

Behavior disorders in children often are reinforced by the parents or the school. If this is the case, behavior-modification techniques may be utilized in conjunction with hypnotherapy to bring about behavioral change. If the behavior disorder is being used to discharge tension, the therapist must uncover what is leading to the anxiety and tension. If the etiological factors are beyond the control of the therapist, hypnosis may be employed in conjunction with supportive therapy or play therapy to allow the child to learn more adaptive ways of coping with these problems. If the child has developed a low self-esteem through environmental crisis, hypnosis may be useful for ego enhancement through posthypnotic suggestions.

Is the Health-Care Specialist Comfortable Using Hypnosis with This Particular Patient?

Child hypnotherapists must first be competent child-development specialists who are comfortable with children in general. Children respond to hypnosis differently than do adults. They are more likely to move about, refuse to close their eyes, open and close their eyes from time to time, and make spontaneous sounds while in a hypnotic state and during hypnotic inductions. The child-health-care giver must also be creative and willing to change an induction in midstream if the child is not responding to the first method. Children respond to a wide array of induction methods.

The successful child hypnotherapist must be knowledgeable and comfortable with many induction and deepening techniques. Methods emphasizing the child's control and active involvement are most effective. A child hypnotherapist may be required to tolerate his or her own regression and allow childlike behavior and feelings to emerge during induction and deepening processes. Many adults find this type of regression frightening.

CASE STUDY OF AN INTERVENTION

J.B., an 8-year-old white boy, was brought to therapy by his mother with the chief complaint of a behavior disorder that evidenced itself on the school bus and in the classroom. Specific problems were defined as physical fighting while on the bus going to and from school and disobeying the bus driver. In the classroom, he was belligerent to the teacher and would not respond to positive reinforcement. J.B. was, however, an excellent student and appeared to be very bright when engaged in conversation. There were no medical problems. In our first two sessions, hypnosis was not officially announced, but hypnotic techniques were utilized. Play therapy was instigated and indirect suggestions embedded in the conversation. In our third session, J.B. complained of a headache. I explained to him that I had a magic way of allowing the discomfort to leave. We talked at length about his likes and dislikes. J.B. enjoyed cowboys and, specifically, their wars with Indians. He had a great admiration for American Indians. I first attempted a TV-movie induction involving cowboys and Indians. J.B. did not wish to imagine cowboys and Indians on the television screen. Instead, he engaged me in a lengthy conversation concerning American Indians.

I had completed my training in clinical psychology in Wyoming near the Little Big Horn River, and we talked at length about American Indians and their history. A Sioux friend had given me a medallion portraying an eagle in the American Indian art style. I have used this medallion successfully for hypnotic inductions in the past. This fascinated J.B., and the medallion, which hangs on a leather string, was utilized as a pendulum for induction with him. We did not talk about hypnosis. We only spoke of the power of the eagle on the medallion. J.B. responded beautifully to this hypnotic induction.

Induction

THERAPIST: This is a really neat necklace that was given to me by a friend who is a Sioux Indian. It has magic power to take away your headache. You told me that your head is uncomfortable and you would like to feel better. This can help.

PATIENT: I like this. It is pretty. How does it work?

THERAPIST: It works by you holding it and staring at it. It will begin to move automatically in your hand—like magic.

PATIENT: It really does move automatically. This is fun.

THERAPIST: Well, just keep holding it and looking at it. You might begin to see, in your imagination, the bird fly. And if you like, you might choose to fly with that bird, feeling lighter and lighter. Just like the bird. Isn't that fun?

PATIENT: Yes, I really like this, it is fun. I feel like I am flying.

THERAPIST: You can see the mountains of Wyoming below with snow on the top, the blue sky, the beautiful green of the evergreen trees, the streams, smelling the fresh, happy, comfortable mountain air as you fly high and free with the other eagles, who accept you, care for you, and *teach* you so much. You can feel the cool breeze against your skin as you move with the eagles as friends. They are so easy to get along with and like you. The eagles feel good with your new friendship and offer love, caring, and kindness. They accept you as one of them. The eagles fly and soar high, free, and happy. They meet Indians in the mountains. They are also friends. The Indians believe the eagles are magical, special, and good, and have strength and intelligence.

The Indians and eagles show love and caring for one another. The eagles gladly share their feathers with the Indians for bonnets to show their friendship. The Indians give the eagles food and water to show their friendship. Both the eagles and the Indians enjoy and feel happy with their ability to work together in peace. The eagles and the Indians find that as they talk and share their feelings, they care more for each other. The eagles feel happy with expressions of trust. The chief of the eagles and the chief of the Indians give their people instructions to continue with the gift of love and caring. *Both the eagles and the Indians love their chiefs and readily accept their instructions.* The two chiefs are happy. The Indian medicine man speaks with the eagle chief and offers to remove any discomfort and unhappiness that any eagle might feel. The eagle chief thanks him and thus begins a ceremony and dance [therapist sings a chant]. The medicine man through this dance brings comfort and well-being with good health to each eagle. The eagles leave the Indians with promises to return and visit their friends once again with an ever-increasing friendship and ever-increasing feelings of goodwill. With each visit, the eagles and the Indians will grow happier and more comfortable with their feelings and find it easier to express feelings.

Assessment of Effectiveness

This hypnotic work was combined with reciprocal inhibition training of the patient's mother to allow her more easily to ignore any inappropriate behavior of the patient at home. The mother was cooperative and hypnotic trance was used for relaxation, combined with a behavioral hierarchy. The mother was also trained with a parenting-skills package similar to the STEP program of Dinkmeyer and McKay (1976).

J.B. exhibited a marked drop in behavioral problems on the bus, at school, and at home after the first hypnotic induction. There was a total remission of all behavior-disorder problems after three hypnotic sessions and four meetings with the patient's mother. These took place over a month, meeting once weekly. The absence of behavior problems had continued at a one-year follow-up. This approach has been utilized successfully in my clinic with over 50 cases during a 10-year period. Empirical research is needed to identify the components of this type of intervention that are essential to a successful outcome.

FUTURE TRENDS

It is clear that there are many difficulties in the empirical study of behavior disorders in children. It is hard to determine an agreed-upon behavioral definition for a behavior disorder. There are also differences in the way researchers and clinicians define hypnosis. Researchers specifically define hypnosis as an altered state of consciousness with characteristics of narrowly focused attention, primary process thinking, and ego receptivity (Fromm, 1977, 1979). Orne (1959) spoke of "trance logic" with deeper levels of hypnosis. He was referring to specific alterations in cognition. Research-oriented people define these by observable behavior and scores on certain tests. Persons more interested in the clinical application of hypnosis to various psychological, medical, and dental problems define hypnosis in a much less restrictive sense and are much less concerned with the depth of hypnotic trance. Clinicians rarely can establish that "successful hypnotherapy" is specifically what brought about change, and not something else. There are, however, many reports of change in people for whom hypnosis was an integral part of the therapeutic intervention. The mere number of clinical case studies reported in the hypnosis literature leads one to ponder what impact hypnosis might have on the treatment of behavior disorders.

It does appear that the area of hypnotherapeutic intervention with children suffering behavior disorders is one where there may be difficulty in integrating research and clinical work. The implementation of a random assignment is not generally feasible in clinical research. Feinstein (1977) points out that when using patients for research material, we must accept those persons who seek us out. The investigator does not have the luxury of choosing an individual and randomly assigning that person to a group, or of having people go without treatment in order to act as a control group. Clearly, more carefully planned experimental research is needed in the area of behavior disorders and the application of hypnotic work in their treatment. Descriptive case studies are important to the increase of knowledge, but there are many more case studies reported with these disorders than there are empirical research studies. A problem arises in finding professionals who are well versed in scientific-research design, statistics, child development, hypnosis, and psychotherapy, and who have the inclination to engage in empirical research. This problem is more difficult to overcome than are the issues surrounding specific definitions of behavior disorder and a hypnotic trance. On the positive side, the resurgence of hypnosis as a therapeutic tool may increase the number of professionals with proper skills to carry out this research.

The renewed interest in hypnosis has already yielded a clearer definition of the "new hypnosis," which Araoz (1981) defines as a state in which the critical mental facilities are temporarily suspended and the person uses mainly imagination or primary process thinking (p. 9). He does not require objective measures for this working definition.

This renaissance of hypnotic work has offered a more thorough understanding of the mind–body interaction in the healing of both emotional and physical wounds (Rossi, 1986). And this renewed focus on body and mind has increased the attractiveness of hypnosis to individuals who previously viewed it as unscientific and not based in theory.

The success of hypnotherapy with children who exhibit behavior disorders depends, to a large degree, on the individual hypnotherapist. Araoz (1981, 1985) talks of TEAM (i.e., trust, expectations, attitudes, and motivation) and its effect on therapeutic outcome. TEAM must be present in both the hypnotherapist and the child for optimum results to be achieved. To assess the presence of TEAM in the child, one must understand the child's role in the family, the school, and the peer group. It is important to create ways of measuring TEAM to determine which children will respond most effectively to direct suggestions, which children will respond to indirect suggestions, which children will benefit from autogenic training, and which children will respond to group hypnosis for maximum benefits.

The most effective way to predict the variances in individual children and then design the most efficient treatment program is certainly a subject for future research considerations. In a time of heightened accountability for medicine, education, and psychology, it is imperative that hypnotherapeutic approaches that show merit be expanded and supported by empirical data. At the same time, those approaches that have little merit will need to be eliminated. We will become clearer as to how to mesh treatment modalities for the most therapeutically effective results with the minimum expenditure of time and money. There will always be a large component of clinical intuition in the application of hypnotherapy (as with any psychological, medical, or educational tool), but it is hoped that a molding of science and art will emerge that will yield the most successful intervention possible for each individual child who suffers the pain and unhappiness that accompany what has become known as a behavior disorder.

REFERENCES

Ambrose, G. (1968). Hypnosis in the treatment of children. *The American Journal of Clinical Hypnosis, 11,* 1-5.

Araoz, D. (1981). *Hypnosis and sex therapy.* New York: Brunner/Mazel.

Araoz, D. (1985). *The new hypnosis.* New York: Brunner/Mazel.

Baker, E. L. (1983). The use of hypnotic techniques with psychotics. *American Journal of Clinical Hypnosis, 24,* 283-288.

Bauman, F. (1970). Hypnosis and the adolescent drug abuser. *American Journal of Clinical Hypnosis, 13,* 17-21.

Coleman, M. C. (1986). *Behavior disorders: Theory and practice.* Englewood Cliffs, NJ: Prentice-Hall.

Coleman, M. C., & Gilliam, J. E. (1983). Disturbing behaviors in the classroom: A survey of teacher attitudes. *Journal of Special Education, 17,* 121-129.

Cooper, G. G. (1966). Sex and hypnosis susceptibility in children. *International Journal of Clinical and Experimental Hypnosis, 14*, 79-92.

Corter, B. F., Whiteside, R., & Haizlip, T. (1986). Biofeedback, cognitive training and relaxation techniques as multimodal adjunct therapy for hospitalized adolescents: A pilot study. *Adolescence, 21*, 339-346.

DeLuca, R. V., & Holborn, W. (1984). A comparison of relaxation training and competing response training to eliminate hair pulling and nail biting. *Journal of Behavioral Therapy and Experimental Psychiatry, 1*, 67-70.

Denowski, K. M., & Denowski, G. C. (1984). Is group progressive relaxation training effective with hyperactive children as individual EMG biofeedback treatment? *Biofeedback and Self-Regulation, 9*, 353-364.

Dinkmeyer, D., & McKay, G. (1976). *Parent's handbook: Systematic training for effective parenting.* Circle Pines, MN: American Guidance Services.

Erickson, M. H. (1958). Naturalistic techniques. *American Journal of Clinical Hypnosis, 1*, 3-8.

Feinstein, A. R. (1977). *Clinical biostatistics.* St. Louis: Mosby.

Fromm, E. (1977). An ego psychological theory of altered states of consciousness. *International Journal of Clinical and Experimental Hypnosis, 25*, 372-387.

Fromm, E. (1979). The nature of hypnosis and other altered states of consciousness: An ego psychological theory. In E. Fromm & R. E. Shor (Eds.), *Hypnosis: Development in research and new perspectives* (2nd ed.). Hawthorne, NY: Aldine.

Gardner, G. G. (1973). Use of hypnosis for psychogenic epilepsy in a child. *American Journal of Clinical Hypnosis, 15*, 166-169.

Gardner, G. G. (1974). Hypnosis with children. *International Journal of Clinical and Experimental Hypnosis, 22*, 20-38.

Gardner, G. G. (1976). Attitudes of child health professionals toward hypnosis: Implications for training. *Journal of Clinical and Experimental Hypnosis, 24*, 63-73.

Gardner, G. G., & Olness, K. (1981). *Hypnosis and hypnotherapy with children.* New York: Grune & Stratton.

Guyer, N., & Guyer, C. (1984). Implementing relaxation in training in counseling emotionally healthy adolescents: A comparison of three modes. *American Mental Health Counselors Association Journal, 6*, 79-87.

Haberman, M. A. (1986). Spontaneous trance or dissociation: A suicide attempt in a schizophrenic Vietnam veteran. *American Journal of Clinical Hypnosis, 28*, 177-182.

Hatzenbuehler, L. C., & Schroeder, H. E. (1978). Desensitization procedures in the treatment of childhood disorders. *Psychological Bulletin, 85*, 831-844.

Helton, G. B., & Oakland, T. D. (1977). Teachers' attitudinal responses to differing characteristics of elementary school students. *Journal of Educational Psychology, 64*, 261-264.

Hobbs, N. (1975). *The future of children: Categories, labels and their consequences.* San Francisco: Jossey-Bass.

Kaffman, M. (1968). Hypnosis as an adjunct to psychotherapy in child psychiatry. *Archives of General Psychiatry, 18*, 725-738.

Kazdin, A. (1987). Treatment of antisocial behavior in children: Current status and future directions. *Psychological Bulletin, 102,* 187-203.

Kohen, D. P., Olness, K. N., Colwell, S. O., & Heimel, A. (1984). The use of relaxation/ mental imagery (self hypnosis) in the management of 505 pediatric behavioral encounters. *Journal of Developmental and Behavioral Pediatrics, 5,* 21-25.

Lawlor, E. D. (1976). Hypnotic intervention with "school phobic" children. *International Journal of Clinical and Experimental Hypnosis, 24,* 74-86.

London, P. (1962). Hypnosis with children: An experimental approach. *International Journal of Clinical and Experimental Hypnosis, 10,* 79-92.

Mack, J. H. (1980). *An analysis of state definitions of severely emotionally disturbed.* Reston, VA: Council on Exceptional Children Policy Research Center. (ERIC Document Reproductive Service No. ED 201 135.)

Murray-Jobsis, J. (1988). Hypnosis as a function of adaptive regression and transference: An integrated theoretical model. *American Journal of Clinical Hypnosis, 30,* 241-247.

Olness, K., & Gardner, G. G. (1978). Some guidelines for uses of hypnotherapy in pediatrics. *Pediatrician, 62,* 228-233.

Orne, M. T. (1959). The nature of hypnosis: Artifact and essence. *Journal of Abnormal and Social Psychology, 58,* 277-299.

Owens, D. (1980). A study in the viability of the hypnotic process with institutionalized adult mentally retarded males. *Dissertation Abstracts International, 41,* 1519-1520.

Petty, G. L. (1976). Desensitization of parents to tantrum behavior. *American Journal of Clinical Hypnosis, 19,* 95-97.

Protinsky, H. (1983). The strategic use of hypnosis in family therapy. *Journal of Strategic and Systemic Therapies, 2,* 23-30.

Raymer, R. & Poppen, R. (1985). Behavioral relaxation training with hyperactive children. *Journal of Behavior Therapy and Experimental Psychiatry, 16,* 309-316.

Richter, N. C. (1984). The efficacy of relaxation training with children. *Journal of Abnormal Child Psychology, 2,* 319-344.

Rigler, D. (1982). Ericksonian approaches with children and adolescents. In J. D. Zeig, (Ed.), *Ericksonian Approaches to Hypnosis and Psychotherapy* (pp. 301-309). New York: Brunner/Mazel.

Rossi, E. (1986). *The Psychobiology of Mind-Body Healing.* New York: W.W. Norton & Company, Inc.

Sarles, R. M. (1975). The use of hypnosis with hospitalized children. *Journal of Clinical Child Psychology, 4,* 36-38.

Scagnelli-Jobsis, J. (1982). Hypnosis with psychotic patients: A review. *Journal of Clinical Hypnosis, 25,* 33-45.

Silber, S. (1980). Induction of hypnosis by poetic hypnogram. *American Journal of Clinical Hypnosis, 24,* 214-216.

Solovey de Melechnin, G. (1955). Conduct problems in children & hypnosis. *Diseases of the Nervous System, 16,* 249-253.

Stein, C. (1963). The clinical first technique as a hypnotic procedure in clinical psychotherapy. *The American Journal of Clinical Hypnosis, 6,* 113-119.

Taboada, E. L. (1975). Night terrors in a child treated with hypnosis. *The American Journal of Clinical Hypnosis, 17*, 270-271.

Werbel, C. S., Mulhern, T. J., & Dubi, M. (1983). The use of hypnosis as therapy for the mentally retarded. *Education and Training of Mentally Retarded, 18*, 321-323.

West, L. J., & Decker, G. H. (1965). Dangers of hypnosis. *Journal of the American Association of Child Psychiatry, 192*, 9-12.

Williams, D. T., & Singh, M. (1976). Hypnosis as a facilitating therapeutic adjunct in child psychiatry. *Journal of the American Academy of Child Psychiatry, 15*, 326-342.

Williams, D. T. (1979). Hypnosis as a therapeutic adjunct. In J. D. Noshpitz (Ed.), *Basic handbook of child psychiatry* (p. 108). New York: Basic Books.

Wood, F. W. (1979). Defining disturbing, disordered and disturbed behavior. In F. H. Wood & K. C. Lankin (Eds.), *Disturbing, disordered or disturbed? Perspectives in the definition of problem behavior in educational settings*. Minneapolis: Advanced Training Institute, University of Minnesota.

12 Hypnotic Treatment of Learning Disorders

Susan R. Eppley, Ed.D.

The rubric of learning disorders is generally understood to refer to any diagnosable constellation of symptoms that prevent children from acquiring a normally expected amount of academic knowledge in an educational environment. Further, the term is generally understood to include cognitive deficits of either physiological or psychological etiology and to exclude lack of achievement attributable exclusively to behavioral disorder. The most frequent disorders are learning disabilities and attention-deficit hyperactivity disorder.

Traditionally, these disorders have been treated through various remedial techniques and strategies, including individual or small-group instruction, behavior modification, modality matching, multisensory experience, language restructuring, modeling, strategy training, and even medication. Most researchers familiar with learning disabilities agree that education in general, as well as remedial techniques, is dominated by left-brain curricula, that is, language, symbols, talking and reciting, listening, and locating details and facts. Vitale (1982) and McCarthy (1981), among others, point out the importance of a right-brained approach—creativity, spatial relationships, color sensitivity, shapes and patterns, and visualization—in education and remediation. These right-brained approaches sound strangely similar to hypnosis.

FOUNDATIONS

Hypnotherapy with learning disorders in children has not been studied extensively. A review of the literature reveals varied results. Several researchers have found a positive correlation between hypnosis and the treatment of learning disorders; others have not. Of additional concern are methodological flaws in some studies that prevent conclusive interpretation. Several authors, including Gardner and Olness (1981) and Russell (1984), have recommended the continued use of hypnosis with learning disorders, as well as continuing research.

Learning Disabilities

Learning disability is a term that is widely known but not well understood. Historically, the term has been associated with the medical model of brain dysfunction. Numerous disciplines and professions have since contributed to the concept of learning disability, however. Currently, the etiology may include generic, neurological, environmental, and psychological factors. Estimates are that between 3 and 10 percent of the school-age population have learning disabilities.

Two definitions of learning disabilities are currently receiving widest acceptance. Public Law 94-142 and the National Joint Committee for Learning Disabilities, though differing somewhat in philosophy, agree that learning-disabled (LD) children (1) have at least average intelligence, (2) show a discrepancy between their actual academic achievement and their expected achievement based on intelligence level, and (3) do not exhibit these problems as a direct result of other handicapping conditions. Learning disabilities may be experienced in reading (dyslexia), arithmetic (dyscalculia), handwriting (dysgraphia), or the spoken language.

Children with learning disabilities often experience concomitant difficulties with low self-esteem, negative attitudes toward learning and school, and related emotional problems. This constellation of symptoms and behaviors would seem amenable to hypnotherapy. Although a plethora of studies does not exist, many researchers have chosen to investigate the use of hypnosis with LD children.

Studies have investigated various aspects of learning disabilities, including general hypnotizability of LD children; actual academic achievement; improvement in comprehension, memory, motor performance, and reversals; and changes in attitude toward learning and self-esteem. The hypnotizability of LD children seems to be one area in which researchers have reached consistent conclusions: these children appear to be at least as hypnotizable as non-LD children. Johnson (1979) explored the effect of group hypnotic and self-hypnotic training on the academic performance of LD children and reported that the children were significantly more hypnotically susceptible than a normative sample.

Most of the literature has centered around the actual measurement of academic achievement when suggestions were given under hypnosis. Russell (1980) assimilated and critically reviewed the reports from 1960 to 1980 of cases in which hypnosis was used with LD children. He concludes that, in spite of methodological problems, hypnosis can facilitate improvement in academic achievement. Crasilneck and Hall (1975) described the successful treatment of an 8-year-old LD girl whose report-card marks rose an average of one letter grade in nine weeks. The treatment consisted of hypnosis and suggestions that grades would improve and concentration would be more sustained.

Jampolsky and Haight (1975) reported that a small group of third- and fourth-graders improved their reading skills and had maintained progress when measured one year later. His hypnotherapy included visualization of an ideal self by the subjects and imagery techniques with parents and teachers whereby they visualized the children as successful readers. Illovsky (1963) compared male adolescents who were nonreaders and concluded that those learning hypnotherapy enhanced and maintained their reading ability. Ambrose (1961) concluded that hypnosis was of benefit to children with learning difficulties.

In contrast to these researchers who provide a measure of optimism regarding the benefit of hypnotherapy in academic achievement, others report less encouraging results. Johnson, Johnson, Olsen, and Newman (1981) studied 15 LD children. Three hypnotic training sessions were employed and instructions were given for six weeks of daily self-hypnotic practice containing suggestions for imagery related to improvement in reading. No overall differences were noted when this group was compared with an untreated control group. And Huff (1980) found that hypnosis used with sixth- and seventh-grade LD students was not more effective than relaxation training or suggestion in improving reading skills.

Reversals of letters and numbers are a frequent symptom of learning disabilities. Jampolsky (1970) studied the combined use of hypnosis and sensory substitution for visual input. Five children in an experimental group had the total number of reversals reduced from an initial 10 to zero. Under hypnosis, these subjects were given the suggestion that they would learn their numbers through feel and then given one hour of instruction daily for 10 days.

Baum (1987) studied the effect of hypnosis on motor performance and auditory memory of LD children. The children, aged 7–12, were divided into three groups, with one group receiving a treatment of hypnosis, one a treatment of relaxation only, and one receiving no treatment. Findings of this investigation suggested that auditory short-term recall was significantly improved in the hypnotic group when compared with both the relaxation and the control group. Perceptual motor skills were not significantly improved, although a positive trend indicating higher scores was found for both the hypnotic group and the relaxation group when compared with the control group.

Attention-Deficit Hyperactivity Disorder

Attention-deficit hyperactivity disorder (ADHD) is the terminology for a cluster of symptoms that have been circumscribed during the 1980s, and though primarily behavioral, have come to be associated with learning disorders. Common features among various definitions include a lack of sustained concentration, impulsiveness, restlessness, noncompliance, onset in early childhood, pervasiveness of symptoms across settings, and exclusion of brain damage, psychosis, mental retardation, and severe sensory deficits as causal. Many children outgrow these symptoms by adolescence. Barkley (1981) states that 25 percent of all ADHD children also have learning disabilities.

The revised third edition of the *Diagnostic and Statistical Manual of Mental Disorders* (DSM-III-R) (American Psychiatric Association, 1987) lists 14 possible symptoms of ADHD, eight of which must be noted as disturbing for at least six months. Onset before the age of 7 and exclusion of the pervasive developmental disorder are also criteria. Severity may be listed as mild, moderate, or severe.

The literature reviewed provided a measure of optimism in considering the use of hypnosis with children who have ADHD. The largest study reviewed was conducted by Illovsky and Fredman (1976), in which 48 hyperactive children received recorded hypnotic suggestions. Results suggested that the addition of this modified hypnotic technique enabled 45 of the 48 to function better in class in terms of attention span and frustration level. Their study, however, lacked a control group. It seems possible that maturity alone could have accounted for the improvement within the group of 6- to 8-year-olds studied. Also, simply receiving special attention may have positively affected the children's behavior.

Dunn and Howell (1982) reported that after receiving relaxation training for 10 sessions, hyperactive boys demonstrated reduced muscle tension and significant changes in behavior that were readily observable by researchers and parents. This study seemed promising in that neutral training sessions were offered prior to treatment, and some anecdotal reports of long-term effects also were received. The subject group, however, was small (only 10 boys), making generalization of results difficult. Calhoun and Bolton (1986) reported that significant improvement in hyperactive behavior was noted from pre- to posthypnotic treatment. In their study, eight ADHD children were hypnotized three times over a two-week period. The problem was that all children in the study were being given methylphenidate (Ritalin), making it difficult to conclude that improvement was the result of hypnosis alone. Additionally, the subject group was small and there was no control group. And in a single-case study, Crasilneck and Hall (1975) described the successful treatment of a 3-year-old who experienced what was termed extreme overactivity and other behavioral problems. Although methodology in this study was adequate, generalization of results from a single-case study can hardly be made.

Self-Esteem

One often-noted consequence of learning disabilities in children is lowered self-esteem. Chronic feelings of frustration and being different from other children exact a psychological toll. Negative feelings about themselves interfere with LD children's further motivation to do well.

Several researchers have investigated the effect of hypnosis on the self-esteem of LD children and their results warrant a degree of optimism. Russell's 1984 critical review of 10 studies on the effect of hypnosis and self-concept of children with dyslexia concludes that hypnosis did enhance self-concept. Johnson and colleagues (1981) explored the impact of group hypnotic and self-hypnotic training on the self-esteem of LD children and suggested that important predictors of self-esteem improvement were the child's hypnotic susceptibility score and self-hypnotic practice by the children and parents. The study concluded that hypnotherapy is of potential benefit to self-esteem improvement. Jampolsky and Haight (1975) reported that self-esteem was markedly increased in third- and fourth-grade LD children who received hypnotherapy. They compared the experimental group with a control. Parents and teachers visualized the children in the experimental group as successful readers. Fahey (1984) reviewed the literature in an effort to provide school counselors with intervention techniques that would be effective in improving the self-esteem of children with learning disabilities and concluded that hypnotherapy has gained support as a viable method.

In Summary

There is no large body of literature regarding hypnotherapy with children who have learning disorders, and the studies that do exist report mixed results. Given the paucity, and sometimes conflicting nature, of research in this area, only cautious statements can be made on the use of hypnotherapy with children who have learning disorders. Additionally, a word must be said regarding the majority of studies cited. Methodological flaws were prevalent, and were detected by either the researcher or subsequent investigators. Although not all flaws were of great importance, they did weaken the impact of this body of literature in general. Optimism regarding the use of hypnotherapy in children with learning disorders must, of necessity, remain guarded. As is so often the case, a need for methodologically sound research exists.

ASSESSMENT

Assessing children with learning disorders for possible hypnotherapy involves the assemblage of information from three sources: the child, the parent, and the teachers.

An interview with the child provides much information, while also permitting the establishment of rapport. Through relatively informal conversation, many details can be gleaned that will be helpful during the actual hypnosis sessions. Information about the child's favorite fairy tales, movies, television shows, toys, or even video games can be helpful in personalizing an induction. An assessment of personality and energy level can be made in order to better tailor the hypnotic suggestions. A formal measure of hypnotizability, such as the Children's Hypnotic Susceptibility Scale or the Stanford Hypnotic Clinical Scale for Children, may be administered at this time if desired.

Another area that is felt to be of critical importance is the initial interview with the child. Most likely, the child has been presented for hypnotherapy at the behest of his or her parents or teachers. It is important to discuss the reason for referral with the child, who should be asked what he or she thinks about the problem. Most important, the child's willingness to work on the problem and to engage in hypnosis should be assessed.

The parents can provide two types of information regarding the child. First, their description of both the child and the problem is useful. Again, information can be deduced regarding imagination, hypnotizability, personality, and cooperation. Another, less obvious body of information involves the parents' expectations. How do the parents see the child in general, and what are their expectations of the hypnosis? Finally, they should be asked about their willingness to be involved. As parents are such an integral part of a child's life, they are likely to be a major factor in influencing the child's attitudes and expectations about the hypnotherapy, as well as in monitoring practice and achievement. In many hypnotherapy programs with children, parents also receive and practice positive imagery regarding their child. If this is to be the case, their willingness to participate should be evaluated.

The child's teachers provide the essential body of information regarding the child's achievement and learning disorder. The importance of a thorough diagnostic workup cannot be overstated lest the target behavior for the hypnotic sessions be missed or misunderstood. Critical information would include the child's areas of cognitive strengths and weaknesses, preferred and less preferred learning styles, modality preference, and specific area of deficit. Most frequently, a psychoeducational evaluation will have been conducted by the school psychologist and will be helpful in circumscribing these areas.

Standardized, norm-referenced testing is obviously of prime importance if empirical data are to be collected through a pre- and posttest design. Tests such as the Woodcock Reading Mastery Tests (Woodcock, 1973), Diagnostic Reading Scales (Spache, 1972), Key-Math Diagnostic Arithmetic Test (Connolly, Nachtman, & Pritchett, 1971), and Stanford Diagnostic Mathematics Test (Beatty, Madder, Gardner, & Karlsen, 1976) are used fairly often in educational settings.

Behavior-rating scales are also useful in measuring progress. A number of hyperactivity-rating scales have had considerable use by psychologists and teachers. The most common are the Werry-Weiss-Peters Activity Scale (Werry, 1968), which is designed for parents to fill out, and the Conners (1969, 1973) checklists, which are completed by teachers.

A more recent development to measure ADHD is the computerized test system by Gordon (1983). This system measures attention and self-control and allows for normative comparison.

INTERVENTION

Case Study

Brian is a 10-year-old boy who has been diagnosed as having dyslexia. He is in the fourth grade and testing has revealed that he has average intelligence. His achievements in math, art, music, and physical education are grade-level appropriate. His reading and spelling achievements are at second-grade level. He experiences difficulty in science and social studies, probably because those subjects depend on language skills. Similarly, his handwriting is poor.

Brian is a rather typical LD child. He is male and of average intelligence. His achievements in language-based areas represent a significant deficit. He is left-handed, left-eyed, and right-footed, suggesting that the right hemisphere of his brain is dominant. Certain academic skills are associated with each hemisphere. Language (i.e., handwriting, reading, phonics, and spelling) is believed to be a specialized area in the left hemisphere of most people, and such would seem to be the case with Brian.

It appeared that Brian would be a good candidate for hypnotherapy. Many of the features that make up hypnosis are specialized within the right hemisphere: visualization, creativity, color sensitivity, feelings and emotions, artistic expression, spatial relationships, fantasy orientation, and a sense of nontemporal processing.

Brian's parents were interviewed just before Brian's initial interview. Following their initial referral contact, they had mailed school records and testing results. During the interview, they provided further information about Brian's personality and likes and dislikes. Their expectations were discussed, as was the hypnotic process in general. Finally, they were asked about their willingness to participate themselves. Upon agreeing to do so, they were asked to spend three minutes three times a day visualizing Brian as a successful and happy student. They felt it an interesting request and restated their willingness to acquiesce.

An initial interview was conducted with Brian with the primary goals of (1) establishing rapport, (2) assessing his view of the problem, (3) assessing his view of the need for intervention, (4) assessing his willingness to engage in hypnotic treatment, and (5) acquiring further information about his personality and interests. Additionally, hypnosis and the pending treatment process were explained to Brian, and he was told that he would be taught a technique that he would practice at home. It had earlier been learned that he enjoyed sports, and particularly followed baseball. He was told how professional ball players often incorporate the very same treatment into their playing regimen—that power hitters, for example, use a similar mastery technique. Brian was intrigued by this, especially since he assumed that practice was the only way to improve. (Practicing the same material over and over is rarely helpful for LD children.) Near the end of the session, Brian was asked if he would prefer to wait until the next session to begin or would rather begin immediately. He excitedly chose to begin at once. A relaxation exercise was employed, followed by visualization of a safe, pleasant place. Ideomotor signaling was used to indicate when he had achieved relaxation and when he had visualized himself in his safe place. Brian was asked to practice relaxation and visualizing himself in his safe place daily until the first training session.

First Training Session

From information provided by Brian and his parents, important facts were learned and woven into the hypnotic design. First, Brian very much enjoyed seeing movies in movie theaters. Second, Brian enjoyed playing video games.

Academically, Brian had difficulty in all language areas. A decision was made to begin with one area, and preferably one in which a degree of mastery could be recognized within a relatively short time. In Brian's case, it was decided to begin with spelling.

Finally, it had been hypothesized that Brian's preferred processing hemisphere was his right. Therefore, a hypnotic design was created that included visualization, color, and fantasy.

DOCTOR: Good morning, Brian. How are you?

BRIAN: Fine. I've been practicing what you taught me.

DOCTOR: That's good. Tell me what you've been doing.

BRIAN: Well, I close my eyes and I think about relaxing.

DOCTOR: Tell me how that feels to you.

BRIAN: It feels good.

DOCTOR: That's good. And you are practicing this every day?

BRIAN: Yes. Two times. I usually go to my bedroom.

DOCTOR: I can tell that you are a hard worker. Are you ready to learn more today?

BRIAN: Yes. I want to know what the ball players do.

DOCTOR: Well, it is very similar to what I am going to be teaching you. You see, the job of ball players is to hit the ball well. That is not the only job they have, of course, but it is an important job. And you have many jobs, too. Schoolwork is one of your jobs. I thought that perhaps we might start with spelling. Would that be all right with you?

BRIAN: Yes. Spelling is hard.

DOCTOR: What is it that makes it so hard?

BRIAN: I don't know. I keep trying and trying but I goof up on tests. Sometimes I can spell them to my mom, and then I go to school and mess up the test.

DOCTOR: You know, different hitters use different ways to learn to hit. Some of them watch videos. Some of them go to the batting cage. Some of them read books about hitting. People learn things in different ways. The same is true in spelling. Some children learn by spelling the word aloud several times. Some children learn by writing the word several times.

BRIAN: I've tried both of those ways.

DOCTOR: Those ways work for some children but not for all. That's OK. Perhaps today we can find a way that works for you. Are you ready to begin?

BRIAN: Yes.

DOCTOR: Good. Let's begin with some things we did last time. Do you remember how to signal me by moving your finger?

BRIAN: Yes.

DOCTOR: Good. OK, Brian, I'd like you to close your eyes just like you've been practicing and begin to relax yourself. Think of your head and all of your body parts all the way down to your toes. Think of them being relaxed. Very relaxed. That's good. Your breathing is very relaxed. Very calm. Your muscles are loosening. Just let them loosen all the way from your head down to your toes. Follow your own speed. Allow them to loosen as you are ready. Calm, relaxed. When you are ready, when you are relaxed, let your imagination take you to your safe place. Floating, relaxed. When you are there, give me a signal so I know. [Ideomotor signal]

That's good. I can see by your signal that you are in your special safe place. Just enjoy it. [Brian was guided through a hot-air balloon ride to a movie theater.] Now you see a movie theater with many seats and a huge movie screen. You walk to a seat, your favorite place to sit. You sit down and almost immediately the huge maroon-colored curtain begins to open and the lights go dim. The movie projector comes on and the screen is a silvery white. When you are settled in your seat and able to see the screen, Brian, let me know. [Ideomotor signal] Very good. Now you notice something very unusual. This is not an ordinary movie. We talked earlier about spelling and how different people learn spelling in different ways. This is one of the ways. I have the list you gave me of your spelling words for this week. We will take one word at a time and I will tell you the word and spell it. As I spell it, you will see the letters go onto the big white screen. But each letter of the word will have a different color. The colors are up to you. But in a word, a letter always gets the same color. Put each word on a new white screen. After you get a clear picture of the word on the screen, open your eyes and reach over to the chair on your left. There are white paper and crayons. Write the word the same way you see it on the screen. Do you understand? [Brian nods his head.] Good. Then let's begin. You can ask me to say a word again or spell a word again if you like. The first word is "remove." That is, r-e-m-o-v-e. Remove. R-e-m-o-v-e. See each letter in color on the screen and then open your eyes and write it in the same color on the paper. You can look up at the screen. [Brian had eight spelling words. His list had been shortened by his teacher. He asked to have three words respelled.]

Very good, Brian. You did a very nice job. That is what you will practice at home. First you will see the words in color on the movie screen. Then you will copy them in color onto your paper.

There is one more thing before we leave the movie theater to catch your balloon home. Watch the screen again. Now the projector comes on. Now you see an image of a person on the screen. A boy. A happy boy. Smiling. It is you. You are smiling, happy. You are happy because you have received a good grade in spelling. You are happy because you worked hard to reach a goal and you did it. You are confident, feeling good, feeling good about yourself. You see yourself doing well in spelling. Spelling with ease and confidence. This is what the baseball hitters do. Just as you imagine, actually seeing yourself doing well at your job of spelling, so do they see themselves in their imagination doing well at their job of hitting. You are doing well at spelling, smiling, successful, happy. Just enjoy that for a while, Brian. [After about 20 seconds] OK, Brian. You have done very well.

The development of the visualization used with Brian was partially based on ideas and material from Jacobs and Jacobs (1966), Levine (1980), Oldridge (1982), Shorr and Sobel (1980), and Tilton (1984).

Brian is brought out of trance by retracing his path and a count from one to five. He comes out of trance and stretches in his seat.

At the end of the session, Brian was instructed to practice the movie-screen color-words technique four times a week.

Brian returned for three sessions, at the end of weeks 1, 3, and 7. Each follow-up lasted approximately 50 minutes and included a 10- to 15-minute period at the beginning in which Brian and his parents were together. Progress was discussed and questions answered. Following this period, Brian was seen alone to discuss his practice. During the third session, he was taught another induction: relaxation coupled with a "melting" similar to the character in one of his favorite video games. The movie screen was used consistently. At the conclusion of the fourth session, Brian and his family were told that since they were doing so well they need not come in for further appointments; however, they could phone if necessary.

ASSESSMENT OF EFFECTIVENESS

The effectiveness of the treatment was assessed in the areas of spelling achievement and self-esteem. Spelling achievement was assessed by self-rating, parental rating, teacher rating, and the WRAT Spelling Subtest. All three subjective ratings were very favorable, with Brian, his parents, and his teacher indicating much progress. More objectively, his teacher reported that on weekly spelling tests he had begun getting As (missing zero or one word) and that she was preparing to raise his word list to 10 words. Before treatment, his teacher estimated that he missed approximately 50 percent of the words on the weekly tests. The WRAT Spelling Subtest was administered by his teacher pre- and posttreatment with four months' progress noted over a two-month period. This was not felt significant, especially when practice effect is considered. Moreover, the treatment was specific for a given set of spelling words. It would be more enlightening to measure long-term recall of the specific words studied.

Self-esteem was measured by the subjective ratings of Brian, his parents, and his teacher. All concurred that he was proud of himself, was beginning to develop confidence, and was happier. His parents' perceptions were quite positive, and they indicated that the family as a whole was feeling better. More objectively, the Piers-Harris Childrens Self-Concept Scale was administered pre- and posttreatment. Improvement was evidenced by increased scores in intellectual and school status, behavior, and happiness and satisfaction. These increases ranged from nine percentile points in behavior to 15 percentile points in intellectual and school status to five percentile points in behavior.

FUTURE TRENDS

The history of research combining the variables of hypnosis and learning disorders does not yield a large number of studies, and the relatively few studies that do exist provide mixed results at best. Methodological flaws exist in some studies. The combination of these factors is likely to discourage further investigation by would-be researchers. Only a handful of studies have been conducted within the past 10 years, and these ''newer'' studies exhibit the same difficulties as those that preceded them. Given this history of discouraging results, the topic is not likely to become a ''hotbed'' of research.

Just as research has not convincingly shown that hypnosis is helpful in the treatment of learning disorders, neither has it convincingly shown that it is not. It is to be hoped that such study will continue.

Certainly one area of difficulty is in teasing out the relevant variables. Even within a population of persons who have similar diagnoses, so many individual variations exist that methodological control is difficult. Children process information differently and have even more varying levels of maturity than adults. Another variable is inconsistency. By definition, children with learning disorders are characterized by inconsistent levels of attention, understanding, and performance. Another variable that cannot be underestimated in work with children is the effect of their parents. Parental involvement and expectations often lead children into self-fulfilling prophecies. To view parents as peripheral when controlling for variables would overlook an essential consideration.

According to many experts, most LD children are right-brained whereas educational instruction is directed toward the left-brained students. (Hemispheric dominance can vary but the result is a mismatch.) In essence, education is geared toward language, symbols, listening, following directions, sequencing and logic, while the LD child's innate processing preference is for shape and patterns, visualization, feelings and expression, spatial relationships, color, intuition, and fantasy. Most of these features are compatible with hypnosis. But if hypnosis is, in fact, to maximize effectiveness, the features need to be further acknowledged and matched. Not all LD children process the world best visually. Many have trouble with visualization and require more emphasis on auditory or kinesthetic input. A good diagnostic evaluation prior to hypnotherapy is essential.

Another consideration in working with children who have learning disorders is that the remediation should not be "more of the same." Creativity in approach, once the individual case is known, should provide a different format than what has previously been attempted at school. Certainly, offering more of the same—when it didn't work to begin with—is an exercise in futility.

Finally, emphasis should be placed on providing the child with something that gives him or her a sense of control. Children who experience learning disorders often *feel* out of control and often *are* out of control. Practicing specific techniques or assignments helps to provide the child with this much-needed sense of control over behavior.

REFERENCES

Ambrose, G. (1961). *Hypnotherapy with children* (2nd ed.). London: Staples.

American Psychiatric Association (1987). *Diagnostic and Statistical Manual of Mental Disorders*, Third Edition, Revised. Washington, D.C.

Bakan, P. (1969). Hypnotizability, laterality of eye-movements and functional brain asymmetry. *Perceptual and Motor Skills, 28,* 927-932.

Barkley, R. (1981). *Hyperactive children: A handbook for diagnosis and treatment.* New York: Guilford.

Baum, J. (1987). The effect of hypnosis on the motor performance and auditory memory of learning disabled children. *Dissertation Abstracts International, 48*(6-B), 1825-1826.

Beatty, L. S., Madden, R., Gardner, E. G., & Karlsen, B. (1976). *Stanford diagnostic mathematics test.* New York: Harcourt Brace Jovanovich.

Calhoun, G., & Bolton, J. (1986). Hypnotherapy: A possible alternative for treating pupils affected with attention deficit disorder. *Perceptual and Motor Skills, 63*(3), 1191-1195.

Cole, R. (1977). Increasing reading and test-taking skills with hypnosis and suggestion. *Dissertation Abstracts International, 37*(8-A), 4859.

Conners, C. K. (1969). A teacher rating scale for use in drug studies with children. *American Journal of Psychiatry, 126,* 884-888.

Connolly, A., Nachtman, W., & Pritchett, E. (1971). *Key-math diagnostic arithmetic test.* Circle Pines, MN: American Guidance Service.

Crasilneck, H., & Hall, J. (1975). *Clinical hypnosis: Principles and applications.* New York: Grune & Stratton.

Dunn, F. M., & Howell, R. J. (1982). Relaxation training and relationship to hyperactivity in boys. *Journal of Clinical Psychology, 38,* 92-100.

Fahey, D. (1984). School counselors and psychological aspects of learning disabilities. *The School Counselor, 31,* 433-440.

Gardner, G., & Olness, K. (1981). *Hypnosis and hypnotherapy with children.* New York: Grune & Stratton.

Gordon, M. (1983). *The Gordon diagnostic system.* Dewitt, NY: Gordon Systems.

Huff, P. (1980). The use of hypnosis in remediating reading in children diagnosed learning disabled. *Dissertation Abstracts International, 40*(8-A), 4491.

Illovsky, J. (1963). An experience with group hypnosis in reading diability in primary behavior disorders. *Journal of Genetic Psychology, 102,* 61-67.

Illovsky, J., & Fredman, N. (1976). Group suggestions in learning disabilities of primary grade children: A feasibility study. *International Journal of Clinical and Experimental Hypnosis, 24*(2), 87-97.

Jacobs, L., & Jacobs, J. (1966). Hypnotizability of children as related to hemispheric reference and neurological organization. *American Journal of Clinical Hypnosis, 8,* 269-274.

Jampolsky, G. (1970). Hypnosis and sensory motor stimulation to aid children with learning problems. *Journal of Learning Disabilities, 3*(11), 570-575.

Jampolsky, G., & Haight, M. (1975). A special technique for children with reading problems. *Academic Therapy, 10*(3), 333-337.

Johnson, L. (1979). Group hypnotherapy with learning disabled children. Paper presented at the Annual Convention of the Rocky Mountain Psychological Association, Las Vegas, April 1979.

Johnson, L., Johnson, D., Olson, M., & Newman, J. (1981). The uses of hypnotherapy with learning disabled children. *Journal of Clinical Psychology, 37*(2), 291-299.

Levine, E. (1980). Indirect suggestion through personalized fairy tale for treatment of childhood insomnia. *American Journal of Clinical Hypnosis, 23,* 57-63.

London, P. (1963). *Children's hypnotic susceptibility scale.* Palo Alto, CA: Consulting Psychologists Press.

McCarthy, B. (1981). Brain function and learning styles. *School Administrator, 38,* 12-13.

McCord, H. (1962). Hypnosis as an aid to increasing adult reading efficiency. *Journal of Developmental Reading, 6,* 64-65.

Oldridge, O. (1982). Positive suggestion: It helps students learn. *Academic Therapy, 17*(3), 279-287.

Piers, E. V. (1984). *Piers-Harris children's self-concept scale.* Los Angeles: Western Psychological Services.

Russell, R. (1984). The efficacy of hypnosis in the treatment of learning problems in children. *International Journal of Psychosomatics, 31*(1), 23-32.

Shorr, J., & Sobel, G. (1980). *Imagery: Its many dimensions and applications.* New York: Plenum.

Spache, G. D. (1972). *Diagnostic reading scales* (rev. ed.). Monterey, CA: Test Bureau.

Tilton, P. (1984). The hypnotic hero: A technique for hypnosis with children. *International Journal of Clinical and Experimental Hypnosis, 4,* 366-375.

Vitale, B. M. (1982). *Unicorns are real: A right-brained approach to learning.* Rolling Hills Estates, CA: Jalmar Press.

Werry, J. S. (1968). Studies of the hyperactive child. IV: An empirical analysis of minimal brain dysfunction syndrome. *Archives of General Psychiatry, 19,* 9-16.

Woodcock, R. W. (1973). *Woodcock reading mastery tests.* Circle Pines, MN: American Guidance Service.

PART III

MEDICAL APPLICATIONS

13 Hypnosis in the Treatment of Nausea and Vomiting in Children

Claudia Hoffmann, Ed.D.

Within medical settings, the children most frequently referred for the treatment of nausea and vomiting (NV) are pediatric oncology patients who are experiencing chemotherapy-related NV. Most children have significant NV following chemotherapy, and many experience anticipatory NV, prior to chemotherapy, as well. Children may also be referred for the treatment of NV associated with other disease processes and of psychogenic NV as a response to stress. Clinically, children presenting with anticipatory NV and psychogenic NV are highly responsive to hypnotherapy. However, a review of the experimental literature provides a more cautious perspective about the "unique effectiveness" of hypnosis in treating these patients.

A number of controlled studies have shown that a variety of behavioral interventions, in addition to hypnosis, are effective in treating both anticipatory and postchemotherapy NV. The variables that account for the success of various behavioral interventions are debated among investigators (Morrow & Dobkin, 1988; Jacobsen & Redd, 1988) and are likely to be the focus of future research. A review of the hypnotic treatment of NV highlights the critical issue of assessing the therapeutic gains attributable specifically to hypnosis in contrast to those derived from nonspecific therapeutic factors in both clinical and experimental settings (Frankel, 1987; Wadden & Anderton, 1982). Although investigators attempt to isolate specific interventions to compare their effectiveness, the knowledgeable clinician can combine behavioral interventions, including hypnosis, as needed, to increase the likelihood of successful treatment for an individual patient.

NATURE AND PREVALENCE OF NAUSEA AND
VOMITING ASSOCIATED WITH CHEMOTHERAPY

The NV associated with chemotherapy pose significant problems for a majority of cancer patients. Severe NV can contribute to a general deterioration of the cancer patient's physical condition owing to such complications as anorexia and electrolyte imbalance. In addition, significant psychological distress is often experienced, with cancer patients expressing as much apprehension and dread about the adverse side effects of treatment as they do about the disease process itself.

Zeltzer, LeBaron, and Zeltzer (1984a) cite studies in which 19 percent of an adult oncology sample and 33 percent of a pediatric oncology sample prematurely terminated chemotherapy because of severe NV. In addition, 59 percent of the adolescents in the pediatric study had compliance problems. These results suggest that severe NV may compromise survival for patients who cannot tolerate these distressing symptoms. Although antiemetics are widely used to control chemotherapy-related emesis, one survey cited found that only 15 percent of pediatric oncologists believed that they were effective. In addition, a study by Zeltzer, LeBaron, and Zeltzer (1984b) suggested that some children may experience more NV when antiemetics are administered than when no antiemetics are used.

Postchemotherapy Nausea and Vomiting

In a prospective assessment of postchemotherapy-related NV, Zeltzer, LeBaron, and Zeltzer (1984c) analyzed the symptoms of 30 children and adolescents who were treated by a total of 18 different chemotherapy regimens over two or more matched courses of chemotherapy without antiemetics. In all, 166 courses of chemotherapy were assessed. The results showed that none of the commonly used chemotherapeutic agents assessed in this study consistently produced or, on the other hand, never produced NV. There was no significant relationship between the severity of vomiting and either the number of agents in a chemotherapy regimen or the addition or subtraction of agents from the regimens. In addition, the extent of NV fluctuated during repeated courses of the same agents, despite no changes in chemotherapy dosage, no use of antiemetics, and no changes in disease course. Only 4 percent of the total study population of 49 children never had nausea or vomiting at any time, and no children always experienced moderate to severe symptoms. In general, approximately two thirds of pediatric cancer patients will experience significant chemotherapy-related NV (Zeltzer, LeBaron, & Zeltzer, 1984a).

Zeltzer, LeBaron, and Zeltzer (1984c) hypothesize that postchemotherapy-related emesis might result from the combined interaction of physiological, environmental, and psychological stimuli that affect each patient's vomiting threshold. They suggest, "The stimulation of target emesis areas of the central nervous system by chemotherapeutic agents may be enhanced or counteracted by a variety of behavioral factors which also stimulate these target areas via cortical pathways" (p. 12). In addition, there may be individual differences in vomiting thresholds, causing some people to be more reactive than others to a small amount of stimulation.

Anticipatory Nausea and Vomiting

Many chemotherapy patients experience NV in anticipation of treatment, prior to the actual infusion of chemotherapeutic agents—perhaps for the entire day before treatment, when approaching the hospital, upon seeing the oncology nurses, or even when talking about chemotherapy. As Jacobsen and Redd (1988) note, the reported prevalence of anticipatory nausea and vomiting (ANV) in chemotherapy patients ranges from 18 percent to 57 percent. They attribute this marked variability to three methodological issues that are specific to the study of ANV. First, anticipatory reactions are defined by the presence of nausea or vomiting prior to chemotherapy by some investigators, whereas others have limited their definition to include only vomiting. In a study by Van Komen and Redd (1985), 33 percent of their sample developed anticipatory nausea (AN), whereas only 11 percent developed anticipatory vomiting (AV). Second, the risk of development of ANV tends to increase with each chemotherapy treatment. Accordingly, the prevalence of ANV would tend to be low if assessed during the initial courses of chemotherapy and higher later in the course of treatment. Finally, the prevalence of ANV appears to vary considerably depending on the emetic properties of the drug protocol. According to Andrykowski, Redd, and Hatfield (1985), while only 20 percent of patients receiving a mildly emetic drug (e.g., fluorouracil) developed ANV, 80 percent of patients on drug regimens considered more highly emetic (e.g., cyclophosphamide, doxorubicin, vincristine, prednisone) developed ANV. Jacobsen and Redd conclude that an individual patient's risk of developing ANV will be greater when treated with the more emetic chemotherapy protocols and will increase with each additional infusion of chemotherapy.

In an excellent review of ANV, Morrow and Dobkin (1988) noted that the prevalence data from 28 studies, published since 1979, show that approximately 25 percent of cancer patients receiving chemotherapy develop ANV by their fourth treatment. For AN, Morrow's (1986) own data show a prevalence rate of 23 percent when 1,480 consecutive chemotherapy patients were assessed prior to the fourth chemotherapy cycle.

Dolgin and his colleagues (Dolgin, Katz, McGinty, & Seigel, 1985) conducted structured interviews with 80 pediatric cancer patients (ages 2–14) with a mean age of 9 years. The results showed that 29 percent of the children reported AN and 20 percent experienced AV. Sixty-two percent of those reporting ANV developed it during the initial four months of treatment.

ETIOLOGY OF ANTICIPATORY NAUSEA AND VOMITING

Learned-Etiology Model

Although a variety of theories have been proposed to explain the development of ANV (Morrow & Dobkin, 1988), the available evidence suggests that it follows the principles of learning by means of classical conditioning. According to the learned-etiology model, during the initial chemotherapy sessions, the administration of chemotherapy drugs (an unconditioned stimulus) is followed by posttreatment NV (an unconditioned response) in the context of potentially conditionable stimuli (sensations, thoughts, images of the oncology clinic). After several chemotherapy treatments (repeated learning trials), previously neutral stimuli (e.g., the presence of the chemotherapy nurse or the smell of the oncology clinic) may become conditioned stimuli and elicit the conditioned response of ANV, independently of the chemotherapy treatment.

In classical conditioning, the intensity of an unconditioned response affects the development of the conditioned response. In the eight studies, reviewed by Morrow and Dobkin, that assessed the severity of posttreatment NV, all found that the greater the severity of posttreatment NV, the higher was the incidence of ANV. Some postchemotherapy NV may have a conditioned component as well, in addition to pharmacological effects. There have been instances in which patients have not received their scheduled chemotherapy treatment for medical reasons, yet still report experiencing "postchemotherapy" NV after leaving the clinic (Lyles, Burish, Krozely, & Oldham, 1982).

HYPNOTIC TREATMENT OF NAUSEA AND VOMITING

Investigating the effectiveness of hypnosis in reducing chemotherapy-related NV in children has become more sophisticated in the past decade. Initial reports on the use of hypnosis to treat NV effectively were in the form of case studies (Dash, 1980; Ellenberg, Kellerman, Dash, Huggins, & Zeitzer, 1980; Hilgard and LeBaron, 1984; LaBaw, Holton, Tewell, & Eccles, 1975; Olness, 1981; Olness & Gardner, 1988; LaClave & Blix, 1989;

Zeltzer, 1980). Subsequently, several controlled studies have assessed the effectiveness of hypnotherapy in alleviating chemotherapy-related NV.

Self-hypnosis was used in a study by Cotanch, Hockenberry, and Herman (1985) to treat pediatric cancer inpatients experiencing chemotherapy-related NV. This study was unique in that the children were receiving chemotherapy that required at least a 48-hour hospitalization; thus, the quantity of emesis was routinely measured by staff nurses. The 12 children, ages 10–18 years, were randomly assigned to either the experimental or the control group. On the day of chemotherapy, the six children in the experimental group received 30–40 minutes of individualized self-hypnosis training consisting of helping the child become intensely involved in imagery or fantasy. Suggestions were given to promote feelings of safety, comfort, and restful sleep. Posthypnotic suggestions were given to feel alert, refreshed, and ready to eat some special favorite food when administration of the chemotherapy was completed. Children in the control group received standard care during the chemotherapy session, consisting of having a trusted person (parent or nurse) hold the child's hand, talk to the child, and/or distract the child's attention to other objects in the treatment room.

The groups were followed through two consecutive courses of chemotherapy. Based on objective measures, the child's self-report, and nurses' observations, the experimental group showed a significant decrease in the frequency, amount, severity, and duration of vomiting as compared with the control group. However, since the children in the control group did not meet with the nurse-therapist for an equivalent time prior to the administration of chemotherapy, it is unclear to what degree these results can be attributed to the extra therapeutic attention children in the experimental group received, rather than to the hypnosis training itself. Replication of this study with an attention–control group would rule out this alternative hypothesis.

Zeltzer and LeBaron have conducted a series of investigations of hypnosis and other behavioral interventions for alleviating the frequency and severity of postchemotherapy-related NV in children and adolescents. An initial study (Zeltzer, Kellerman, Ellenberg, & Dash, 1983) of 12 adolescents assessed symptoms during baseline courses prior to intervention and then with hypnotic intervention, and found a reduction in the frequency and severity of emesis with hypnosis. This study was limited in that it lacked a control group and assessed only a single course of chemotherapy before and during intervention.

It is interesting to note that one of the 12 adolescents studied by Zeltzer and her colleagues (Zeltzer et al., 1983) was experiencing NV secondary to a brain tumor rather than to chemotherapy. While the patient reported a reduction in emesis, her qualitative pattern of change differed from those patients with chemotherapy-related vomiting. Patients with postchemotherapy NV had an immediate positive response following hypnotic training; in contrast, this patient showed no response for two weeks. Nevertheless, after continued hypnotic sessions and practice, a steady decrease in emesis was noted over a seven-week period and her vomiting was completely alleviated eventually, despite no change in her medical status.

Another study (LeBaron & Zeltzer, 1984) was then conducted with eight pediatric patients, ages 10–17, using a multiple-baseline design in which subjects served as their own controls. As shown by the prospective study of NV previously cited, the use of a multiple-baseline design was important since children's symptoms can vary widely even during repeated courses of the same agents and dosages. Using the chemotherapy form (see Fig. 13.2a p. 200), patients rated the severity of postchemotherapy NV and the extent to which it bothered them for two to three baseline courses and two to three courses during which behavioral interventions were provided. While behavioral interventions produced significant reductions in postchemotherapy NV, subjects were treated with a combination of hypnotic and nonhypnotic distraction techniques so that hypnosis could not be identified as the sole effective treatment variable.

In a follow-up study, Zeltzer, LeBaron, and Zeltzer (1984a) compared hypnotherapy with supportive counseling using nonhypnotic distraction techniques. Of the 51 children, ages 6–17 years, rating the severity of postchemotherapy side effects, 16 children had few or no symptoms, another 16 had symptoms, but did not receive matched courses of chemotherapy necessary for study requirements. Following baseline assessment of two matched courses, the remaining 19 patients were randomized to receive hypnosis or supportive counseling during two more matched courses. The hypnotic intervention consisted of helping the child to become as absorbed as possible in vivid imagery and fantasy. Posthypnotic suggestions were given to help the children use imagery at home and to promote appetite and restful sleep. The supportive-counseling intervention consisted of distracting the child from attending to the chemotherapy by focusing on interesting objects in the treatment room, jokes, guessing games, and deep breathing. The use of imagery, fantasy, or other hypnotic techniques was avoided with this group. The child was encouraged to remain as active as possible at home to avoid focusing attention on possible symptoms.

Although there was no significant reduction of symptoms prior to intervention, both the hypnosis and supportive-counseling interventions were associated with significant reductions in NV and the extent to which these symptoms bothered patients. No statistically or clinically significant differences in outcome were found between the two approaches. After the termination of the interventions, symptom ratings of NV remained significantly lower than baseline ratings, although continued reduction of NV following thera-pist-directed interventions usually had not been found in behavioral studies of adults (Burish & Lyles, 1981; Lyles et al., 1982; Redd, Andersen, & Minagawa, 1982; Redd & Andrykowski, 1982). It is suggested that the children were able to maintain symptom reductions because of the active involvement of nurses and parents in the intervention procedures, which then enabled these caretakers to continue to provide effective interventions in the therapists' absence.

Hypnotic responsiveness was assessed by means of the Stanford Hypnotic Clinical Scale for Children (Morgan & Hilgard, 1978/1979) in the hypnosis-treatment group. No significant relationship was found between hypnotic susceptibility and the reduction of NV with hypnosis. Accordingly, Zeltzer and her colleagues (1984a) suggest that "the most effective components of intervention may not be derived from a specific technique, such as hypnosis. Perhaps any intervention that directs the child's attention away from chemo-therapy might be effective" (p. 688).

In contrast, according to the preliminary results presented by Zeltzer, Dolgin, LeBaron, and LeBaron (1989), hypnosis was found to be signifi-cantly more effective than supportive counseling (nonimagery distraction) in decreasing both anticipatory and postchemotherapy NV in a randomized, controlled-design study of 54 pediatric oncology patients (5–17 years of age). Following baseline assessment, subjects were randomly assigned to one of three groups—hypnosis, nonhypnotic distraction, or delayed intervention (control)—during the next identical chemotherapy course. Following inter-vention, the duration and severity of NV decreased by 31 percent in the hypnosis group and 13 percent in the supportive-counseling group. However, there was a 50 percent increase in these symptoms in the control group. The authors observe that there was considerable within-group variability in children's responses to interventions and suggest that further research is needed to identify salient intervening variables, such as the family's and child's coping styles.

NONHYPNOTIC BEHAVIORAL INTERVENTIONS

Other behavioral interventions investigated for their effectiveness in con-trolling NV have included progressive relaxation, systematic desensitization, and cognitive diversion techniques. Progressive relaxation training combined with guided imagery has been used to control NV in studies by Burish and his colleagues (Burish & Lyles, 1981; Lyles, Burish, Krozely, & Oldham, 1982; Burish, Carey, Krozely, & Greco, 1987). In the 1982 study, patients in the progressive-relaxation-training group were found to be significantly less anxious and nauseated both during and following their chemotherapy treatment sessions compared with the patients in a therapist contact group, in which emotional support and encouragement were provided, and a no-treatment control group.

In the 1987 study, Burish and his colleagues investigated whether progressive relaxation training prior to the initiation of chemotherapy and during the first three chemotherapy sessions could prevent or delay conditioned NV. The results showed that by the fifth chemotherapy session, only 10 percent of the patients in the progressive-relaxation-training group experienced post-chemotherapy nausea in contrast to 54 percent of the patients in the control group. The authors suggest that the effectiveness of relaxation training may be attributable, in part, to attention diversion; that is, the patient's attention is diverted away from the chemotherapy and toward more pleasant and relaxing thoughts.

Morrow and his colleagues (Morrow, 1986; Morrow & Dobkin, 1988; Morrow & Morrell, 1982) have investigated the use of systematic desensitization in treating ANV. According to the results of the 1982 study by Morrow and Morrell, there was a significant reduction in the frequency, severity, and duration of AN and the frequency and severity of AN for patients in the systematic-desensitization group compared with patients in the supportive-counseling or no-treatment control group.

In a follow-up study (Morrow, 1986), patients in the systematic-desensitization group showed a significant decrease in the severity and duration of AN in contrast to patients in the relaxation-only, counseling, and no-treatment control groups. Morrow concludes that the components of the cognitive-stimulus hierarchy and relaxation are both necessary for the successful treatment of ANV.

Studies (Kolko & Rickard-Figueroa, 1985; Redd, Jacobsen, Die-Trill, Dermatis, McEvoy, & Holland, 1987) have investigated interventions based on cognitive/attentional-distraction techniques, using commercially available video games to distract pediatric and adolescent patients. In the Kolko and Rickard-Figueroa (1985) study, access to video games during the administration of chemotherapy was associated with the reduction of self-reported and observer-recorded anticipatory symptoms as well as posttreatment distress.

In a study by Redd and his colleagues (1987) that used a combined ABAB withdrawal and repeated-measures analysis-of-variance design, availability of video games produced a significant reduction in the patient's nausea; likewise, withdrawal of the video games resulted in a significant exacerbation of nausea. Decreases in conditioned nausea were not accompanied by a significant reduction in self-reported anxiety or by decreases in physiological arousal, lending support to the hypothesis that cognitive distraction, and not relaxation, was the critical component of this intervention.

SIGNIFICANT VARIABLES IN THE TREATMENT
OF NAUSEA AND VOMITING

The relative efficacy of a variety of behavioral interventions in the treatment of NV suggests the difficulty in identifying the critical components contributing to positive outcomes. In a critical review of the use of hypnosis to treat NV, Stam (1989) observes, "In almost all reports there are indications that the induction and suggestions are meant to enhance relaxation and that suggestions are aimed at distraction (e.g., Kaye, 1984) or used in conjunction with a modified systematic desensitization approach (e.g., Hoffman, 1982)" (p. 326). The overlap of progressive relaxation training (especially with imagery) or systematic desensitization with hypnosis is considerable and other differences in the treatments are difficult to distinguish. Lyles and associates (Lyles et al., 1982) acknowledge, "The relaxation and imagery procedures we use appear to be very similar to the 'hypnosis' procedures used by Redd, et al. (1982), and it may be that they differ more in name than in substance or effect" (p. 511).

Other investigators (Morrow & Dobkin, 1988; Redd et al., 1987) disagree about the essential components of effective treatment for NV. Redd and his colleagues (1987) and Kolko and Rickard-Figueroa (1965) identify cognitive distraction as the critical component. In addition, hypnotherapy and progressive relaxation training use guided imagery to divert the patient's attention away from the aversive chemotherapy experience. However, Morrow and Dobkin (1988) concluded that it is not simply distraction that accounts for effective intervention with NV since systematic desensitization focuses the patient's attention on the aversive chemotherapy-related stimuli.

Increased relaxation is also identified as a critical component (Burish et al., 1987; Lyles et al., 1982). However, Morrow and Dobkin (1988) conclude that relaxation itself is a necessary but not sufficient treatment component for reducing ANV. Counterconditioning appears to be a necessary element in the treatment package since ANV symptoms are thought to be learned, maladaptive responses. Through systematic desensitization, involving both relaxation and cognitive elements, the patient learns a new, adaptive response. In cognitive/attentional-distraction studies (Redd et al., 1987), decreases in conditioned nausea were not accompanied by significant reductions in self-reported anxiety or by decreases in physiological arousal. In fact, patients occasionally became more physiologically aroused while playing video games. According to the authors, "These results suggest that reductions in conditioned nausea can be achieved with a distracting task independent of physiological relaxation" (p. 395).

Additional research is needed to identify further the critical components that contribute to significant improvement in the control of aversive chemotherapy-related side effects.

ASSESSING THE ROLE OF HYPNOSIS IN THE
TREATMENT OF NAUSEA AND VOMITING

In a comprehensive review of the clinical use of hypnosis, Wadden and Anderton (1982) observe, "Authorities disagree on what distinguishes hypnotic from nonhypnotic therapy or on the circumstances under which an induction may add leverage to cognitive-behavioral treatments" (p. 215). It is often unclear from both a theoretical and a practical standpoint what criteria are used to identify a treatment as uniquely hypnotic. In many studies, the principal factors that distinguish a situation as such are the therapist's labeling the treatment as hypnosis and the use of a hypnotic induction. Often no formal assessment of hypnotic susceptibility is conducted. Individuals are often said to have been treated with hypnosis, although no evidence is available to confirm that they were hypnotized.

In contrast, hypnosis may not be defined in terms of what the therapist does, but may instead be regarded as a stable characteristic (trait) of the individual (Hilgard, 1977). According to Bowers (1983), there is a 0.65 correlation between waking and hypnotic suggestibility. Waking suggestibility provides a high base level of responsiveness to suggestion, but suggestibility in the hypnotic state leads to slight but significant increases over this waking baseline. As Wadden and Anderton (1982) note, for a subject with high susceptibility, any communication from the practitioner can be turned into a therapeutic suggestion, regardless of whether the situation has been labeled as hypnosis or an induction has been employed.

> Treatment outcome is examined to determine whether there is a positive relation between therapeutic improvement and hypnotizability. If a relation is found, the treatment (regardless of what it is or how it is presented) is probably exploiting the subject's hypnotic talent. In the absence of a relation, then regardless of how successful a hypnotic treatment has been, the outcome probably has little to do with genuine hypnotic effects. Nonhypnotic factors such as expectancy or placebo effects are likely to be responsible for the success. What is questioned in this case is not treatment efficacy but only whether the effectiveness is hypnotically based. (p. 217)

Some therapists believe that hypnotic responsiveness is irrelevant to clinical outcome and that virtually anyone can benefit from hypnotic treatment. Although a hypnotic induction can be used with almost anyone, only persons possessing hypnotic talent will experience the alteration in consciousness commonly known as the hypnotic state. But even subjects with limited hypnotic responsiveness are likely to benefit from the nonspecific aspects of hypnosis, which may include relaxation and reduced anxiety. These issues highlight the importance of assessing hypnotic responsiveness. If therapeutic improvement does not correlate with measured hypnotic responsiveness, "it is doubtful if hypnosis is the primary causal factor responsible for the changes that occurred" (Hilgard, 1987, p. 253).

ASSESSMENT ISSUES

For the health professional, expertise in one's primary health profession, knowledge of child development, and the ability to establish good rapport with children are prerequisites to the effective use of hypnotherapy with children. A health professional should not attempt to treat a problem with hypnotherapy unless he or she is also competent to assess the problem and to recommend other therapies if necessary (O'Grady & Hoffmann, 1984). In considering the use of hypnotherapy to treat a child or adolescent experiencing distress related to NV, a routine assessment should be conducted of factors associated with positive therapeutic outcome, including (1) the psychological functioning of the child and parents, (2) the status of the child's medical condition and treatment milieu, (3) hypnotic responsiveness, and (4) severity of NV.

Assessment of the Psychological Functioning of the Child and Parents

Although it is not always possible to conduct a comprehensive assessment of child and parental functioning in acute-care situations, the information gathered through such an evaluation is often important in developing the therapeutic relationship and enhancing positive treatment outcomes.

It is important to meet initially with parents to obtain a developmental history and information about the child's coping both prior to and following the diagnosis of the illness.

Objective assessment measures such as the Personality Inventory for Children (Wirt, Lacher, Klinedinst, & Seat, 1977) or the Child Behavior Checklist (Achenbach, 1981) are helpful in assessing significant anxiety, depression, or other serious emotional problems that may impede successful hypnotherapy. Parents can complete the Brief Symptom Inventory (Derogatis & Spencer, 1982) and the Impact on Family Scale (Stein & Riessman, 1980) to assess their functioning and evaluate the need for supportive counseling to enable the family to cope better with the prolonged stress of caring for a seriously ill child. As noted in the study by Dolgin and his colleagues (1985), parental anxiety is significantly correlated with the development of ANV in their children.

During this initial meeting, parents' attitudes and possible misconceptions about hypnosis are explored. Hypnosis is defined in familiar terms, such as being mesmerized while driving a car on a highway or being so totally absorbed in a movie that one is oblivious to one's surroundings. How hypnosis may be of benefit to their child in reducing NV is discussed. The parents' interest in using hypnosis and/or other behavioral interventions to promote their own relaxation and an increased sense of mastery is also explored. Ideally, parents are viewed as cotherapists who can assist the therapist in engaging the child in guided imagery during procedures and coach their child in hypnotic strategies in the therapist's absence (Hoffmann, O'Grady, & Harris, 1986).

During an initial meeting with the child or adolescent, it is important to begin to establish a positive therapeutic relationship. Clinically, many children experiencing ANV present as anxious, perfectionistic individuals who are "slow to warm up." As with the parent interview, other sources of stress should be explored. Social isolation is a frequent problem for many of these children and the planning of enjoyable activities with peers within a reasonable time after the completion of chemotherapy can be a powerful incentive to practice strategies to reduce NV. The child's attitudes toward hypnosis should be discussed and possible benefits of using hypnosis and other behavioral interventions to reduce NV can be presented.

Assessment of the Status of the Child's Medical Condition and Treatment Milieu

Consultation with other members of the oncology treatment team on a regular basis will enable the therapist to become readily aware of any change in the child's medical condition and to promote their cooperation in the use of hypnosis with the patient. Many clinic nurses establish long-term relationships with the children during their prolonged course of treatment. They are often very supportive of the children's efforts to control their NV and may be willing to coach them in hypnotic strategies if the therapist and parents are unavailable.

Although most of the children referred for treatment of NV may be experiencing chemotherapy-related distress, children may also be referred for psychogenic vomiting. In these cases, it is important to inquire whether an organic explanation for the vomiting has been thoroughly investigated. Olness and Gardner (1988) cite a case of cyclic vomiting that was thought to be psychogenic and, after one year of intricate testing by a pediatric neurologist and endocrinologist, was found to be due to an urea-cycle abnormality.

The vomiting was eliminated by controlling the 10-year-old girl's intake of protein.

Assessment of Hypnotic Responsiveness

Recent studies (Apfel, Kelly, & Frankel, 1986; Stam, 1989) suggest that patients with high hypnotic responsiveness or absorption in imaginative involvements may be at a greater risk for developing ANV. Children, as a group, are highly responsive to hypnosis. Most normative studies have concluded that hypnotizability is limited in young children, achieves its apex during the middle childhood years, and then decreases somewhat in adolescence, remaining stable through midlife before decreasing again in the older population (Olness & Gardner, 1988). In children, hypnotic responsiveness is significantly related to the ability to become absorbed in imaginative involvements, vividness of imagery, and fantasy play (Plotnick, 1988).

Hypnotic responsiveness in children can be formally evaluated by means of two scales: the Children's Hypnotic Susceptibility Scale (London, 1963) and the Stanford Hypnotic Clinical Scale for Children (SHCS: C) (Morgan & Hilgard, 1978/1979a). The SHCS: C was designed for clinical use and can be administered in 20 minutes, in contrast to 45–60 minutes for the London scale. In our experience, the SHCS: C can easily be incorporated into initial hypnotherapy sessions owing to its brevity and the generally appealing selection of items (Hodel, Hoffman, O'Grady, & Steffen, 1982). (For a detailed review of hypnotic responsiveness in children, see Chapter 2 in this book.)

Assessment of Nausea and Vomiting

Among the key issues in the assessment of NV are the definition of response terms, questions of self-report versus observer-rated assessment, the usefulness of both direct and indirect assessments of NV, and whether combining NV responses into overall measures is justified. Morrow (1984b) recommends the assessment of nausea separate from vomiting.

Currently, the Morrow Assessment of Nausea and Emesis (MANE) (see Fig. 13.1) is the most comprehensive and widely used measure for assessing treatment-related NV in patients 19 years old and older (Carnrike et al., 1988). According to Morrow (personal communication), it has been informally modified by some clinicians to be used with younger populations.

The MANE was developed to be administered at the time of the fourth chemotherapy treatment and is used to assess all previous chemotherapy administrations. The MANE-FU is used for all subsequent chemotherapy treatment, as it assesses only one treatment at a time. Test–retest reliability

Continued on p. 199

MORROW ASSESSMENT OF NAUSEA AND EMESIS

These questions will ask about nausea and vomiting separately. NAUSEA is feeling sick to your stomach; VOMITING is actually throwing up.

The word "treatment" will refer to any drugs you are given here or to take home.

1.   **I have experienced NAUSEA: (please circle one)**

   1.   during or after every treatment
   2.   after many of my treatments
   3.   after only about half my treatments
   4.   rarely after a treatment
   8.   never after a treatment (if never, please skip to question #2)

   When I have NAUSEA after a treatment it usually lasts _____ hours.

   I would describe the NAUSEA as:

   1.   very mild
   2.   mild
   3.   moderate
   4.   severe
   5.   very severe
   6.   intolerable

   The NAUSEA is usually the worst:

   01.   during treatment
   02.   0-4 hours after treatment
   03.   4-8 hours after treatment
   04.   8-12 hours after treatment
   05.   12-24 hours after treatment
   06.   24 or more hours after treatment
   07.   no time is more severe than any other time

2.   **I have experienced VOMITING:**

   1.   during or after every treatment
   2.   after many of my treatments
   3.   after only about half of my treatments
   4.   rarely after a treatment
   8.   never after a treatment (if never, please skip to question #3)

   When I VOMIT after a treatment, I usually vomit for _____ hours.

   I would describe the VOMITING as:

   1.   very mild
   2.   mild
   3.   moderate
   4.   severe
   5.   very severe
   6.   intolerable

   The VOMITING is usually the worst:

   01.   during treatment
   02.   0-4 hours after treatment
   03.   4-8 hours after treatment
   04.   8-12 hours after treatment
   05.   12-24 hours after treatment
   06.   24 or more hours after treatment
   07.   no time is more severe than any other time

3. I have experienced NAUSEA:

    1. before every treatment
    2. before many of my treatments
    3. before about half of my treatments
    4. rarely before a treatment
    8. never before a treatment (if never, please go on to question #4)

    I would describe the NAUSEA I have before my treatment as:

    1. very mild
    2. mild
    3. moderate
    4. severe
    5. very severe
    6. intolerable

    When I have NAUSEA before a treatment it usually begins _____ hours before my treatment.

    I experienced NAUSEA before my last treatment:

    1. yes
    2. no

4. I have experienced VOMITING:

    1. before every treatment
    2. before many of my treatments
    3. before about half of my treatments
    4. rarely before a treatment
    8. never before a treatment (if never, please go on to question #5)

    I would describe the VOMITING before my treatment as:

    1. very mild
    2. mild
    3. moderate
    4. severe
    5. very severe
    6. intolerable

    When I have VOMITING before a treatment, it usually begins _____ hours before my treatment.

    I experienced VOMITING before my last treatment:

    1. yes
    2. no

5. I have experienced motion sickness at some time (riding in cars, boats, planes):

    1. yes
    2. no

MORROW ASSESSMENT OF NAUSEA AND EMESIS FOLLOW UP

These questions will ask about nausea and vomiting separately. NAUSEA is feeling sick to your stomach; VOMITING is actually throwing up. Please circle or fill in the corresponding number.

1. Did you experience NAUSEA *during or after* your *last* chemotherapy treatment?

    1. yes
    2. no (*if no, please skip to question #2*)

Continued

How long did the NAUSEA last? _____ hours

How would you describe the NAUSEA at its worst?

      1.   very mild
      2.   mild
      3.   moderate
      4.   severe
      5.   very severe
      6.   intolerable

When was the NAUSEA the worst?

      01.   during treatment
      02.   0-4 hours after treatment
      03.   4-8 hours after treatment
      04.   8-12 hours after treatment
      05.   12-24 hours after treatment
      06.   24 or more hours after treatment
      07.   no time more severe than any other

2.   **Did you experience VOMITING *during or after* your *last* chemotherapy treatment?**

      1.   yes
      2.   no (*if no, please skip to question #3*)

How long did the VOMITING last? _____ hours

How would you describe the VOMITING at its worst?

      1.   very mild
      2.   mild
      3.   moderate
      4.   severe
      5.   very severe
      6.   intolerable

When was the VOMITING the worst?

      01.   during treatment
      02.   0-4 hours after treatment
      03.   4-8 hours after treatment
      04.   8-12 hours after treatment
      05.   12-24 hours after treatment
      06.   24 or more hours after treatment
      07.   no time more severe than any other

3.   **Did you experience NAUSEA *before* your *last* chemotherapy treatment?**

      1.   yes
      2.   no (*if no, please skip to question #4*)

How would you describe the NAUSEA before treatment?

      1.   very mild
      2.   mild
      3.   moderate
      4.   severe
      5.   very severe
      6.   intolerable

How many hours before treatment did it first occur? _____ hours

4. **Did you experience VOMITING *before* your *last* chemotherapy treatment?**

    1. yes
    2. no (*if no, please skip to question #5*)

How would you describe the VOMITING at its worst before treatment?

    1. very mild
    2. mild
    3. moderate
    4. severe
    5. very severe
    6. intolerable

How many hours before treatment did the VOMITING first occur? _____ hours

5. **Did you take medication for NAUSEA and/or VOMITING for your last treatment?**

    1. yes
    2. no

If yes, was it useful?

    1. very
    2. somewhat
    3. works a little
    4. doesn't seem to help

FIGURE 13.1. *Morrow assessment of nausea and emesis.* (Reprinted with permission.)

of the MANE was assessed in a study by Morrow (1984b). The concurrent validity of the MANE and continuous self-monitoring of patients was evaluated in a study by Carnrike and his associates (Carnrike et al., 1988).

The Chemotherapy Self-Report Form (see Fig. 13.2a) was developed by LeBaron and Zeltzer (1984) to assess postchemotherapy NV in children. For children who are 10 years of age and younger, there is an accompanying ''Faces Form,'' a visual analogue scale consisting of six faces (with ratings of even numbers from 0 to 10 beneath them) that portray increasing amounts of distress (see Fig. 13.2b). The Faces Form is placed above the numbers of the scales on the Chemotherapy Self-Report Form and used as signposts for the younger children.

The Chemotherapy Self-Report Form is used initially to interview the patient about his or her most recent chemotherapy course. Parents are interviewed separately. Each family is given a copy of the Chemotherapy Self-Report Form and the Faces Form, if appropriate, to take home. The patients and their parents are contacted by telephone within two to five days following the adminstration of each course of chemotherapy and interviewed about their responses to form items.

CHEMOTHERAPY FORM

NAME _____ DATE _____

CHEMOTHERAPY

1. Did you have any nausea and vomiting this time before you got your medicine (i.e., at home, coming to clinic, or while the needle was being put in)? yes   no   n

2. When was the last time you felt nauseated?
   _____ minutes   _____ hours   _____ days

3. How much of the time did you have nausea during or after this course?

   none   a little   half the   much of   constantly
           bit   time   the time

   0 1 2 3 4 5 6 7 8 9 10

4. When was the last time you vomited?
   _____ minutes   _____ hours   _____ days

5. How much of the time did you have vomiting during or after this course?

   none   a little   half the   much of   constantly
           bit   time   the time

   0 1 2 3 4 5 6 7 8 9 10

6. How much did this course of chemotherapy bother you?

   none   the worst that
                                               I can imagine

   0 1 2 3 4 5 6 7 8 9 10

COMMENT: Describe in what way the n/v bothered you (worry, discomfort, pain, thoughts, feelings, changes how people treat them). Also, what helped you to do well? (thoughts, people, activities).

7. How much did this course stop you from going to school? (check one)
   none   two days
   half a day   more than two days
   one day   (how many?   )

8. How much did this course of chemotherapy stop you from doing things with friends?
   none   two days
   half a day   more than two days
   one day   (how many?   )

9. How much did this course of chemotherapy stop you from sleeping?
   none   two nights
   half a night   more than two nights
   one night   (how many?   )

10. How much did this course of chemotherapy stop you from eating?
    none   two days
    half a day   more than two days
    one day   (how many?   )

11. Antiemetics:

Type _____

Number of times taken _____

Who suggested taking them (i.e., patient, parent, nurse) _____

FIGURE 13.2a. *Chemotherapy form*. [From Lebaron and Zeltzer (1984). Reprinted by permission.]

"FACES FORM"

CHEMOTHERAPY

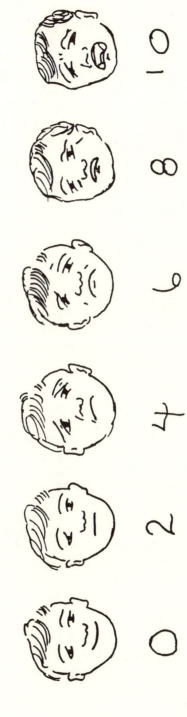

FIGURE 13.2b. *Faces form.* [From LeBaron & Zeltzer (1984). Reprinted by permission.]

INTERVENTION PROCESS

Despite most children's high hypnotic responsiveness, parents must be educated about the potential benefits of hypnotherapy for their child. O'Grady and Hoffmann (1984) have presented a six-phase approach to hypnotherapy with children that will be only briefly reviewed here. The use of hypnosis can be divided somewhat arbitrarily into six phases: (1) preparation, (2) induction, (3) deepening, (4) therapeutic suggestions, (5) posthypnotic suggestions, and (6) termination.

Preparation of the Parent

During the preparation phase, the therapist introduces parents to the potential use of hypnosis as a treatment modality for their child or adolescent. As previously discussed, much of the preparation is accomplished during the initial session in which the child's and parents' psychological functioning are assessed. It is helpful to view parents as therapeutic allies, since they will be in the position of coaching their child in hypnosis in the therapist's absence (Gardner, 1974). In my experience, both fathers and mothers have been able to guide their children successfully in the use of hypnosis to relieve distress associated with illness or medical procedures (Hoffmann, O'Grady, & Harris, 1986). As Zeltzer and LeBaron (1984a) have noted, children and adolescents tend to regress during acute-stress situations and are often unable to soothe themselves. They may require active therapist-directed intervention to reduce their distress. However, "the majority of children can maintain their reduced symptomatology with nurse and parent support or, for adolescents, through their own efforts and positive expectations" (p. 20).

Often the parent is encouraged, with the child's permission, to observe the child practicing hypnosis. This usually occurs after several training sessions with the child when he or she is proud to demonstrate his or her hypnotic skills. Additionally, having the parents experience hypnosis for themselves is offered as an option; however, few parents avail themselves of this opportunity. It is usually the parents of hospitalized children who have chosen to learn self-hypnosis as a coping strategy to enhance feelings of relaxation and a sense of mastery during their child's variable medical course.

Preparation of the Child

Preparation of the child varies with age. For children in the 5–6-year-old age group, hypnosis is introduced through play. According to Morgan and Hilgard (1978/1979a), children in this age group respond more readily to what they named "protohypnosis," that is, external distraction, such as listening to a story, in contrast to distraction through self-controlled fantasy. These children often resist suggestions for eye closure.

Preparation for this age is brief and concrete and induction begins as the therapist engages the child in stories about his or her favorite activities, television, heroes, or pets. For children 7 years of age and older, means that they currently use to distract themselves from distress can be explored (e.g., television shows, video games). Hypnosis can be introduced as a talent most children have to use their imagination to become fully absorbed in fantasies and favorite activities, enabling them to "get away" from discomfort and to become more the "boss of their body." It is described as a skill, much like athletic or musical ability, that improves with frequent practice. The Stanford Hypnotic Clinical Scale for Children—revised (Zeltzer & LeBaron, 1984b), for children 6–16 years of age, or the Stanford Hypnotic Clinical Scale (Morgan & Hilgard, 1978/1979b), for adolescents older than 16 years, is usually administered during the second session with the child. The administration of the scale is easily integrated into the therapy session and most children find the experience enjoyable.

Induction

The choice of the method of induction depends on the child's age, the therapist's preference, and the situation. A list of induction techniques for different age groups can be found in Olness and Gardner (1988). As previously noted, young children are unlikely to close their eyes during the induction phase. It is not until age 11 that 90 percent of the children prefer to close their eyes, and those who close their eyes do not always keep them closed (Morgan & Hilgard, 1978/1979a). Involving the young child in imaginative play with a favorite character or pet is often sufficient for the child to enter hypnosis. At approximately age 7 and older, children begin to enjoy ideomotor techniques, such as arm lowering, coin dropping, or index fingers moving together when hands are clasped. Because the ultimate goal is to teach self-hypnosis, the child is usually taught a number of induction techniques and is encouraged to select the one he or she prefers.

Deepening

During this phase, the child is helped to dissociate further and become more and more involved in his or her imagination. With some children, the therapist may simply count backwards and suggest to the child that with each number he or she will take a step down a hill or staircase and become more and more relaxed. Many children become more fully involved in the hypnotic experience as the therapist focuses on the sights, sounds, and tactile sensations they are experiencing in their imaginative play or absorbing fantasy. Since children as a group are able to make the necessary shift to the hypnotic state more readily than adults, the deepening phase is usually shorter than with adults.

Suggestions

Since the goal of hypnosis is to help the child become as intensely involved in imagery and fantasy as possible, it is important to interview the child about his or her choice of favorite images from past experiences, fantasy, television, or movies that can be incorporated into the hypnotic experience. It is important to select the precise words that the child finds meaningful to describe the sights, sounds, and sensations in his or her images. As Olness (1981) and Zeltzer and LeBaron (1984a) have noted, behavioral interventions in adults are generally aimed at relaxing the patient, whereas with pediatric patients, hypnosis is often more effective if it is action-oriented. Most children have great difficulty maintaining their attention span long enough to relax during periods of distress. This reflects my experience that most children and adolescents select active fantasies in which they are energetically participating in a sport (e.g., swimming, horseback riding, soccer) or engaged in exciting adventures (e.g., landing an airplane on a carrier). Often it is helpful to rehearse the child in momentarily losing control (i.e., swallowing some water while swimming, riding a horse that is running too fast, falling down on a playing field) and then regaining control, so that the patient realizes that he or she can regain control even if he or she does become nauseated or vomits.

Direct suggestions can be given for being "the boss of your body," and for having a sense of well-being. As Zeltzer and her colleagues (1983) note, suggestions can be given concerning the refreshing nature and antiemetic properties of patients' imagery, "notice the cool, clear air and taste the snow" (p. 79). Many children respond to suggestions that they are hungry for their favorite foods, which can then be incorporated into their imagery. Focusing on the smells and tastes of the selected foods (most often pizza and coke) distracts many children from the smell of the chemotherapy. Dash (1980) provides specific hypnotic suggestions for symptom amelioration in pediatric cancer patients.

Posthypnotic Suggestions and Termination

Posthypnotic suggestions are given to the child during hypnosis to increase the likelihood of desirable behavior after hypnosis is terminated. Frequently, children are given posthypnotic suggestions to practice self-hypnosis at home; to have a continuing sense of well-being prior to, during, and following the scheduled chemotherapy appointment; to have a good appetite; and to have a restful night's sleep. In addition, suggestions can be given to promote ease in reentering a hypnotic state using treatment- or symptom-related visual cues, such as, "When you see the nurse, you can feel reassured, and this feeling will remind you to become deeply relaxed and comfortable" (Zeltzer et al., 1983).

After termination, all the hypnotic strategies, images, and suggestions are reviewed with the child in order to select the most effective or preferred ones for subsequent use.

Summary of Intervention

In the treatment of chemotherapy-related NV with hypnosis, if possible, it is advisable to schedule at least three treatment sessions with the child and his or her parents prior to the scheduled chemotherapy appointment. During the initial session, preparation of the parents and child can be introduced. Parents can be given personality inventories to complete. Forms assessing NV can be completed as the therapist interviews the child and parents. During the second session, the child's hypnotic responsiveness can be assessed and the child can be introduced to specific induction and deepening techniques. In addition, the child is interviewed for favorite activities and fantasies in order to develop appropriately detailed suggestions and images. During the third session, the child practices hypnosis, with the therapist helping the child to become intensely involved in imagery. The session can be audiotaped for the child's use at home and in the car en route to the hospital. Occasionally, a child with ANV reports becoming nauseated while listening to the tape, providing another example of conditioned learning. Obviously, in such cases, the use of the audiotape is discontinued.

The therapist conducts another practice session with the child one half hour prior to the scheduled chemotherapy session and usually remains with the child for the first half hour of treatment, continuing to engage the child in imagery. If chemotherapy is administered intravenously over several hours, many children will attempt to go to sleep during the treatment. If possible, the therapist can check back with the patient during the course of the treatment. Parents and clinic nurses are encouraged to engage the child in hypnotic imagery, as needed.

Case Study

The following case study illustrates several treatment issues.

M.T., a 19-year-old adolescent with recurrent osteogenic sarcoma, originally diagnosed at age 15, had had severe ANV for several years at the time of her referral for hypnotherapy. Merely reading a birthday card sent to her by the Children's Hospital staff would cause her to vomit. She would usually start vomiting two weeks before a scheduled chemotherapy treatment and she would experience severe vomiting during the five-hour car trip from her home to the hospital. She was unable to discuss her disease without feeling nauseous and vomiting. Despite an amputated leg and recurrent disease, M.T. attended college and achieved high grades. She presented as an unusually pleasant young woman. Both she and her mother appeared to have difficulty expressing negative affect despite a difficult and prolonged course of treatment, including repeated surgeries.

With regard to hypnotic responsiveness, she scored in the high range on the Stanford Hypnotic Clinical Scale, passing four out of five items, and proved to be a good hypnotic subject. Although an eye-roll induction was initially introduced to M.T., she preferred simply to close her eyes and focus on her breathing. She was encouraged to inhale and exhale slowly and deeply and given suggestions to "breathe in relaxation" and "exhale all worries and concerns." To increase her relaxation, she enjoyed the suggestion to have a golden, yellow light slowly move up her body, warming and relaxing her muscles. Walking down a boardwalk was used to promote further deepening of the hypnotic experience since M.T.'s "favorite place" to be was a Florida beach with several of her friends. M.T.'s absorption in her imagery was encouraged by focusing on the sensations she was experiencing, such as the warmth of the sun on her body, the sound of the waves, and the smell of steak being barbecued. More active imagery that was sometimes used was M.T. playing basketball, an activity she had enjoyed prior to her amputation. M.T. also responded to direct suggestions to reduce distress, visualizing her stomach as changing in color from red (i.e., wobbly) to pink (i.e., calm) as she became more relaxed. Posthypnotic suggestions were given for a continued sense of well-being (e.g., feeling that she was "boss of her body") prior to, during, and following chemotherapy and of ease at reentering the hypnotic state by simply closing her eyes and breathing deeply. An audiotape of a therapy session was prepared to promote practice at home and en route to the hospital.

M.T. was treated for 10 sessions, over a five-month period, as an inpatient at the time of her scheduled chemotherapy treatments. As therapy sessions progressed, she was able to talk about her disease with family and friends without NV, and vomiting gradually decreased en route to the hospital until all symptoms were eliminated. This case is interesting in that the ANV symptoms were very severe and had been experienced for several years at the time of the referral. Because of M.T.'s high hypnotic responsiveness, it is likely that the positive therapeutic outcome can be attributed, in part, to the hypnotherapy employed; nevertheless, it is unclear to what degree other common therapeutic factors may have contributed to treatment success.

SUMMARY AND FUTURE TRENDS

In summary, a review of the literature on the hypnotic treatment of NV in children suggests that hypnosis, as well as other behavioral interventions, is effective in this treatment. The critical components that have characterized successful therapies have included relaxation, distraction, and/or counterconditioning. Many interventions have a number of components and investigators disagree about which variables are necessary and sufficient to alleviate symptoms. Additional research is needed further to identify the relative contribution of these critical components.

Furthermore, there is a need for studies in which hypnotic responsiveness is assessed for all subjects in all conditions (i.e., hypnosis, no-treatment control, and contrasting interventions) in order to evaluate better the efficacy of hypnosis in treating NV. A patient assessed as having high hypnotic responsiveness may have spontaneously employed hypnosis although the treatment intervention was not labeled as such. If a patient is assessed as having low hypnotic responsiveness, a positive outcome would not be attributed to hypnosis (i.e., dissociative ability or absorption in imaginative fantasy), but rather to common therapeutic factors (i.e., relaxation or distraction). It is likely that a child low in hypnotic responsiveness would be more successfully treated using cognitive/attentional-distraction techniques (e.g., video games). Accordingly, it is important for the health professional interested in using hypnotherapy to be competent to use other therapies, if necessary.

As discussed earlier in this chapter, absorption in imagery is conceptualized as a component of hypnotic responsiveness that describes the ability to set ordinary reality aside temporarily while engaging in fantasy. There is a significant relationship between measured hypnotic responsiveness and absorption in children (Plotnick, 1988). Findings from several studies (Apfel, Kelly, & Frankel, 1986; Stam, 1988) suggest that patients with high hypnotic responsiveness or absorption in imaginative involvements may be at greater risk for developing ANV. Stam (1989) suggests that patients scoring high in absorption may ruminate about their upcoming chemotherapy treatments and the associated side effects, thereby facilitating the development of the conditioned ANV response. Prospective studies are needed to explore further the possible relationships among hypnotic responsiveness, the severity of postchemotherapy side effects, and the development of ANV.

According to LeBaron and Zeltzer (1983), major studies are still needed in which there are multiple baseline and intervention assessments, postintervention follow-up, appropriate controls, and comparisons of hypnosis and other behavioral techniques in the treatment of aversive chemotherapy side effects. This is difficult research to conduct. On the basis of their pilot studies, LeBaron and Zeltzer found that about 30–40 percent of patients in their clinic population do not have significant NV, and an additional 30 percent may be expected to go off treatment, experience changes in their chemotherapy protocols, or die before they complete the study. Thus, only approximately one third of their total clinical population 5 years of age or older are available for baseline, intervention, and postintervention follow-up.

Finally, a recurrent problem in the behavioral treatment of NV with adults has been the failure to maintain positive treatment effects in the therapist's absence. In contrast, children have been able to maintain their therapeutic gains (Zeltzer, LeBaron, & Zeltzer, 1984a), and it is hypothesized that this is due to the active participation of parents and oncology nurses. Parents of pediatric cancer patients have been trained to engage their child in hypnosis during painful procedures and in alleviating NV, resulting in an increased sense of mastery for both parents and children (Hoffmann, O'Grady, & Harris, 1986).

In addition, it is likely that the participation of the oncology nurse as a resource in the treatment of NV has been underutilized. A study by Cohen and her associates (Cohen, Blanchard, Ruckdeschel, & Smolen, 1986) found that treatment centers differed significantly in the prevalence of both post-treatment and anticipatory NV, despite the use of similar treatment protocols. Future studies are needed to examine specific factors that differentiate treatment facilities, including the role of the attending nurse prior to, during, and following the chemotherapy session. Many oncology nurses are highly motivated to employ interventions to alleviate adverse side effects. Consideration should be given to training oncology nurses in guiding children in hypnotic strategies, thereby increasing their confidence that they can assist children in maintaining therapeutic gains following formal hypnotherapy training sessions.

REFERENCES

Achenbach, T. (1961). *Child behavior checklist for ages 4-16*. Burlington, VT: University of Vermont.

Altmaier, E., Ross, W., & Moore, K. (1982). A pilot investigation of the psychologic function of patients with anticipatory vomiting. *Cancer, 49*, 201-204.

Andrykowski, M. A., & Redd, W. H. (1987). Longitudinal analysis of the development of anticipatory nausea. *Journal of Consulting and Clinical Psychology, 55*, 36-41.

Andrykowski, M. A., Redd, W. H., & Hatfield, A. K. (1985). Development of anticipatory nausea: A prospective analysis. *Journal of Consulting and Clinical Psychology, 53*, 447-454.

Apfel, R. J., Kelly, S. G., & Frankel, F. H. (1986). The role of hypnotizability in the pathogenesis and treatment of nausea and vomiting of pregnancy. *Journal of Psychosomatic Obstetrics and Gynaecology, 5*, 179-166.

Bowers, K. (1983). *Hypnosis for the seriously curious.* New York: Norton.

Burish, T. G., Carey, M. P., Krozely, M. G., & Greco, A. (1987). Conditioned side effects induced by cancer chemotherapy: Prevention through behavioral treatment. *Journal of Consulting and Clinical Psychology, 55*, 42-48.

Burish, T. G., & Lyles, J. H. (1981). Effectiveness of relaxation training in reducing adverse reactions to cancer chemotherapy. *Journal of Behavioral Medicine, 4*, 65-78.

Carnrike, C., Brantley, P., Bruce, B., Faruqui, S., Gresham, F., Buss, R., & Cocke, T. (1988). Test-retest reliability and concurrent validity of the Morrow Assessment of Nausea and Emesis (MANE) for the assessment of cancer chemotherapy-related nausea and vomiting. *Journal of Psychopathology and Behavioral Assessment, 10*, 107-116.

Cohen, R. E., Blanchard, E. B., Ruckdeschel, J. C., & Smolen, R. C. (1986). Prevalence and correlates of posttreatment and anticipatory nausea and vomiting in cancer chemotherapy. *Journal of Psychosomatic Research, 30*, 643-654.

Cotanch, P., Hockenberry, M., & Herman, S. (1985). Self-hypnosis as antiemetic therapy in children receiving chemotherapy. *Oncology Nursing Forum, 12*, 41-46.

Dash, J. (1980). Hypnosis for symptom amelioration. In J. Kellerman (Ed.), *Psychological aspects of childhood cancer* (pp. 215-230). Springfield, IL: Charles C. Thomas.

Derogatis, L. R., & Spencer, P. (1982). *Brief symptom inventory manual.* Baltimore: Clinical Psychometric Research.

Dobkin, P., Zeichner, A., & Dickson-Parnell, B. (1985). Concomitants of anticipatory nausea and emesis in cancer chemotherapy. *Psychological Reports, 56*, 671-676.

Dolgin, M. J., Katz, E. R., McGinty, K., & Seigel, S. E. (1985). Anticipatory nausea and vomiting in pediatric cancer patients. *Pediatrics, 75*, 547-552.

Ellenberg, L., Kellerman, J., Dash, J., Huggins, C., & Zeltzer, L. (1980). Use of hypnosis for multiple symptoms in an adolescent girl with leukemia. *Journal of Adolescent Health Care, 1*, 132-136.

Frankel, R. (1987). Significant developments in medical hypnosis during the past 25 years. *International Journal of Clinical and Experimental Hypnosis, 35*, 231-247.

Gardner, G. G. (1974). Parents: Obstacles or allies in child hypnotherapy? *American Journal of Clinical Hypnosis, 17*, 44.

Hilgard, E. R. (1977). *Divided consciousness: Multiple controls in human thought and action*. New York: Wiley.

Hilgard, E. R. (1987). Research advances in hypnosis: Issues and methods. *International Journal of Clinical and Experimental Hypnosis, 35,* 248-265.

Hilgard, J. R., & LeBaron, S. (1984). *Hypnotherapy of pain in children with cancer*. Los Altos, CA: Kaufmann.

Hodel, T. V., Hoffmann, C., O'Grady, D. J., & Steffen, J. (1982). Hypnosis for leukemic children for coping with medical procedural distress. Presented at the American Psychological Association Annual Meeting, Washington, DC.

Hoffman, M. (1982). Hypnotic desensitization of the management of anticipatory emesis in chemotherapy. *American Journal of Clinical Hypnosis, 25,* 173-176.

Hoffmann, C., O'Grady, D. J., & Harris, R. (1986). Hypnosis with parents and children for coping during bone marrow transplantation. Presented at the Annual Scientific Meeting of the Society for Clinical and Experimental Hypnosis, Chicago.

Ingle, R. J., Burish, T. G., & Wallston, K. A. (1984). Conditionability of cancer chemotherapy patients. *Oncology Nursing Forum, 11,* 97-102.

Jacobsen, P. B., & Redd, W. H. (1988). The development and management of chemotherapy-related anticipatory nausea and vomiting. *Cancer Investigation, 6,* 2329-2336.

Kaye, J. (1984). Hypnotherapy and family therapy for the cancer patient: A case study. *American Journal of Clinical Hypnosis, 27,* 38-41.

Kolko, D., & Rickard-Figueroa, J. (1985). Effects of video games on the adverse corollaries of chemotherapy in pediatric oncology patients: A single-case analysis. *Journal of Consulting and Clinical Psychology, 53,* 223-225.

LaBaw, W., Holton, C., Tewell, K., & Eccles, D. (1975). The use of self-hypnosis by children with cancer. *American Journal of Clinical Hypnosis, 17,* 233-238.

LaClave, L. J., & Blix, S. (1989). Hypnosis in the management of symptoms in a young girl with malignant astrocytoma: A challenge to the therapist. *International Journal of Clinical and Experimental Hypnosis, 37,* 6-14.

LeBaron, S., & Zeltzer, L. (1983). Children on chemotherapy: Behavioral treatment of emesis. Unpublished manuscript.

LeBaron, S., & Zeltzer, L. (1984). Behavioral intervention for reducing chemotherapy-related nausea and vomiting in adolescents with cancer. *Journal of Adolescent Health Care, 5,* 178-182.

London, P. (1963). *Children's Hypnotic Susceptibility Scale*. Palo Alto, CA: Consulting Psychologists Press.

Lyles, J. N., Burish, T. G., Krozely, M., & Oldham, R. K. (1982). Efficacy of relaxation training and guided imagery in reducing the aversiveness of cancer chemotherapy. *Journal of Consulting and Clinical Psychology, 50,* 509-524.

Morgan, A. H., & Hilgard, J. R. (1978/1979a). The Stanford Hypnotic Clinical Scale for Children. *American Journal of Clinical Hypnosis, 21,* 148-169.

Morgan, A. H., & Hilgard, J. R. (1978/1979b). The Stanford Hypnotic Clinical Scale for Adults. *American Journal of Clinical Hypnosis, 21,* 134-147.

Morrow, G. R. (1982). Prevalence and correlates of anticipatory nausea and vomiting in chemotherapy patients. *Journal of the National Cancer Institute, 68,* 585-588.

Morrow, G. R. (1984a). Clinical characteristics associated with the development of anticipatory nausea and vomiting in cancer patients undergoing chemotherapy treatment. *Journal of Clinical Oncology, 10,* 1170-1176.

Morrow, G. R. (1984b). The assessment of nausea and vomiting. *Cancer, 53* 2267-2280.

Morrow, G. R. (1985). The effect of a susceptibility to motion sickness on the side effects of cancer chemotherapy. *Cancer, 55,* 2766-2770.

Morrow, G. R. (1986). Behavioral management of chemotherapy-induced nausea and vomiting in the cancer patient. *Clinical Oncologist, 113,* 11-14.

Morrow, G., & Dobkin, P. (1988). Anticipatory nausea and vomiting in cancer patients undergoing chemotherapy treatment: Prevalence, etiology, and behavioral interventions. *Clinical Psychology Review, 6,* 517-556.

Morrow, G. R., & Morrell, C. (1982). Behavioral treatment for the anticipatory nausea and vomiting induced by cancer chemotherapy. *New England Journal of Medicine, 307,* 1476-1480.

O'Grady, D. J., & Hoffmann, C. (1984). Hypnosis with children and adolescents in the medical setting. In W. Wester & A. Smith (Eds.), *Clinical hypnosis: A multidisciplinary approach* (pp. 181-209). Philadelphia: Lippincott.

Olness, K. (1981). Imagery (self-hypnosis) as adjunct therapy in childhood cancer: Clinical experience with 25 patients. *American Journal of Pediatric Hematology/ Oncology, 3,* 313-321.

Olness, K., & Gardner, G. (1988). *Hypnosis and hypnotherapy with children.* Philadelphia: Grune & Stratton.

Plotnick, A. (1988). Hypnotic responsiveness in children: Absorption, vividness of imagery, fantasy play and social desirability. Master's thesis, University of Cincinnati.

Redd, W. H., Andersen, G. U., & Minagawa, R. V. (1982). Hypnotic control of anticipatory emesis in patients receiving cancer chemotherapy. *Journal of Consulting and Clinical Psychology, 50,* 14-19.

Redd, W. H., & Andrykowski, M. A. (1982). Behavioral intervention in cancer treatment: Controlling aversion reactions to chemotherapy. *Journal of Consulting and Clinical Psychology, 50,* 1018-1029.

Redd, W. H., Jacobsen, R. B., Die-Trill, M., Dermatis, H., McEvoy, M., & Holland, J. C. (1987). Cognitive/attentional distraction in the control of conditioned nausea in pediatric cancer patients receiving chemotherapy. *Journal of Consulting and Clinical Psychology, 55,* 391-395.

Stam, H. J. (1989). From symptom relief to cure: Hypnotic interventions in cancer. In N. P. Spanos & J. F. Chaves (Eds.), *Hypnosis: The cognitive-behavioral perspective* (pp. 313-339). Buffalo, NY: Prometheus.

Stein, R., & Riessman, C. (1980). The development of an impact-on-family scale: Preliminary findings. *Medical Care, 18,* 465-472.

Van Komen, R., & Redd, W. (1985). Personality factors associated with anticipatory nausea/vomiting in patients receiving cancer chemotherapy. *Health Psychology, 4,* 189-202.

Wadden, R., & Anderton, C. (1982). The clinical use of hypnosis. *Psychological Bulletin, 91*, 215-243.

Wirt, R. D., Lachar, D., Klinedinst, J. K., & Seat, P. D. (1977). *Multidimensional description of child personality: A manual of the Personality Inventory for Children.* Los Angeles: Western Psychological Services.

Zeltzer, L. (1980). The adolescent with cancer. In J. Kellerman (Ed.), *Psychological aspects of childhood cancer* (pp. 70-99). Springfield, IL: Charles C. Thomas.

Zeltzer, L. K., Dolgin, M. J., LeBaron, S., & LeBaron, C. (1989). A randomized, controlled study of behavioral intervention for chemotherapy-related distress. Presented at the Annual Meeting of the Society for Behavioral Pediatrics, Boston.

Zeltzer, L., Kellerman, J., Ellenberg, L., & Dash, J. (1983). Hypnosis for reduction of vomiting associated with chemotherapy and disease in adolescents with cancer. *Journal of Adolescent Health Care, 4*, 77-84.

Zeltzer, L., & LeBaron, S. (1984a). Behavioral intervention for children and adolescents with cancer. *Behavioral Medicine Update, 5*, 17-22.

Zeltzer, L., & LeBaron, S. (1984b). The Stanford Hypnotic Clinical Scale for Children—revised. Unpublished scale.

Zeltzer, L., LeBaron, S., Richie, D., Reed, D., Schoolfield, J., & Prihoda, T. (1988). Can children understand and use a rating scale to quantify somatic symptoms? Assessment of nausea and vomiting as a model. *Journal of Consulting and Clinical Psychology, 58*, 567-572.

Zeltzer, L., LeBaron, S., & Zeltzer, P. (1984a). The effectiveness of behavioral intervention for reduction of nausea and vomiting in children and adolescents receiving chemotherapy. *Journal of Clinical Oncology, 2*, 683-690.

Zeltzer, L., LeBaron, S., & Zeltzer, P. (1984b). Paradoxical effects of prophylactic phenothiazine antiemetics in children receiving chemotherapy. *Journal of Clinical Oncology, 2*, 930-936.

Zeltzer, L., LeBaron, S., & Zeltzer, P. (1984c). A prospective assessment of chemotherapy-related nausea and vomiting in children with cancer. *American Journal of Pediatric Hematology/Oncology, 6*, 25-37.

14   Hypnosis and Pain Management in Children

Donald J. O'Grady, Ph.D.

The use of hypnosis for pain relief has a long history in both clinical and experimental settings (Hilgard & Hilgard, 1975). Pain control is one of the few areas where evidence to date strongly suggests unique benefits of hypnosis beyond nonspecific therapeutic effects (Wadden & Anderton, 1982). Although the relationship between hypnotizability and pain reduction is not perfect, there is a much increased probability of successful pain reduction for those persons highly responsive to hypnosis, at least with experimentally induced pain (Hilgard & Hilgard, 1975). The Hilgards also estimate that about 50 percent of clinical-pain cases show marked improvement with hypnosis.

Studies of its applications to pain management in children have been less evident than with adults (Olness & Gardner, 1988). This discrepancy is surprising in light of the fact that children generally are more hypnotically responsive than adults (London & Cooper, 1969; Morgan & Hilgard, 1973). Although the number of studies with children is small, recent excellent reviews suggest the efficacy of use of hypnosis in the treatment of children in pain (Hilgard & LeBaron, 1984; Olness & Gardner, 1988; Zeltzer & LeBaron, 1986).

The purpose of this chapter is to review the use of hypnosis for pain management in children and to illustrate techniques and considerations for different ages and types of pain. Initially, some comments on issues in pain management in general are made to place the use of hypnosis in a broader context. Following this, uses of hypnosis in acute- and then chronic-pain management in children will be reviewed and illustrated.

ISSUES IN PAIN MANAGEMENT

Childhood pain is a complex, multidimensional phenomenon with sensory, affective, cognitive, and interpersonal components (Ross & Ross, 1988). Although there has been an increase in research on pain in children in the past decade, Schecter's (1985) review concluded that it is "woefully inadequate" in relation to the problem. The need for an integrated biopsychosocial approach is increasingly being recognized, as suggested by the recent development of multidisciplinary pediatric pain clinics (Berde, Sethna, Masek, Fosburg, & Rocklin, 1989).

Current principles of pain management include a comprehensive model of pain that allows the clinician to conceptualize the remarkable individual differences in response to similar pain stimuli. Dolgin and Jay (1989), in an excellent review of pain management in children, emphasize the importance of mediating variables between varying pain stimuli and varying ways of responding to or expressing pain. These mediating variables include differences in three areas: (1) a child's cognitive/affective status; for example, developmental level, degree of anxiety and depression, expectations, and past coping experience; (2) operant environments, for example, degree of positive and negative reinforcement and sociocultural and familial demands for pain expression or suppression; and (3) constitutional factors, for example, differences in age and pain threshold. Keeping these variables in mind allows the child hypnotherapist not only to individualize the application of hypnosis, but also to realize the limitations of hypnosis and the need for a multimodal treatment for other mediating variables not affected by hypnosis.

This model is also a guide for the initial assessment of the child's pain. In addition to assessing the child's cognitive and affective status; operant features, including responses of parents and health providers to the child's pain; and constitutional factors; the clinician needs to assess the source of the pain or pain stimuli, as well as the different modes of response to the pain. Olness (1987) reviewed the cases of 80 children consecutively referred specifically for hypnotherapy and found 20 (25 percent) to have unrecognized organic bases for their symptoms. In reinforcing the biopsychosocial model for assessment, she cautions, "It is prudent for child health professionals to assume that there are behavioral components to every biologic disease and biological components to every behavioral condition. . . ." (p. 8).

Methods for assessing pain response in children have been well reviewed by a number of authors (Beyer & Wells, 1989; Ross & Ross, 1988; Savedra & Tesler, 1989). What is important for the hypnotherapist is to recognize that pain responses are multiple and may vary in the same child. Katz, Kellerman, & Ellenberg (1987) found significant decreases in self-report of procedural pain and fear related to hypnotic treatment, but little change in observed behavior, suggesting the need for multimodal assessment. Assessment of both overt behavioral responses to pain (verbal and nonverbal) and covert responses (the child's self-report of pain intensity and distress) seems necessary, not only for treatment planning, but also for accurately assessing the effectiveness of treatment.

Psychological interventions in pain management generally are focused on pain perception and pain behavior (Dolgin & Jay, 1989). Strategies to help the child's self-regulation of pain are usually directed toward pain perception, but may also gradually help the child with pain behavior. These strategies include hypnosis, relaxation, distraction, and information.

In the remainder of the chapter, the role of hypnosis, as one of a number of self-regulation strategies, will be emphasized for helping children cope with acute and chronic pain.

GENERAL GUIDELINES FOR USING HYPNOSIS
WITH CHILDREN

The process of hypnosis conceptually can be divided into six phases: (1) preparation, (2) induction, (3) deepening, (4) therapeutic suggestions, (5) posthypnotic suggestions, and (6) termination (O'Grady & Hoffmann, 1984). Developmental differences may demand different strategies in each phase, as summarized in Table 14-1. The growth or changes in hypnotic ability from the preschool years through adolescence are well described by Hilgard and LeBaron (1984). They introduced the concept of "protohypnosis" to describe the early signs of hypnotic ability as seen in "fantasy portrayed in action" (p. 191) by children talking to their dolls and moving trains and planes about. The change from the pretend, enacted play of protohypnosis to the "peak" hypnosis of 9- to 12-year-olds is characterized by more eye closure and internalization of fantasy. These differences are reflected in the characteristic inductions of preschool as compared with school-aged children. It is also helpful to the hypnotherapist to keep in mind the positive relationships between hypnotic ability and pretend play, fantasy, humor, and parent–child relationships. Children who are unusually active often will have trouble letting fantasy happen and, along with those children who have a long history of anxious overdependence on their parents, may be low in hypnotic ability.

An excellent discussion of the need for the preparation of parents, a variety of induction and deepening techniques, and relative and absolute contraindications for the use of hypnosis, can be found in Olness and Gardner (1988). In addition, the rationale for the use of scales of hypnotic responsiveness in the clinical setting is discussed in Chapter 2 of this book. The

TABLE 14-1 Age Differences for Each Phase of Hypnosis

	4–6 Years	*7–11 Years*	*12 + Years*
Preparation	Parents with child. Short discussion. Fear—doubt guilt, if misbehave.	Parents and patient. Separate and together. Focus on skills. Fear—embarass; can't do.	Usually alone. Focus on identity—fit with perception of self. Fear—loss of control or being different.
Induction	Play/imagine. Eyes not always closed. Move less. *"Protohypnosis."*	Relax/imagine. Eyes close. Move less. Protohypnosis to peak hypnosis.	Eyes stay closed. move less. More dissociation.
Deepening	Involvement in play. More questions.	Further relaxation. Increased involvement in fantasy, visually quicker than at 4–6 years.	Direct, active imagery. Dissociate. Fractionate.
Suggestions	Short, flexible, embedded in imaginative play and/or stories.	Key words, favorite heroes and TV shows. Mastery/overcoming odds.	Active imagery. Choice. Develop preferred key words.
Posthypnotic suggestion	Reminders of positive features of story or pretend play.	Practice. Cues for easy reentry. Mastering skill.	Practice. Cues for easier reentry. Increased self-control.
Terminate	Spontaneous, natural.	Skill, usually enjoy ritual counting (5–1). Debrief.	Permissive, slower, counting. Debrief. Make audiotapes.

*(See Hilgard & LeBaron, 1984.)

scale is usually introduced in the preparation phase, and sometimes the induction from the scale may be the easiest one to begin with in the induction phase. Inquiry with the child regarding his or her experience of realness and involuntariness on the scale can be helpful in developing therapeutic suggestions. Special hypnotic approaches for preschool children, such as the use of favorite stories, are also discussed in Chapter 4 of this book.

Finally, in addition to special consideration regarding age, hypnotic responsiveness, and target symptom, there are some general cautions. First, the importance of taking a thorough history to determine whether hypnosis is indicated cannot be overemphasized. For example, an 8-year-old girl was referred for hypnotherapy to help her cope with acute pain related to a tractor-mower accident. She was initially cooperative with the hypnotherapist, being involved with favorite imagery for distraction and relaxation. However, on subsequent visits, she seemed very distressed and unable to concentrate on the hypnotic induction or suggestions. Further interviews with her parents, nurses, and, finally, with her, revealed that she refused to take her oral pain medications because her father had inadvertently suggested that she would not recover as fast if she were "drugged." He had misunderstood some comments from the attending physician and nurses. Rather than try hypnosis further, it seemed more prudent to clarify the misconceptions of the father and he, in turn, those of his daughter. She began taking her pain medication regularly and seemed much less emotionally depressed. Additionally, hypnotherapy was not felt to be needed. Failure with hypnotherapy is likely if the emotional meaning of the child's pain is not considered.

Second, hypnosis is not therapy itself, but a phenomenon that can be used with children to help them change their perceptions, cognitions, and feelings that mediate their behavior. Numerous factors influence the degree to which hypnosis is effective. Golden, Dowd, and Friedberg (1987) discuss factors influencing "resistance" to hypnotherapy and related treatment failures in three broad categories: (1) therapist factors, such as the failure to establish rapport or the improper use of technique; (2) environmental factors, such as secondary gains; and (3) patient or client factors, such as physical limitation or low motivation. These "sources of resistance" in hypnotherapy apply to the parents as well as the children and to other therapies as well as hypnotherapy. Nevertheless, careful attention to these factors can prevent or lessen treatment failures.

HYPNOSIS FOR PAIN RELIEF IN CHILDREN

Studies in children demonstrating pain relief with hypnosis can be divided according to whether the pain is acute or chronic and to the source of the pain—for example, related to injury, disease, medical procedures, or unknown causes, such as in recurrent abdominal pain. Obviously, these variables will affect the meaning of the pain for the child and parents. The history taking will be quite different for the child accidentally run over by a tractor mower driven by her father than for a child of the same age receiving a bone-marrow aspiration. Providing hypnotherapy to a child with chronic, benign headaches will be much less stressful for the therapist than using hypnosis with a child suffering from chronic, malignant pain. However, the previous guidelines will generally apply, that is, the need for careful preparation of the child and parents and for age-appropriate techniques of induction and deepening.

The role of parents in acute- and chronic-pain management that involves hypnosis has not been systematically studied. However, generalizing from studies using other cognitive-behavioral strategies, inclusion of parents as allies who are well prepared with information on the procedure and the intervention, as well as on stress-reduction strategies, and encouragement of participation, is strongly recommended (Dolgin & Phipps, 1989).

In our own work with children undergoing bone-marrow aspirations and lumbar punctures, the parents have been trained in the hypnotic procedures, experienced hypnosis themselves if they wished, and assisted their child and therapist on an individual basis during the procedures (Hodel, 1983). In addition, parents have been taught self-hypnosis to reduce stress associated with bone-marrow transplantation for their child (Hoffmann, O'Grady, & Harris, 1986). Whether self-hypnosis is more beneficial than other cognitive-behavioral therapies for reducing parental stress in these situations is unclear, but it merits further study.

Before reviewing selected studies of hypnosis for acute- and then chronic-pain relief, a discussion of the typical suggestions used for pain relief might be helpful as there are numerous techniques in practice.

There is some evidence that suggestions are more effective for pain relief if they include both analgesic and relaxation dimensions. Intensity of pain seems to respond to hypnotic suggestions of analgesia, but the "unpleasantness" of the pain responds better to hypnotic suggestions of relaxation (Malone, Kurtz, & Strube, 1989). Two components have been proposed by Hilgard and Hilgard (1975) for pain reduction. The first component, involving less altered consciousness, consists of suggestions for relaxation and anxiety reduction. This component is effective for practically all subjects, whether in a waking or hypnotic condition. The second component involves dissociations in the information-processing subsystems related to the pain experience and is usually available only to the more hypnotizable subjects. Whether both components are needed for children is unclear at this time.

Strategies for coping with pain have recently been categorized in an easy-to-remember fashion by Brown and Fromm (1987) to include (1) avoidance, (2) alleviation, (3) alteration, and (4) awareness. These categories and corresponding strategies from two other authors are illustrated in Table 14.2. It is important to note that these categories are conceptually rather than empirically based. Patients, adults or children, are likely to use a mix of these strategies when experiencing pain, whether in hypnosis or not. Also, it has been observed by this author that patients may use one strategy while the hypnotherapist is suggesting another. These categories, however, do help the therapist and the investigator communicate better about what is being suggested to the patient. One striking conclusion from the following review of studies using hypnosis with children for pain relief is that there is wide variation in actual suggestions made.

Hypnosis and Acute-Pain Relief

A comprehensive review of psychological and pharmacological interventions for pain associated with pediatric procedures recently was completed by Zeltzer, Jay, and Fisher (1989). This article is important because it discusses the issues involved in choosing and combining psychological (including hypnosis) and pharmacological interventions.

Studies related to hypnotic treatment of children in pain were reviewed by Zeltzer and LeBaron (1986). They reported on 38 studies, including 13 that did not specifically label their interventions as hypnotic but used play therapy or guided imagery. Of the 25 studies with hypnosis labeled as the intervention, 21 were case reports. These case studies have contributed to the advancement of knowledge of clinical hypnosis with children by providing excellent descriptions of techniques and by encouraging investigators to pursue the systematic study of hypnosis with children. However, only seven published studies have been found that have designs and measurements to control for threats to internal and external validity. Three of these were published after the review of Zeltzer and LeBaron (1986).

These selected studies are summarized in Table 14-3. All but one, of a child with burns (Wakeman & Kaplan, 1978), concern children undergoing painful procedures, such as bone-marrow aspirations and lumbar punctures, related to the treatment of cancer. These studies clearly demonstrate significant reduction of pain and anxiety in those children participating. Results, however, are notably mixed, with some interventions showing pain relief by self-report and not by observer ratings (Katz, Kellerman, & Ellenberg, 1987) and another study giving opposite results (Kuttner, 1988). Some interventions seem to affect anxiety and pain differentially as measured. A few of the studies (Katz et al., 1987; Wall and Womack, 1989) found hypnosis to

TABLE 14-2 Classifying Hypnotic Suggestions for Pain Relief

Brown & Fromm, 1987	Golden et al., 1987	Olness & Gardner, 1988
Avoidance Distraction, internal and external Age regression Time distortion	Hypnotic relaxation and distraction techniques	Distraction techniques Attention to "unrelated material" Discussion of details of injury or procedure
Alleviation Direct suggestion Numbness Imagined analgesia	Direct and indirect suggestions for analgesia	Direct suggestions for hypnoanesthesia Numbness Topical anesthesia Local anesthesia
Alteration Altered memory, meaning, or anticipation Dissociation	Transformation of pain to other body part or other type of sensation Dissociative techniques and cognitive restructuring	Distancing suggestions Moving pain away from self Transferring pain to another body part
Awareness Focussing on sensations and reactions		Paying attention to pain itself—"lighted globe"

TABLE 14-3   Selected Controlled Studies of Acute Pain Relief with Hypnosis in Children

Reference	Subjects	Pain Source*	Design and Measurement	Hypnosis	Results
Hilgard & LeBaron (1982)	24, ages 6–19 yrs. with cancer	BMAs	One group, pre- and post self- and observer ratings (two judges) on 10-point scale. Hypnotizability measured.	Individualized, fixation, fantasy induction with hypnotic rehearsal/simulation before BMA. Hypnoanalgesic suggestions.	15 of 24 patients significantly reduced self-reported pain and observer-rated pain from baseline to treatment. High hypnotizables more successful.
Zeltzer & LeBaron (1982)	33 children ages 6–17	BMAs (27) LPs (22)	Two groups (16 hypnotized and 17 nonhypnotized) randomly assigned pre- and post. Both pain and anxiety rated (1–5) by patient and observer separately, data not collected by therapists. No hypnotizability measured.	Individualized, involvement in pleasant imagery and fantasy, deep breathing, practice suggestions. Therapist present for procedure. No hypnoanalgesic suggestions.	Significant pain reduction for both hypnotic and nonhypnotic techniques with hypnosis more effective.
Kellerman et al. (1983)	18 adolescents	BMAs, LPs, and injections	One group, multiple baselines across subjects. Anxiety and discomfort, measured by self-report ratings, measured pre and post (6 months) trait anxiety, self-esteem, health locus of control, and illness impact. No hypnotizability measured.	Individualized, eye-fixation or hand-levitation induction suggestions for relaxation, favorite place, well-being, reduced discomfort, and increased mastery.	16 patients showed significant anxiety and "discomfort" reduction before, during, and after procedure.
Wakeman & Kaplan (1978)	42 patients, ages 7–70	Burns	Two groups, matched on age and extent of burns, random assignment. Attention/support control group. Percent maximum allowable medication used was measured. No hypnotizability measured.	Inductions were eye fixations, eye roll or relaxation. Suggestions for hypnoanalgesia, dissociation, and the reduction of anxiety. Individualized time spent varied.	Significantly lower use of pain medications by hypnosis group. Children and adolescents significantly less use than adults (19–70 years).

Continued

Study	Sample	Procedure	Design/Methodology	Results
Katz, Kellerman, & Ellenberg (1987)	36 children, ages 6–12	BMAs	Two groups, hypnosis vs. play, random assignment, attention control, multiple measures (PBRS-R), only distressed included. Response to hypnosis noted for each intervention. No hypnotizability measured.	Eye fixation with or without closure. Individualized active imagery and relaxation suggestions to "reduce or reframe" sensory/pain experience. Posthypnotic suggestions for practice and reentry cues. Nonverbal cue only for hypnosis in BMA room.	Significant reduction in self-reported distress with both—no differences between them. Behavioral (PBRS-R) not significant. Response to hypnosis correlated with reduced fear and pain self-reports.
Kuttner (1988)	25 children, ages 3–6	BMAs and LPs	Three groups, random assignment; hypnosis, behavior, and standard multiple measures, including self-report and observer rating (PBRS-R). No hypnotizability measured.	Imagination, favorite-story induction; suggestions for comfort, decrease "pain" awareness, increased coping.	Significant reduction in observer-rated pain (PBRS-R) for hypnosis. No differences on self-report.
Wall & Womack (1989)	20 children, ages 5–18	BMAs and LPs	Two groups, random assignment, hypnosis vs. active cognitive (distraction) multiple measures of pain and anxiety. Visual analogue ratings (VAS). Hypnotizability measured.	Standardized hypnotic instructions. Audiotapes used to cue. No therapist present.	Significant pain reduction by self-report and observer rating. Anxiety mixed results. No difference for hypnosis. Hypnotizability not related.

*BMA = bone-marrow aspiration; LP = lumbar puncture

be of significant benefit, but no greater than that from nonhypnotic cognitive-behavioral interventions.

In summary, a careful reading of these studies leads this author to conclude that hypnosis has not yet been clearly demonstrated to add a significant increment to the therapeutic outcome for acute pain as compared with other cognitive-behavioral therapy techniques with children. Spinhoven (1987), in a review of hypnosis and behavior therapy with adults, came to a similar conclusion. He challenges hypnotherapists to "demonstrate either that hypnosis has an additional nonspecific effect or that for certain patients it yields a far more favorable therapeutic outcome" (p. 26).

On a positive note, these challenges have been met to a notable degree in the laboratory setting (Hilgard & Hilgard, 1975). It would, therefore, seem reasonable to expect that, with robust suggestions delivered with enough potency and practice and in a way appropriate to the severity of the pain, it should be possible to meet the challenge in the clinical situation. One problem to be overcome is how to avoid sacrificing the potency of the hypnotherapy for methodological improvements. For example, it is not surprising to many clinicians that the substitution of audiotapes for a live therapist; the absence of an active, experienced, hypnotherapist; and limited or no suggestions when a child is undergoing a bone-marrow aspiration result in no incremental benefit from the hypnosis.

Although Hilgard and LeBaron's (1982, 1984) study did not control for the attention of the therapist or nurse awareness of treatment, the rich and varied suggestions by experienced, supportive therapists both before and during simulated and actual painful procedures continue to be an excellent model for developing a treatment package. Training manuals used in other studies may also be helpful to clinicians, as well as to investigators, in developing their own hypnotic treatment (Wall & Womack, 1989; Hodel, 1983).

Hypnosis and Chronic-Pain Management

Because of the complexity of chronic pain, the knowledge and use of general assessment and management strategies for chronic pain seem critical before hypnosis is considered. Although even with acute pain there is not a one-to-one correlation between the stimulus and the response, with chronic pain its meaning and its consequences often become more problematic than its intensity. The classic work by Fordyce (1976) on the role of learning in the disabling aspects of chronic pain should be required reading for anyone working with such patients. More recently, Karoly and Jensen (1987) have provided a conceptual framework for understanding chronic-pain management in its broader, multiple contexts, allowing greater application of self-regulation theory and research to the problems of chronic pain.

Excellent recent reviews of chronic-pain management in children and adolescents are also available (Varni, Walco, & Katz, 1989; McGrath, 1987; Dolgin & Jay, 1989). Reviews focusing on hypnosis in chronic-pain management, both specific to children (Zeltzer & LeBaron, 1986) and more generally with adults (Evans, 1987; Brown & Fromm, 1987), emphasize the importance of multimodal treatment; that is, attention not only to reducing the intensity of the pain, but also to decreasing associated anxiety and depression and increasing the activities of daily living.

Chronic pain can be further categorized as either episodic or persistent and as either benign or malignant. Unfortunately, many chronically ill children can experience all categories of pain, suggesting that hypnosis may be useful for them in different ways at different times in their illness. For example, a child with hemophilia might experience acute episodic pain from bleeds into joints and chronic persistent pain caused by chronic arthritis, to say nothing of the possibility of acute pain from medical procedures.

Studies of hypnosis with children experiencing chronic episodic pain have primarily focused on those with hemophilia or sickle cell anemia. The multimodal treatment described has clearly been beneficial to children and adolescents for both hemophilia (Olness & Singher, 1967; LaBaw, 1975; LeBaron & Zeltzer, 1984) and sickle cell anemia (Zeltzer, Dash, & Holland, 1979; Vichinsky, Johnson, & Lubin, 1982). Hypnotic suggestions included relaxation and pleasant imagery with instructions for use at the onset of painful episodes. In addition, suggestions focused on imagined peripheral vasodilation in the cases of sickle cell anemia and reduced bleeding in hemophiliac children. Although these studies with their descriptions of hypnotic treatment have helped clinicians use hypnosis for such patients, the lack of systematic, controlled studies warrants caution in recommending its routine use (Zeltzer & LeBaron, 1986). In individual children with episodic pain and related social disability, hypnosis should be considered. The possibility of benefit from the components of relaxation, analgesia, and hypnotic context (Evans, 1987) seems to outweigh the cost of uncertain scientific validity at this time.

For chronic persistent pain in children, hypnotic treatment has been reported for juvenile rheumatoid arthritis (Cioppa & Thal, 1975), cancer (LaBaw, 1975; Olness, 1981; Ellenberg, Kellerman, Dash, Huggins, & Zeltzer, 1980; Hilgard & LeBaron, 1984), hemophilia (Olness & Singher, 1967; LaBaw, 1975), and migraine headaches (Olness, MacDonald, & Uden, 1987). Again, these studies strongly suggest that hypnosis is beneficial.

Encouragingly, systematic, controlled study has begun in this area with the excellent study by Olness and colleagues (1987) comparing hypnotic treatment with medication and placebo for migraine headaches in children. Thirty school-aged children with migraine headaches were randomized to propranolol or placebo for three months and then crossed over for three months. Following this crossover, the children received three months of training and practice in self-hypnosis. Only the self-hypnosis condition showed significant reduction in the frequency of headaches. Treatment involved five sessions. Random assignment and comparison with placebo and propranolol put the hypnotic treatment to a robust test. Future studies should include measurement of hypnotizability and comparison with nonhypnotic cognitive-behavioral therapy to separate specific hypnotic effects from nonspecific therapeutic factors.

Because controlled studies such as that of Olness and colleagues (1987) are difficult to implement, most clinicians will continue to use their own judgment and experience in integrating hypnosis into the multimodal treatment of chronic pain in children. The necessary components of an effective multimodal treatment program for chronic pain may vary somewhat among clinicians, but all would include (1) a biopsychosocial assessment and (2) a rehabilitative rather than curative model for selecting interventions (Hawkins, 1988). Specific guidelines for using hypnosis in a multimodal treatment program are well described by Brown and Fromm (1987) for adults and could easily be adapted to children and adolescents in chronic pain. In their experience, patients initially benefit from hypnotic strategies of avoidance and alleviation with a shift to hypnotic alteration and awareness strategies (see Table 14.2) as the patient gains a sense of self-efficacy, decreased despair, decreased avoidance of responsibilities, and increased interest in social activities.

Finally, hypnosis is used by some clinicians to assist patients with chronic pain to change their self-image and life-style via ego-strengthening suggestions as well as posthypnotic suggestions to reinforce involvement in responsible and enjoyable activities (Brown & Fromm, 1987; Hawkins, 1988). Whether these additional hypnotic suggestions offer any benefits beyond the nonspecific effects of reassurance and optimism is difficult to know at this time. Until proved otherwise, however, most hypnotherapists working with children and adolescents in chronic pain are likely to be observed using variations of Hartland's (1965) ego-strengthening suggestions to counter the possible "benefits" or "secondary gains" of chronic nonmalignant pain (Meilman, 1984).

SUMMARY AND CONCLUSIONS

The use of hypnosis for acute- and chronic-pain management in children has continued to grow, perhaps as a result of the broader movement in the culture toward holistic, biopsychosocial, and self-regulatory emphases in the delivery of health care.

Future studies are needed to demonstrate whether or not hypnosis facilitates the outcome of cognitive-behavior therapy for pain relief and for which children it is suited. Progress is likely to be slow owing to "conceptual, ethical, and pragmatic constraints" (Karoly & Jensen, 1987) on studying pain in children. Results are also likely to be conflicting as methods of measuring pain are refined and interventions are combined. Differences in results are likely to be related to differences in the origin and severity of the pain, as well as to variation in treatment components, including the nature of suggestions, the "dose," and the context of delivery of treatment.

In any case, while awaiting progress in the scientific investigation of the phenomenon of pain, the challenge of pain and suffering in children continues to be enormous. Any clinician who is involved with children in a health-care setting quickly becomes aware of the unmet needs for pain relief and pain management, ranging from infants and toddlers undergoing procedures to teenagers with sickle cell anemia, recurrent abdominal pain, hemophilia, juvenile rheumatoid arthritis, inflammatory bowel diseases, and cancer.

This chapter has emphasized the need for an integrated, interdisciplinary approach to pain management that includes the use of hypnosis as a tool that is beneficial to children and their families and also to clinicians who wish to provide relief, comfort, and an increased sense of personal control to their patients. Our hope is that training children in self-hypnosis will become a routine consideration in the treatment of acute and chronic pain, not only to afford relief and comfort, but also to prevent disabling chronic-illness behavior.

REFERENCES

Berde, C., Sethna, N. F., Masek, B., Fosburg, M., & Rocklin, S. (1989). Pediatric pain clinics: Recommendations for their development. *Pediatrician, 16*(1-2), 94-102.

Beyer, J. E., & Wells, N. (1989). The assessment of pain in children. In N. L. Schechter (Ed.), Acute pain in children. *Pediatric Clinics of North America, 36*(4), 837-854.

Brown, D. P., & Fromm, E. (1987). *Hypnosis and behavioral medicine*. Hillsdale, NJ: Erlbaum.

Cioppa, J. B., & Thal, A. D. (1975). Hypnotherapy in a case of juvenile rheumatoid arthritis. *American Journal of Clinical Hypnosis, 17*, 160-169.

Dolgin, M., & Jay, S. M. (1989). Pain management in children. In E. Mash & R. Barkley (Eds.), *Treatment of childhood disorders* (pp. 383-404). New York: Builford.

Dolgin, M. J., & Phipps, S. (1989). Pediatric pain: The parent's role. *Pediatrician, 16,* 103-109.

Ellenberg, L., Kellerman, J., Dash, J., Huggins, C., & Zeltzer, L. (1980). Use of hypnosis for multiple symptoms in an adolescent girl with leukemia. *Journal of Adolescent Health Care, 1,* 132-136.

Evans, F. J. (1987). Hypnosis and chronic pain management. In G. D. Burrows, D. Elton, & G. V. Stanley (Eds.), *Handbook of chronic pain management* (pp. 285-299). Amsterdam: Elsevier Science Publishers.

Fordyce, W. E. (1976). *Behavioral methods for chronic pain and illness.* St. Louis: Mosby.

Golden, W. L., Dowd, E. T., & Friedberg, F. (1987). *Hypnotherapy: A modern approach.* New York: Pergamon.

Hartland, J. (1965). The value of "ego strengthening" procedure prior to direct symptom removal under hypnosis. *American Journal of Clinical Hypnosis, 8,* 89-93.

Hawkins, R. (1988). The role of hypnotherapy in the pain clinic. *Australian Journal of Clinical and Experimental Hypnosis, 16*(1), 23-30.

Hilgard, E. R., & Hilgard, J. R. (1975). *Hypnosis in the relief of pain.* Los Altos, CA: Kaufmann.

Hilgard, J. R., & LeBaron, S. (1982). Relief of anxiety and pain in children and adolescents with cancer: Quantitative measures and clinical observations. *International Journal of Clinical and Experimental Hypnosis, 30,* 417-442.

Hilgard, J. R., & LeBaron, S. (1984). *Hypnotherapy of pain in children with cancer.* Los Altos, CA: Kaufmann.

Hodel, T. V. (1983). Hypnosis for relief of pain and anxiety in leukemic children undergoing bone marrow aspirations. Unpublished master's thesis, University of Cincinnati.

Hoffmann, C., O'Grady, D. J., & Harris, R. (1986). Hypnosis with parents and children for coping during bone marrow transplantation. Presented at the Annual Scientific Meeting of the Society for Clinical and Experimental Hypnosis, Chicago.

Karoly, P., & Jensen, M. P. (1987). *Multimethod assessment of chronic pain.* New York: Pergamon.

Katz, E. R., Kellerman, J., & Ellenberg, L. (1987). Hypnosis in the reduction of acute pain and distress in children with cancer. *Journal of Pediatric Psychology, 12*(3), 379-394.

Keefe, F. J., & Williams, D. A. (1989). New directions in pain assessment and treatment. *Clinical Psychology Review, 9,* 549-568.

Kellerman, J., Zeltzer, L., Ellenberger, L., & Dash, J. (1983). Adolescents with cancer: Hypnosis for the reduction of the acute pain and anxiety associated with medical procedures. *Journal of Adolescent Health Care, 4,* 76-81.

Kuttner, L. (1988). Favorite stories: A hypnotic pain-reduction technique for children in acute pain. *American Journal of Clinical Hypnosis, 3,* 30-34.

LaBaw, W. L. (1975). Auto-hypnosis in hemophilia. *Haematalogia, 9,* 103-110.

LaBaw, W. L., Holton, C., Tewell, K., & Eccles, D. (1975). The use of self-hypnosis by children with cancer. *American Journal of Clinical Hypnosis, 17,* 233-238.

LeBaron, S., & Zeltzer, L. (1984). Research on hypnosis in hemophilia: Preliminary success and problems. *International Journal of Clinical and Experimental Hypnosis, 32,* 130-134.

London, P., & Cooper, L. M. (1969). Norms of hypnotic susceptibility in children. *Developmental Psychology, 1,* 113-124.

Malone, M. D., Kurtz, R. M., & Strube, M. J. (1989). The effects of hypnotic suggestion on pain report. *American Journal of Clinical Hypnosis, 31*(4), 221-230.

McGrath, P. A. (1987). The management of chronic pain in children. In G. D. Burrows, D. Elton, & G. V. Stanley (Eds.), *Handbook of chronic pain management* (pp. 205-216). Amsterdam: Elsevier Science Publishers.

Meilman, P. W. (1984). Chronic pain: The benefits of being sick. *Journal of Orthopedic and Sports Physical Therapy, 6,* 7-9.

Morgan, A. H., & Hilgard, E. R. (1973). Age differences in susceptibility to hypnosis. *International Journal of Clinical and Experimental Hypnosis, 21,* 65-78.

O'Grady, D. J., & Hoffmann, C. (1984). Hypnosis with children and adolescents in the medical setting. In W. Wester and A. Smith (Eds.) *Clinical Hypnosis: A Multidisciplinary Approach,* (181-209). Philadelphia: Lippincott.

Olness, K. N. (1981). Imagery (self-hypnosis) as adjunct therapy in childhood cancer: Clinical experience with 25 patients. *American Journal of Pediatric Hematology/Oncology, 3,* 313-321.

Olness, K. N. (1987). Unrecognized biologic bases of behavioral symptoms in patients referred for hypnotherapy. *American Journal of Clinical Hypnosis, 30*(1), 1-8.

Olness, K., & Gardner, G. (1988). *Hypnosis and hypnotherapy with children.* Philadelphia: Grune & Stratton.

Olness, K., MacDonald, J. T., & Uden, D. L. (1987). Comparison of self-hypnosis and propranolol in the treatment of juvenile classic migraine. *Pediatrics, 79.*

Olness, K. N., & Singher, L. J. (1967). Effects of self-hypnosis in the management of hemophilia in children. *Thrombosis and Haemostasis, 38*(1), 366.

Ross, D. M., & Ross, S. A. (1988). *Childhood pain: Current issues, research and management.* Baltimore: Urban & Schwarzenberg.

Savedra, M. C., & Tesler, M. D. (1989). Assessing children's and adolescents' pain. *Pediatrician, 16,* 24-29.

Schecter, N. L. (1985). Pain and pain control in children. *Current Problems in Pediatrics, 15,* 1-67.

Shapiro, B. S. (1987). Hypnosis and behavior therapy: A review. *International Journal of Clinical and Experimental Hypnosis, 35*(1), 8-31.

Spinhoven, P. (1987). Hypnosis and behavior therapy: A review. *The International Journal of Clinical and Experimental Hypnosis, 35,* 1, 8-31.

Varni, J. W. (1983). *Clinical behavioral pediatrics: An interdisciplinary biobehavioral approach.* New York: Pergamon.

Varni, J. W., Walco, G. A., & Katz, E. R. (1989). Assessment and management of chronic and recurrent pain in children with chronic diseases. *Pediatrician, 16,* 56-63.

Vichinsky, E. P., Johnson, R., & Lubin, B. H. (1982). Multidisciplinary approach to pain management in sickle cell disease. *American Journal of Pediatric Hematology/Oncology, 4,* 328-333.

Wadden, T. A., & Anderton, C. H. (1982). The clinical use of hypnosis. *Psychological Bulletin, 91*(2), 215-243.

Wakeman, R. J., & Kaplan, J. Z. (1978). An experimental study of hypnosis in painful burns. *American Journal of Clinical Hypnosis, 21,* 3-12.

Wall, V. J., & Womack, W. (1989). Hypnotic versus cognitive strategies for alleviation of procedural distress in pediatric oncology patients. *American Journal of Clinical Hypnosis, 31*(3), 181-191.

Zeltzer, L. K., Dash, J., & Holland, J. P. (1979). Hypnotically induced pain control in sickle cell anemia. *Pediatrics, 64,* 533-536.

Zeltzer, L. K., Jay, S. M., & Fisher, D. M. (1989). The management of pain associated with pediatric procedures. In N. L. Schecter (Ed.), Acute pain in children. *Pediatric Clinics of North America, 36*(4), 941-961.

Zeltzer, L., & LeBaron, S. (1986). The hypnotic treatment of children in pain. In D. K. Routh & M. Wolraich (Eds.), *Advances in developmental and behavioral pediatrics* (197-234). Greenwich, CT: JAI Press.

15 *Eating Disorders*

Moshe S. Torem, M.D.

FOUNDATIONS

Review of the Recent Literature

The revised third edition of the *Diagnostic and Statistic Manual of Mental Disorders* (DSM-III-R) (American Psychiatric Association, 1987) classifies eating disorders as including the following: anorexia nervosa, bulimia nervosa, pica, rumination disorder of infancy, and eating disorder not otherwise specified. It is rather conspicuous that obesity resulting from overeating is missing from this list.

In this chapter, I plan to focus on anorexia nervosa, bulimia nervosa, and eating disorder not otherwise specified. These three disorders are related to each other, and begin in adolescence, frequently stretching into early adult life. Therefore, most of the illustrations are taken from adolescents and young adults.

The natural history of anorexia nervosa shows a great variability. Some patients may have a single episode, followed by complete and spontaneous recovery. Other patients have multiple episodes occurring over many years with periods of remission associated with symptom relief and an improvement in adaptive daily functioning. Many patients may develop a chronic and unremitting form. About 40 percent of patients may recover completely, 30 percent show partial improvement, and 20 percent remain severely ill with no signs of improvement. The mortality rate for anorexia nervosa may be as high as 22 percent, with suicide reported in 2–5 percent of the chronic cases (Herzog & Copeland, 1985; Hsu, 1980; Theander, 1985; Tolstrup et al., 1985; Toner, Garfinkel, & Garner, 1986; Willi & Grossman, 1983).

The natural history of bulimia nervosa is influenced by the mechanism used to induce purging. Emetic substances, such as ipecac and baking soda, may lead to coma and death (Friedman, 1984). The use of diuretics and laxatives may lead to a severe electrolyte imbalance, including hypocholemia, cardiac arythmia, and death. The prognosis for this condition is relatively unknown; however, fatalities in patients with bulimia nervosa are not rare, reminding us all of the severity of this condition. Patients who purge only by self-induced vomiting, and never abuse laxatives, diuretics, or other chemicals, seem to have a better prognosis. A report by Garner and Garfinkel (1985) demonstrated a significant increase in the prevalence of anorexia nervosa in the preceding 10 years, which may be approaching one severe case among every 200 adolescent girls. The number of patients with bulimia nervosa appears to be increasing as well. A study by Halmi and her colleagues (Halmi, Falk, & Schwartz, 1981) showed that 13 percent of the college-age population (19 percent of females, 5 percent of males) have distorted body images, report feeling fat regardless of their weight, and are aspiring to a much lower body weight than is medically acceptable. Although many studies have been published regarding these conditions, their etiology remains obscure and their treatment less than satisfactory (Bruch, 1973; Griffith, Touyz, Mitchel, & Bacon, 1987; Gross, 1982a; Garner and Garfinkel, 1985; Herzog and Copeland, 1985; Hsu, 1980; Pope, Hudson, Jonas, & Yurgelum-Todd, 1983, 1985; Steiger, 1989; Thakur, 1980; Theander, 1985; Tolstrup et al., 1985; Torem, 1986c, 1987b, 1988b, 1989a, 1989b; Torem & Curdue, 1988; Vandereycken & Meermann, 1984; Webb, 1988).

Various forms of treatment have been advocated for patients with eating disorders, including biological treatments such as psychotropic medications, electroshock therapy, phototherapy, and sleep deprivation (Anderson, 1985; Brotman, Herzog, & Woods, 1984; Grossa, 1982; Larocca, 1984; Moor & Rakes, 1982; Pope et al., 1983, 1985; Webb, 1988). In addition, various forms of psychotherapy have been used as well, such as psychoanalytic psychotherapy, family therapy, behavior modification, group therapy, relaxation therapy, and hypnotherapy (Fairburn, 1981; Garner & Garfinkel, 1985; Griffith et al., 1987; Long & Cordle, 1982; Steiger, 1989; Stevens & Salisbury, 1984; Torem, 1987b; Vandereycken & Meerman, 1984; Vandereycken, Depreitere, & Probst, 1987). These treatments have been used in a variety of settings (outpatient, inpatient, day hospital) and in various combinations.

However, the results are less than satisfactory, and unfavorable outcomes, including the mortality rate, seem to be rather high (Hsu, 1980; Tolstrup et al., 1985; Toner et al., 1986; Willi & Grossman, 1983).

Hypnosis in the Treatment of Eating Disorders: Literature Review

A review of the literature regarding the use of hypnosis in the treatment of eating disorders may be classified, according to Vanderlinden and Vandereycken (1988), into three eras: (1) before 1975, (2) from 1975 to 1984 (the anorexic phase), and (3) from 1984 to the present (the bulimic phase).

Before 1975: The Preanorexic Phase

This era began with the French psychiatrist Pierre Janet, who reported detailed descriptions of patients with anorexia nervosa and bulimia, and was probably the first to use hypnotherapy with eating disorders (Janet, 1907, 1919). Janet used hypnosis to manipulate the patient's dissociated, fixed ideas, and promote general mental synthesis (*la synthèse mentale*). Janet also applied cognitive restructuring techniques in these patients.

Birnie (1936) reported the successful treatment of anorexia nervosa by means of hypnosis. A decade later, Brenman and Knight (1945) and Brenman and Gill (1947) described a case of a 14-year-old anorexic girl who benefited from the use of hypnosis. Meignant (1948), Delay (1949), and Scouras (1959) published their beliefs that using intravenous barbiturates (narcoanalysis) would create a hypnoticlike state that would allow the physician to analyze the patient's subconscious fantasies, and block the patient's pathological thoughts about body image, food, and eating.

From 1975 to 1984: The Anorexic Phase

Crasilneck and Hall (1975, 1985) used hypnotherapy with 70 patients who had anorexia nervosa and reported that more than half showed a marked improvement. The hypnotherapy included direct hypnotic suggestions to increase eating and, in some cases, the use of hypnoanalytic techniques to explore underlying conflicts that might be responsible for the anorexic symptoms. Kroger and Fezler (1976, 1977) promoted the combination of behavior modification and hypnosis. Hypnotic suggestions were used to increase food intake. These were associated with pleasant memories and images designed to enhance feelings of hunger and emptiness in the stomach. David and Herbert Spiegel (1978) emphasized the importance of hypnosis as a diagnostic and therapeutic tool in the management of anorexia nervosa. Milton Erickson (Erickson & Rossi, 1979; Erickson, 1985) reported on a case of an adolescent girl who was treated by hypnotherapy combining indirect and paradoxical strategies. Thakur (1980, 1984) described his experience with 90 patients with anorexia nervosa who were treated with hypnotherapy. In his method, he used several suggestions to modify eating habits and such sensations as appetite and hunger, and suggestions for breast augmentation and menstruation. He also used hypnotic suggestions directed at making patients more assertive in their relationships with others. Thakur reported a rather poor outcome in those patients who had a medical history of over three years of the illness. Gross (1982b, 1983a&b, 1984, 1986) stated that he had treated more than 500 anorexia nervosa patients. Only 10 percent of the patients were motivated to use hypnosis, but those who did succeeded in gaining weight and improving their skills in dealing with the responsibilities of daily living. According to Gross, the therapist must first identify the core of the anorexic condition. Then, hypnotherapeutic suggestions can be introduced to counteract the anorexic symptoms, promote separation from the family, and enhance the patient's sense of effectiveness. In patients with bulimia, Gross uses hypnotic suggestions directed at improving the patient's control of eating and eliminating binge eating and purging.

From 1984 to the Present: The Bulimic Phase

Since 1984 we have seen a significant increase in the reported use of hypnosis for the treatment of bulimia. Hall and McGill (1986) described the hypnobehavioral treatment of one bulimic woman for whom they used hypnotic suggestions to facilitate healthy eating habits. These included guided imagery and direct suggestions. Calof (1986) reported the treatment of a 19-year-old woman with chronic bulimia. By producing a dissociative state under hypnosis, the therapist could use suggestions and communicate with the patient's subconscious. In a previous publication (Torem, 1986b), I reported on my work with 60 eating-disorder patients, and found 12 who had dissociated ego states that were in disharmony with each other. I also reported on the likelihood that some patients with an underlying dissociative disorder may present first with pathological eating symptoms. I believe it is important to include hypnosis and hypnoanalytic explorative techniques as a routine part of the diagnostic assessment of eating-disorder patients.

The dissociation hypothesis as a possible etiology of eating disorders was supported by recent research data published by Pettinati, Horne, and Staats (1982, 1985), as well as by Council (1986). These studies found that bulimia patients were significantly more hypnotizable than anorexia nervosa patients and normal age-matched controls. The authors suggest that since hypnosis has been conceptualized as a dissociative process, it is likely that such patients may, in fact, have a dissociative mechanism involved in their pathological eating behavior. Sanders (1986) developed the Perceptual Alteration Scale (PAS) for the measurement of dissociation, and demonstrated that bulimic college students reported a higher degree of dissociation phenomena as compared with normal controls. Yapko (1986) reported on the use of indirect hypnotic suggestions to change the four common dynamics associated with anorexia nervosa—family enmeshment, delay of emotional and physical maturation, low self-esteem, and distorted body image. He recommends the use of metaphors in the hypnotic suggestions, age-progression techniques, and paradoxical behavioral assignments such as symptom prescription and cognitive restructuring, as well as reframing through metaphorical story telling.

Baker and Nash (1987) used hypnosis in the treatment of 36 women (ages 17–31) with anorexia nervosa. The treatment program combined individual and group psychotherapy with occasional use of psychotropic medication. Their follow-up data at six- and 12-month intervals showed that 76 percent of the patients had a remission of symptoms and had stabilized weight gain at an acceptable level. These results were compared with a group of 31 women who were treated identically, but without the use of hypnosis. In this comparison group, only 53 percent achieved the same level of symptom remission and weight stabilization. The use of medication and number of days of inpatient and outpatient treatment were essentially the same for both groups. According to Baker and Nash, their results "although preliminary would seem to indicate that the introduction of hypnosis into the treatment paradigm has improved the treatment response" (p. 192). Griffith (1989) reported the results of a study on the use of hypnobehavioral treatment for bulimia nervosa. The group included 12 patients who were treated for eight weeks in a program that consisted of behavior modification and four sessions of hypnosis and suggestions to enhance their self-control of binge-eating and purging episodes. The patients were assessed at the beginning of treatment, at the end of treatment, and at intervals of six weeks, four months, and nine months after treatment. There was a significant reduction in binge eating and vomiting between pretreatment and the nine-month follow-up assessment.

To summarize the literature review, there is a lack of information regarding the patient's characteristics studied in the use of hypnosis, the presence of specific psychopathology, and detailed elements involved in the hypnotherapy itself. There is also a lack of information regarding the specific type of hypnotic induction that was used, the deepening techniques that were employed, and at what stage of the treatment hypnosis was introduced as an explorative and therapeutic technique. According to Vanderlinden and Vandereycken (1988) the introduction of hypnotherapy in the treatment of anorexia nervosa is extremely difficult in the beginning phase of treatment. Emaciated anorexia nervosa patients also have a hard time relaxing (Vandereycken, Depreitere, & Probst, 1987). On the other hand, patients with bulimia respond better to the initial introduction of relaxation techniques (Mizes & Fleece, 1986). This finding is supported by research data from Pettinati, Horne, and Staats (1985, & Pettinati et al., 1989) who report a higher degree of hypnotizability in patients with bulimia as compared with patients with anorexia nervosa. This finding is also congruent with those of Sanders (1986), Barbasz (1988), and myself (Torem, 1984, 1986b, 1986c, 1988a).

Striking is the fact that in a number of recent publications reviewing eating disorders, the subject of hypnosis is not even mentioned (Larocca, 1984a; Garner & Garfinkel, 1985; Anderson, 1985; Webb, 1988; Steiger, 1989). The remainder of this chapter describes specific issues in the assessment, intervention process, and effectiveness of using hypnosis with eating-disorder patients.

ASSESSMENT

We are all familiar with the old Greek saying, "Well begun, half done." The value of a comprehensive assessment of any patient cannot be overstated in terms of its usefulness to an effective treatment plan. Evaluating the underlying dynamics is part of a comprehensive assessment. The following underlying dynamics have been identified with eating disorders.

1. Family enmeshment and a struggle for autonomy (Minuchin, Rosman, & Baker, 1978).
2. Fear of growing up and sexual maturation (Bruch, 1973, 1974; Gross, 1984).
3. Fear of pregnancy and of hostile impulses, and a need for self-punishment (Evans, 1982).
4. Obsessive perfectionism and distorted body image (Bruch, 1973, 1974, 1978).
5. History of child abuse and unresolved past trauma (Torem & Curdue, 1988; Goodwin, 1988; McFarlane, McFarlane, & Gilchrist, 1988; Damlouji & Ferguson, 1985).
6. Underlying dissociation (Torem, 1986b, 1986c, 1989b; Pettinati et al., 1982, 1985, 1989; Council, 1986; Sanders, 1986; Chandarana & Malla, 1989).
7. Underlying splitting and multiplicity (Torem, 1984, 1988, 1989a, 1990).

As part of an effective assessment, I find it useful to explore in patient's history for the existence of abuse and unresolved past trauma as etiological factors contributing to the patient's eating disorder. This exploration can be done with the use of ideomotor signaling as described by Cheek and LeCron (1968) or other hypnoanalytic techniques (Brown & Fromm, 1986; Barnett, 1981; Watkins, 1971). Many of the patients who are adult survivors of childhood trauma are found to have a high degree of hypnotizability and dissociation. In a previous publication (Torem, 1989b), I delineated the following examples that may serve as clues to an underlying dissociative mechanism in the patient's description of his or her symptoms.

- "I sometimes do not know why I do it. I am so confused . . . it is not like me."
- "A part of me wants to binge and then throw up, and another part of me hates it, and is just plain disgusted."
- "Whenever food is put in front of me, I automatically become frightened like a little kid. I know I need to eat, but it is like the devil gets into me."
- "When I get into a binge . . . it feels so strange, as if I am in a daze . . . I don't know what comes over me. . . ."
- "Eating is so hard. I am torn inside, pulled and pushed. . . ."
- "Sometimes I feel like a Dr. Jekyl and Mr. Hyde about everything . . . not just eating. . . ."
- "Look at this body . . . isn't it a shame? She used to be a fine, attractive girl, and then this awful thing happened. . . . She is afraid of men, all men . . . she hides behind the fat. . . ."
- "Doctor, you may not believe me, but at times I don't even remember bingeing . . . my husband tells me . . . and so did my mother . . . but, I can hardly remember doing it. . . ."
- "I look at my body and I know the scale says I have lost more than 25 pounds . . . but, yet, my body feels too fat. . . . I know it doesn't make sense . . . it is as if I hear this voice in my head telling me I am fat. . . ."
- "You know, at times I am so confused. I feel fat and skinny at the same time. I don't know who I am anymore."

An additional method I use in identifying a possible dissociation mechanism in my patients is the administration of dissociation scales. Currently, I use three scales: (1) the Dissociation Experience Scale (DES) (Bernstein & Putnam, 1986), (2) the Perceptual Alteration Scale (PAS) (Sanders, 1986), and (3) the Questionnaire of Experiences of Dissociation (QED) (Riley, 1988). Since dissociation experiences are highly correlated with the capacity for hypnosis, I learn in advance whether a certain patient will benefit from the use of hypnosis without having to use a more formal assessment for hypnotizability. At times, I use the Hypnotic Induction Profile (Spiegel & Bridger, 1970), which takes about five minutes and is very useful in a clinical setting. These scales are also useful for older adolescents. Similar scales are needed for children.

Many of the patients with eating disorders feel helpless and hopeless, and are ashamed of having this disorder and of having to seek psychological help. I use the principle of "meeting the patient where the patient is at." I allow the patient to talk about any subject he or she wishes to discuss and to choose the priority of his or her concern, even if it first seems only remotely related to the eating disorder. I listen to metaphors in the patient's communication, and I am aware that people communicate simultaneously on two levels—manifest and latent. For example, in the first session, an 18-year-old adolescent girl tells how the house in which she is living is falling apart and needs to be remodeled and renovated, and that she is determined to find the resources to accomplish this goal. On a manifest level, this patient is talking about her house, which may need to be renovated and remodeled; however, on a latent level, she is referring to her own body, which needs to be restored to health. In fact, this girl had lost many of her teeth as a result of repeated self-induced vomiting, and, in addition, had an electrolyte imbalance, abnormal liver functions, and esophageal bleeding requiring immediate medical and psychiatric care. The therapist's recognition that the patient communicates through her subconscious mind and is referring to her own body makes the therapist an ally with the patient's subconscious mind, and creates an ideal setting for the effective use of hypnosis to facilitate the desired change.

INTERVENTION PROCESS

When I see a new patient, I focus on the following goals to be accomplished in the first session: (1) the patient must leave the session feeling that he or she has been listened to, and (2) the patient must leave the session feeling he or she has been understood. This will assure the patient's willingness to follow up with additional sessions, as needed. Moreover, this approach cements a trustful therapist/patient relationship and communicates a message of hope and change.

I introduce the idea of using hypnosis by putting in the context of the patient's symptoms, complaints, or desire for change. For example, a common symptom in patients with eating disorders is that of anxiety or distress. I ask a patient, "Would you like to learn an exercise to reduce your stress and promote a general state of calmness and relaxation?" Most patients respond affirmatively. I then proceed by teaching the patient self-hypnosis. The following is a typical exercise (self-hypnosis for relaxation).

Put yourself in a comfortable position, and let your hands rest on your lap. Now, look up with your eyes all the way toward the top of your head, and as you look up, let your eyelids close all the way down. Let them flutter, if you wish. Now, take a deep breath . . . hold it . . . that's right. Now, exhale. Let your eyes relax . . . let your body float down as if you are on a cushion of air . . . keep on breathing comfortably like this . . . in and out, at your own pace. [Match the words "in and out" to the pace of the patient's breathing.]

Now, as you keep on breathing like this . . . in and out . . . with each breath that you take, this inner calmness is becoming stronger and spreading all the way from your head down to your toes . . . from top to bottom . . . inside out, and outside in. Everywhere in your body, and mind; every cell . . . every tissue . . . every organ . . . every system becoming fully calm and relaxed. In fact, if you wish, you may allow your body to become immersed in an ocean of calmness.

As I do this, I watch any changes in the patient's body posture, and I comment to the patient on what I see. For example, "I notice your head is dropping forward toward your chest, and that is perfectly fine. In fact, it even shows how much deeper you allow yourself to go into this state of self-hypnosis."

I then proceed to give a posthypnotic suggestion as to the patient's ability and confidence in using self-hypnosis in the future, and I practice with the patient during the remainder of the session. For example, I may say:

As you sit here feeling fully calm and relaxed and buoyant, I want you to know that in the future you will be able to do this exercise on your own, if you wish. Anytime you want to go into a state of self-hypnosis, all you need to do is put yourself in a comfortable and safe position, and count in your own mind from one to three. At one, you just look up with your eyes, all the way to the top of your head as you did before. At the count of two, you slowly close your eyelids and take a deep breath. At the count of three, you exhale, let your eyes relax, and let your body float. The more you do this exercise, the easier and easier it will become for you, and the more you do it, the more talented and experienced you will be, and greater and deeper will be the sense of calmness and relaxation. Your mind, body, and spirit will be fully in control. This inner calmness and relaxation will continue to create internal harmony within you, putting in synch various systems and organs in your body, working harmoniously together to promote your healing and recovery. This calmness and relaxation will continue and stay with you as long as you need them. The way to come out of this self-hypnosis is to count back from three to one. Three, you get ready, two with your eyelids closed, you look up with the eyes, and one, the eyes open, they come back

into focus. You are becoming fully alert and awake—oriented to your sur-
roundings as an adult, ready to deal with your tasks of daily living adaptively
and effectively. That's right. Let's go ahead and do it together right now.
Three, get ready in your own mind. Two, with your eyelids closed, look up
with the eyes. That's right, and one, the eyes open, come back into focus.
You are becoming fully alert and awake, and this inner calmness continues
to stay with you as long as you need it. Good. How are you feeling right
now?

Most patients report an immediate response of total calmness and relaxation. Some of them even add spontaneously, "Oh, Doctor, I have never
felt so relaxed in my whole life," or "This is great! I love it! You mean I
can do it on my own anytime I want to?" I then proceed by telling them: "I
am impressed with how well you have learned to use your self-hypnosis. In
fact, you need to know that all hypnosis is self-hypnosis, and yes, you can
do this on your own in the future, if you wish to. You may think that I did
this to you, however, the truth is that you have had this gift for self-hypnosis
all of your life. Today, you have learned how to evoke this self-hypnotic
trance on your own. Now, I would like to do this exercise with you again.
I will serve as your coach, and you will be my student-athlete. Are you
ready?"

I then go through the exercise again, but this time I am less wordy,
allowing the patient to use his or her own clues to count himself or herself
in and out of self-hypnosis, and if necessary, I repeat it a third time. The
patients are instructed to practice this exercise on their own three to four
times a day in a safe environment. In the following session, I spend some
time discussing the patient's practice of self-hypnosis, and allow time for
clarifications and minor "tune-ups." I then ask the patient whether he or she
would be interested in learning how to go to a place that is associated with
great calmness, such as an ocean beach, a state park, an inland lake, or a
mountain trail. Many patients choose an ocean beach. I then proceed with
an additional exercise of self-hypnosis, matched with vivid imagery of the
ocean beach. The following is an example:

Now that you have entered into a state of self-hypnotic trance, if you wish,
open a new channel of concentration whereby you may visualize yourself
being at your favorite ocean beach . . . that's right. Look at the sky. It is
clear: a June day. The skies are blue and clear; maybe some white, patchy
clouds are floating around. The sun is bright and warm. Look at the sky and
compare it with the color of the ocean. Notice where there is a similarity
and a difference. Notice how the ocean and the sky blend together, meeting
each other at the horizon. Now, look at the ocean again, and notice the

waves coming onto the beach, one after the other, in rhythm. White and foamy. That's right . . . look at the sand. Is it white? Is it yellow? Or is it gray, or maybe a blend of all three? Look at the beach. Are there any other people there walking around? Any bushes, any trees at a distance? Look at the sky again. Are there any seagulls floating around? Some may be diving toward the ocean in their attempt to catch some fish for their meal. That's right. Isn't that interesting?

Now, I would like you to move on and experience that ocean beach with your sense of hearing. Listen to the sounds. That's right. The sounds of the ocean waves coming onto the beach, one after the other. That's right. The sounds of the seagulls as they float in the air. Perhaps the sound of a radio playing in the distance, or the sounds of people talking, if you wish. Now, go on and experience that ocean beach with your sense of touch. Allow yourself to touch the sand with your bare feet. I would like you to sense the texture of the granules of this warm and comfortable dry sand under your feet. That's right. Go ahead . . . take a walk on the sand. Walk toward the waters of the ocean, and as you do, notice the change in the firmness of the sand from dry to firm, wet sand as you approach the waves of the ocean. Get a little closer and allow your feet to be touched by the ocean waters as they come onto the beach. Allow yourself to sense the coolness and wetness on your feet from the ocean waters as compared with the rest of your body exposed to the sun . . . feeling the sun rays touching your body with dry warmth, creating inside a comfortable, warm feeling of healing. Keep on walking on the beach and notice if there is a breeze. Notice the air movement touching your hair and your face, clear and clean and comfortable. Keep on walking and notice whether you see on the beach some of the seashells that have been left from the last high tide. You may want to pick one of them up, touch it with your fingers. Notice the sand that covers the seashell. Allow yourself, if you wish, to wash the sand off the shell with the ocean waters. Now, notice the special design on the seashell. Isn't that interesting?

Keep on walking on the beach, and take a deep breath through your nose. Experience the ocean beach with your sense of smell. Notice the special smell of the ocean beach. A blend of fish, seaweed, and salt that you are so familiar with. That's right. Isn't that interesting? Keep on walking on the beach, and get closer, if you wish, to a place where there are lots of big rocks. That's where the waves are breaking with even greater force . . . and throwing into the air a cloud of mist that is made up of billions of tiny droplets of water. Some of them land on your face and on your lips, and quickly dry out, leaving a tiny film of salt on your lips. All you have to do now is experience this ocean beach of yours with your sense of taste, allowing your tongue to lick your lips. That's right. Go ahead, if you wish, and experience this special salty taste of the ocean beach. Now, notice that the more you experience this ocean beach with all your senses, the more relaxed and calm you have become without even noticing it happening.

All you have to do in the future is to focus on your special beach and experience it with all your senses—as if you are actually there. And now you know you can do this exercise on your own anytime you wish to. The more you do it, the easier and easier it becomes for you. The more you do it, the more talented and gifted you become in doing this exercise. Promoting a state of total calmness and relaxation in your mind, body, and spirit. That's right. Now the way to come out of this state of self-hypnosis is to count back from three to one and go right ahead. At three, you get ready. Two, with your eyelids closed, you look up with the eyes, and one, the eyes open, they come back into focus. You are becoming fully alert, awake, oriented, and the inner calmness and relaxation continue to stay with you as long as you need.

Most patients respond very well to this form of guided imagery. It can be tailored to meet the patient's choice, such as an inland lake, a state park, or a mountain trail. Many patients with eating disorders have insomnia. I teach them to use this method to induce natural sleep by instructing them to practice it at home, and when they are in bed, to continue to focus on their nature scene and special hiding place, and not to count back three, two, one, by giving them the suggestion that the next thing they know, they wake in the morning refreshed, alert, and full of energy, since during the night they automatically switched from self-hypnosis to natural sleep.

The success of this method makes the patient an ally and believer in the powers of self-hypnosis as a vehicle for change. It capitalizes on the successful outcome of using self-hypnosis to induce relaxation and natural sleep. These are utilized as a springboard to move the patient to the next level in which further therapeutic change takes place.

To facilitate an even more successful outcome, I add a set of ego-strengthening suggestions. Ego strengthening is a technique that was described in detail by John Hartland (1965, 1971) and elaborated on by Stanton (1975, 1979, 1989). In this technique, the patient is given general suggestions to promote healing, strength, and well-being. According to Hartland, it is designed to increase the patient's confidence in himself or herself and his or her ability to cope. It is analogous to the nutritional support given to an emaciated, anorexic, low-weight patient.

Healing Suggestions—Direct and Indirect

When using general suggestions for calmness and ego strengthening, I find it useful to introduce, at times, direct and indirect suggestions relating to healthy eating and improvement in the patient's body image. However, this needs to be done with great caution since it may be met with resistance from the patient, especially if the patient is rather defiant and rebellious. Yapko (1983, 1984) pointed out that the more resistant the patient is, the less effective direct suggestions will be. Therefore, one should be familiar with and skilled in the use of indirect suggestions. This is especially true for patients with anorexia nervosa and for adolescents in general. Many adolescents use the eating disorder as a metaphor in which they communicate their dissatisfaction with a family setting or their dissociation from an unacceptable, introjected parental object. Their purging is a metaphor for rejecting the parents' value system and ideas and declaring their separateness in finding their own identity. Indirect suggestions for healing may be quite helpful when constructed in a way that allows the patient a choice of whether to continue to cope with the family dynamics in the old ''anorexic'' or ''bulimic'' way or to be creative and find new ways to deal with the predicament. The following is a verbatim example of such suggestions.

As you sit here in this state of self-hypnosis, notice that the central core of your subconscious mind has a great deal of wisdom and intelligence, and is aware of the meaning of your predicament, and how you have coped with it. I know that you, the central core of the subconscious mind, have always been there for Joan [patient's name]. You have helped her to cope with even the most difficult predicaments from the time she was a little girl. Do you want me to help Joan now? [Use ideomotor signaling to get a response.]

If the patient responds affirmatively, move on to say:

Are you willing to cooperate with me in this process of helping Joan, and, in fact, be my partner and ally as we work together to guide Joan on her journey to full healing and recovery? [Use ideomotor signaling to get a response.]

If the patient responds affirmatively, I proceed with the following:

Now that you know you have had a chance to bring Joan into treatment, I trust your creativity with confidence that you are going to find a new healing solution to this puzzle and this predicament so that Joan's body can be respected and protected for the rest of her life while you resolve her internal conflicts and her external disagreements with her parents on a psychological level while her body is respected, protected, and nurtured into health. That's right. I trust you will create for her many healing dreams every night to facilitate her journey of healing and recovery. You know, I don't even have to know how that will happen or what methods you are going to use. You may wish to share it with me in a letter or a postcard or in the next session. You may feel a sense of optimism and resourcefulness about this; however, I want you to know that is a natural response, and to be prepared to expect it, and accept it as a natural outcome.

Cognitive Restructuring and Reframing

Cognitive restructuring, which is discussed in detail by Herbert and David Spiegel in their book *Trance and Treatment* (1978), was also described by cognitive-behavioral therapists such as Meichenbaum (1977) and by Kroger and Fezler (1976). In essence, the method teaches the patient a new way of looking at an old problem and of finding new, creative solutions in situations where the patient was, in fact, cognitively "chasing his own tail" and feeling stuck with no way out. In the case of an eating disorder, the patient is first guided into a state of self-hypnotic trance. In this state, the patient is highly receptive to new ideas and suggestions. The patient is asked under hypnosis, with the use of ideomotor signaling, whether he or she would be willing to cooperate fully in this process of therapy. If the signal is in the affirmative, the therapist may proceed as follows:

As you are sitting in this chair, in this special state of extrareceptivity and self-hypnotic trance, you realize that your subconscious mind has now become your ally, and together you are making the commitment to develop a new relationship between yourself and your body. In this relationship, you, in fact, vow to respect and protect your body for the rest of your life. You are learning to develop a new view of your body as a helpless little creature that is totally dependent on you to be taken care of. In fact, your body is like a precious plant through which you can experience life itself, and to the extent that you want to live your life to the fullest, you owe your body this respect and protection. You also are quite aware that if not for you, for your body, binge eating and purging are, in fact, a poison. [The last is for bulimic patients. For anorexic patients, modify this statement to say: "For your body, if not for you, self-starvation is, in fact, a poison."]

You realize that you cannot live without your body. Your body is this precious plant through which you experience life itself, so you need your body to live, and to the extent that you want to live your life to the fullest, you owe your body this respect and protection. Do you agree [waiting for an ideomotor signal of confirmation]? Now, these are the three principles that reaffirm your commitment to respect and protect your body for the rest of your life. This new commitment is going to be locked in from now on and forever with the urge to binge, to purge, or to self-starve. Anytime the impulse for binge eating, purging, or self-starvation arises, it will be locked in with the new urge to respect and protect your body. Since you and your subconscious have committed to support and strengthen and empower the urge to respect and protect your body, the destructive impulses for binge eating, purging, or self-starvation are going to become weaker, and eventually dissipate, as if they were never there. Are you willing to reaffirm your commitment and your vow to respect and protect your body for the rest of your life?

Wait for the affirmative through ideomotor signaling, or in words. If the answer is yes, proceed in the following way.

Now, repeat after me the following statements, reaffirming your commitment as a whole person on a conscious and subconscious level: (1) for my body, if not for me, binge eating, purging, and self-starvation are, in fact, a poison. [Patient verbally repeats statement.] (2) I need my body to live. [Patient verbally repeats statement.] (3) To the extent that I want to live my life to the fullest, I owe my body this respect and protection. [Patient verbally repeats statement.]

Now that you have reaffirmed your commitment and vow to respect and protect your body for the rest of your life, I suggest you do this exercise once every two hours by first guiding yourself into a relaxed state of self-hypnosis and then opening a new channel of concentration whereby you reaffirm the commitment and vow you have made by repeating in your own mind the three principles, ending with your vow to respect and protect your body. The more you do this exercise, the easier and easier it becomes for you. The more you do it, the stronger your vow and commitment become to respect and protect your body for the rest of your life. This new vow and commitment are translated into action in your day-to-day activities and behavior. They are going to have a positive ripple effect on your self-esteem and your sense of mastery in your life. In fact, you are going to regain a sense of mastery and control in your life as related to activities on your job, your plans for the future, the learning of new things, and your relationships with other people. Now, I would like you to take a moment or so to visualize yourself as fully healed and recovered in the future. Notice the sense of joy and accomplishment as you look at your life and your healthy body. You continue your self-hypnotic exercises, which you are going to do safely and comfortably on a regular basis. Now, whenever you are ready, we are going to count back from three to one. At one, your eyes open, come back to focus. You become fully alert, awake, oriented to the reality around you in time, place, and person; ready to cope with your present reality in the most adaptive way. Now, ready, three, just get ready; two, with the eyelids closed, look up with the eyes; and one, the eyelids open, the eyes come back to focus, and you become fully alert and awake and oriented. That's right. Very good.

This hypnotic session is followed by a discussion with the patient in which he or she learns to avoid self-entrapment using the principle of "don't think about the purple elephant." The patient is asked to engage in a thought exercise where he or she is asked not to think about a purple elephant. Most patients smile and report immediately that they pictured a nice, big, purple elephant. The patient is then told, "You see, people don't like to be told 'don't.' Your subconscious mind does not incorporate the word 'don't', and only hears, 'think about a purple elephant,' and then complies appropriately. The same thing happens when you say to yourself, 'don't binge,' or 'don't purge.' You are, in fact, giving yourself the suggestion to binge and to purge, and thus entrapping yourself in doing exactly what you're wishing to avoid. In this new approach, anytime you get the impulse to binge, purge, or use self-starvation, this is your signal to engage in a state of self-hypnosis, and reaffirm your commitment and your vow to respect and protect your body for the rest of your life. So, now you focus on your vow to respect and protect your body for the rest of your life, and on your future picture of yourself living as a healthy, recovered individual."

In a patient with anorexia nervosa, I set up an additional method of reframing whereby we talk about gaining strength units instead of gaining weight. The patient is instructed that each strength unit is equal to one pound of body weight. Since most patients with anorexia nervosa who are extremely emaciated get into treatment feeling tired and physically weak, I capitalize on these presenting symptoms by asking them, under hypnosis, whether they would be willing to regain their strength. Most patients respond positively to such a suggestion, and this method uses the principle of "meet the patient where the patient is at." Meeting the patient at his or her level means devising a treatment plan that will be accepted by the patient with minimal resistance. The patient with anorexia nervosa, who suffers from a low body weight, tiredness, and physical weakness, engages more readily and is more cooperative in activities that supply the body with healthy nutrition through wholesome meals that help the patient to regain strength.

Symbolic Guided Imagery

In this method, the patient is guided into a state of self-hypnotic trance relaxation and calmness induced in a nature scene of the patient's choice. This is followed by the use of symbolic guided imagery intended to introduce a variety of natural images communicating changes of maturation, differentiation, integration, growth, self-mastery, control, and freedom of choice (Baker & Nash, 1987). I like to use natural images of transformation, such as the metamorphoses of a caterpillar through a cocoon into a mature, well-differentiated butterfly. The butterfly is well differentiated sexually and can fly freely from flower to flower and choose its own mate, while the caterpillar is asexual, cannot fly (is immature), and is limited in its choices of food and resources. This method is especially useful in the immature adolescent patient who struggles with conflicts around gender identity. Another image I like to use is one called the "red-balloon technique" (Walch, 1976), which was adapted by Hammond (1987) as an effective adjunct in helping patients to alleviate guilt. I also use images for gaining a sense of control and mastery by asking the patient to visualize himself or herself driving a car, holding onto the steering wheel with both hands, turning to the right or left whenever he or she wishes to do so, changing the speed of the car, moving forward, or reversing, based on his or her need and travel plans, and using the brakes and other control instruments in the car. All these are suggested in association with a sense of joy and self-mastery.

"Back From the Future" Technique

In this method, I utilize hypnotic age-progression techniques as described by Yapko (1984, 1986), Erickson (1985a), and others. Here, a discussion is held with the patient about a desired future image in which the patient would be interested as representing his or her full recovery. This is particularly important with a developing adolescent patient who is in the process of change and is generally struggling with the question, "Who shall I become?" The patient, in the following example a young woman, is guided into a state of self-hypnotic trance, and such a session may continue as follows:

Now that you have reached the state of self-hypnotic trance, I would like you to continue and breathe comfortably, if you wish, in and out. With each breath that you continue to take, the calmness and total state of peace and serenity, as well as inner harmony, continue and become stronger and stronger. As this takes place, you may allow yourself, if you wish, to experience the very special state of extrareceptivity in which you pay attention—your special commitment for full healing and recovery. Everyone who is committed to a state of full recovery has an image of the future. If you wish, you may follow me on this very special trip, a trip in time into the future where we are moving forward in time now as you continue to mature, turning into the age of 17 [assuming the patient is 16 years old], moving forward into 18, 19, age 20, 21, 22, 23 . . . that's right, and now, age 25.

By this time you have graduated from college and you are working in a job of your choice, gainfully employed, living in your own apartment, enjoying your state of independence. I'd like you to view yourself strolling in a department store, trying on new clothes. How you enjoy your femininity! Find yourself sitting at the counter consulting a cosmetic sales representative regarding the special colors of lipstick and other makeup that fit your skin tone and colors. As you try these on, you look in the mirror and you see with joy how much you like your face, and the rest of your body, and yourself, and your blooming femininity presenting the young woman in you. As this goes on, you may continue with the picture of yourself on a date with a young man who truly accepts you and loves you with respect and dignity for what you are and, if you wish, you may experience the special joy of being liked, the special joy of having a date and wondering about your normal and healthy attraction to the young man that you love, too, wondering about the special compatibility and chemistry that exist between the two of you, trusting the central core of your subconscious mind that has guided you and led you to this point. On the job, you continue to excel and do what you like best, feeling a sense of self-accomplishment and self-actualization . . . going to work every day with a special feeling of looking forward to the day, being assertive, appropriately so, expressing your feelings and your emotions verbally, clearly, representing your own point of view, and at the same time, being flexible, adaptively so, to consider the opinions of other people, as well.

Now, with a sense of wisdom, inner joy, intelligence, and special deep knowledge, I'd like you to come back in time to the present, age 16, and bring with you, back from the future, *all these feelings of confidence and competence, the sense of self-actualization, the joys, the sense of contentment, the sense of maturity that you already have experienced at the age of 25, bringing them with you back to age 16, and let your subconscious guide you and use the special feelings, the joys, the wisdom to guide you in the present in moving you forward on your journey of healing and recovery. That's right, now, you don't have to remember anything that's been discussed and experienced here by you. In fact, even if you don't remember anything at all, your subconscious will continue to do all the work every minute of the hour, every hour of the day, every day of the week, every week of the month, every month of the year, every year for the rest of your life. However, if you wish to remember, you may remember whatever you need to remember to continue and guide you on this special journey of recovery. That's right. Very good. That's right. Now, I'm going to slowly count back from three to one together with you, we get to one, the eyes open, they come back to focus, you're getting fully alert, awake, oriented in the present situation, ready to deal with life and the rest of the day in the most adaptive way. Ready now . . . three . . . that's right . . . two, with the eyelids closed, look with the eyes, and one, the eyes open, back to focus, fully alert and awake. That's right. Very good.*

This is followed by a discussion with the patient as to what the patient remembered of the exercise in future-oriented hypnotic imagery. The patient is then given the assignment of writing in a personal journal all the details of this experience of the trip into the future, and then, specifically, requested to bring the completed assignment to the following session. At that time, I ask the patient to read to me the assignment and I listen carefully to the tense the patient uses in describing the trip into the future. I have found that patients who describe their trip into the future using the past tense throughout usually respond very well to this technique, and I use it as a positive, prognostic indicator. Many times, this has proved to be a turning point in the patient's therapy.

Metaphorical Prescription

As part of the whole treatment program, I also give my patients concrete assignments reinforced with hypnotic suggestions for better compliance. I ask them to complete specific assignments designed for them to experience a sense of success metaphorically and concretely, as well as a sense of gaining mastery and control and exercising new choices and options. Examples of such metaphorical prescriptions are the following.

1. Chart a journey, on a map, from point A to point B. Drive your car in confidence from point A to point B. Choose two different routes—one via the expressway and the other on a country road.
2. Redecorate your own room or remodel the house.
3. Change the linens on your bed.
4. Buy yourself a new item of clothing.
5. Get new glasses (frames). Get contact lenses.
6. Adopt a pet (dog or cat).
7. Do a puzzle (and a picture of a whole person).
8. Plant a vegetable garden or one tomato plant. Watch it grow (be responsible for it) and develop. Pick the tomatoes only when they are ready.
9. Bottle-feed a small human baby; hold it and let it hold you.

Age Regression, Abreactions, and Catharsis

This specific method has been found useful with patients in whom the underlying dynamic for the eating disorder has been found to be related to past trauma. It can be carried out by using hypnosis as a diagnostic tool with such techniques as the affect bridge (Watkins, 1978) and other methods of hypnoanalytic exploration, such as those used with the assistance of ideomotor signaling as was described by Cheek and LeCron (1968), Barnett (1981), and Brown and Fromm (1986). Once this dynamic has been identified, the patient can be led by the use of age regression to the original trauma to which the eating disorder is being related. Many patients then have a chance to fully abreact emotions attached to the original trauma, and the emotional catharsis in the abreaction itself produces relief. At times, a significant improvement in (although not a full cure of) the eating-disorder symptoms is apparent, as has been described with regard to the special subgroup of patients with eating disorders in whom the symptoms may represent an underlying posttraumatic stress disorder (Torem & Curdue, 1988). In order to make this specific technique work, it must be employed together with additional methods, such as cognitive restructuring, as well as other methods that use hypnotic suggestion to foster personal growth, healing, recovery, letting go of the past, and being freed from the traumatic memories (Watkins, 1980).

Ego-State Therapy

Ego-state therapy has become a frequent focus in the hypnosis literature (Watkins, H., 1984; Watkins & Watkins, 1981, 1982; Edelstein, 1982; Beahrs, 1982; Newey, 1986). It is defined by Watkins and Watkins (1982) as the "utilization of family and group treatment techniques for the resolution of conflicts between the different ego states which constitute a 'family of self' within a single individual." This method of therapy is aimed at conflictual resolution and may employ any of the directive, behavioral, psychoanalytic, supportive, existential, and even relaxation or biofeedback techniques of therapy. It involves a notion of how much the individual's behavior is the result of the associated ego states with rigid nonflexible boundaries. According to Watkins and Watkins (1982), experience with ego-state therapy shows that activating, studying, and communicating with various ego states decrease the patient's tendency to dissociate. The patient who once dissociated and experienced these changes as "mood swings," "confusion states," or "lost time" develops an awareness of his or her condition. Confusion is then replaced by greater clarity, understanding, new hope, and a sense of self-mastery. The goal of ego-state therapy is not total fusion of all ego states into one fully "fused" ego, but rather an increased permeability of ego-state boundaries and an improved internal harmony, resulting in better cooperation and congruence among the various ego states. Ego states may be maladaptive; however, the strategy is not to eliminate any ego state, even if it is responsible for maladaptive behavior. Instead, the objective is to change the maladaptive behavior and to make the ego state more adaptive in its behavior.

In previous publications (Torem, 1987b, 1989b), I have described in great detail the use of this method for the treatment of patients with eating disorders. It is especially effective with patients in whom the underlying dynamic for the eating disorder is related to dissociated ego states that are in a state of conflict. This method also has been found useful in patients with eating disorders who had an underlying multiple-personality disorder (Torem, 1989a).

ASSESSMENT OF EFFECTIVENESS

The test of any treatment modality is its outcome. The results of treatment must be compared with the natural history of the illness. There are insufficient data available regarding the natural history of eating disorders in terms of what takes place when no treatment is used. Nevertheless, it is only by comparing a variety of such natural outcomes with a variety of treatment interventions that we can declare a treatment modality effective. The following are the criteria I use to measure the effectiveness of a specific treatment intervention.

1. *Symptom relief.* Patients who come for treatment suffer from various symptoms that can be measured and recorded by way of the psychiatric interview, the mental-status examination, and such scales as the Eating Disorders Inventory (EDI) (Garner, Olmsted, & Polivy, 1983), the Zung Scale for Anxiety (Zung, 1971), and the Zung Scale for Depression (Zung, 1965). I expect to see these symptoms relieved in terms of their intensity, frequency, and effect on the patient's ability to adapt to the activities of daily living.

2. *Behavioral change.* I expect to see a change in the patient's ability to form healthy, interpersonal relationships; in the patient's social skills; and in the patient's ability to hold a job and be gainfully employed (for adults) or to perform academically (for adolescents).

3. *Improvement in self-esteem.* I expect to see a change in the patient's sense and stability of a positive self-image that can be reflected in the sentence-completion test, as well as in the psychiatric interview and specific projective testing such as the Thematic Apperception Test (TAT).

4. *Body image.* I expect to see a change in the patient's body image, moving from a distortion in his or her body image to a realistic assessment and perception of the body. This can be done by the use of the

Mental Status Examination (MSE), the Eating Disorders Inventory (EDI), and the Draw-A-Person test (DAP).

All of these assessments can be implemented by gathering data from close family members who have knowledge of the patient prior to the treatment, during the treatment, and after the treatment intervention has been completed, and so can compare how the patient has changed.

Some of these assessments should also be made with the aid of hypnoanalytic exploratory techniques such as ideomotor signaling.

FUTURE TRENDS

From reviewing the literature on the use of hypnosis with eating disorders, it is clear that the technique has been underutilized by the administrators of formal eating-disorders programs. I predict that the future will see an increase in the number of clinicians who are educated and trained in the use of hypnotic techniques as an aid in the diagnosis and treating of eating disorders. This will be the result of more than three decades of effective educational workshops sponsored by the International Society of Hypnosis and its various constituent societies, such as the American Society of Clinical Hypnosis and the Society for Clinical and Experimental Hypnosis in the United States, as well as professional hypnosis societies in Australia, Brazil, Canada, Finland, Great Britain, India, Ireland, Israel, Italy, the Netherlands, Norway, Sweden, and West Germany. There will be a greater awareness of the importance of a treatment approach that incorporates many modalities in the same patient, such as individual therapy, family therapy, drug therapy, behavioral therapy, and hypnotherapy.

I also predict an increase in our ability to identify earlier the underlying etiology such as seen in dissociative eating disorders or affective eating disorders, allowing clinicians to match treatment interventions with the subtype of eating disorder. And I foresee the emergence of a holistic approach based on the biopsychosocial model that will take into account not only the type of illness the patient has, but also who the patient is in terms of his or her biological, psychological, sociocultural, and spiritual makeup. This will allow clinicians to choose treatment modalities that are compatible with the person who has the illness, as well as with the type of illness the person has.

REFERENCES

American Psychiatric Association (1987). *Diagnostic and statistical manual of mental disorders* (3rd ed., rev.), (pp. 65-71). Washington, DC: Author.

Anderson, A. (Ed.) (1985). *Practical comprehensive treatment of anorexia nervosa and bulimia*. Baltimore, MD: Johns Hopkins University Press.

Baker, E. L., & Nash, M. R. (1987). Applications of hypnosis in the treatment of anorexia nervosa. *American Journal of Clinical Hypnosis, 29,* 185-193.

Barbasz, M. (1988). Bulimia, hypnotizability, and dissociative capacity. Presented at the 11th International Congress of Hypnosis and Psychosomatic Medicine, The Hague, The Netherlands.

Barnett, E. (1981). *Analytical hypnotherapy; principles and practice*. Kingston, Ont.: Junica.

Beahrs, J. O. (1982). Unity and multiplicity: Multilevel consciousness of self in hypnosis. In *Psychiatric disorders and mental health*. New York: Brunner/Mazel.

Bernstein, E. M. & Putnam, F. W. (1986). Development, reliability, and validity of a dissociation scale. *Journal of Nervous and Mental Disease, 174,* 727-735.

Birnie, C. R. (1936). Anorexia nervosa treated by hypnosis in outpatient practice. *Lancet, 2,* 1331.

Brenman, M., & Gill, M. (1947). *Hypnotherapy*. New York: International Universities Press.

Brenman, M., & Knight, P. (1945). Self-starvation and compulsive hopping with para-doxical reaction to hypnosis. *American Journal of Orthopsychiatry, 15,* 65.

Brotman, A. W., Herzog, D. B., & Woods, S. W. (1984). Antidepressant treatment and bulimia: The relationship between bingeing and depressive symptomatology. *Journal of Clinical Psychiatry, 45,* 7-9.

Brown, D. P., & Fromm, E. (1986). *Hypnotherapy and Hypnoanalysis*. Hillsdale, NJ: Earlbaum.

Bruch, H. (1973). *Eating disorders: Obesity, anorexia nervosa and the person within*. New York: Basic Books.

Bruch, H. (1974). Eating disturbances in adolescence. In S. Arieti (Ed.), *American handbook of psychiatry* (pp. 275-286). New York: Basic Books.

Bruch, H. (1978). *The golden cage: The enigma of anorexia nervosa*. Cambridge, MA: Harvard University Press.

Calof, D. L. (1986). Brief hypnotherapy in a case of bulimia nervosa. In E. T. Dowd & J. M. Healy (Eds.), *Case studies in hypnotherapy* (pp. 147-165). New York: Guilford.

Chandarana, P., & Malla, A. (1989). Bulimia and dissociative states: A case report. *Canadian Journal of Psychiatry, 34,* 137-139.

Cheek, D. P., & LeCron, L. M. (1968). *Clinical hypnotherapy*. New York: Grune & Stratton.

Council, J. R. (1986). Exploring the interface of personality and health: Anorexia nervosa, bulimia and hypnotic susceptibility. *Behavioral Medicine Abstracts, 7,* 165-168.

Crasilneck, H. B., & Hall, J. A. (1975). *Clinical hypnosis: Principles and applications*. New York: Grune & Stratton.

Crasilneck, H. B., & Hall, J. A. (1985). *Clinical hypnosis: Principles and applications* (2nd ed.) (pp. 214-220). Orlando, FL: Grune & Stratton.

Damlouji, N. F., & Ferguson, J. M. (1985). Three cases of post-traumatic anorexia nervosa. *American Journal of Psychiatry, 142,* 362-363.

Davis, H. K. (1961). Anorexia nervosa treatment with hypnosis and ECT. *Diseases of the Nervous System, 22,* 627-631.

Delay, J. (1949). La narco-analyse d'une anorexie mentale. *La Presse Medicale, 59,* 577.

Edelstein, M. G. (1982). Ego-state therapy in the management of resistance. *American Journal of Clinical Hypnosis, 25,* 15-20.

Erickson, M. (1985). The case of Barbie: An Ericksonian approach to the treatment of anorexia nervosa. *Transactional Analysis Journal, 15,* 85-92. [Originally published in J. K. Zeig (Ed.) (1980). *A teaching seminar with Milton H. Erickson.* New York: Brunner/Mazel.]

Erickson, M., & Rossi, E. (1979). *Hypnotherapy: An exploratory casebook.* New York: Irvington.

Evans, J. (1982). *Adolescent and pre-adolescent psychiatry.* New York: Academic Press.

Fairburn, C. (1981). A cognitive behavioural approach to the treatment of bulimia. *Psychological Medicine, 11,* 707-711.

Fairburn, C. (1982). Binge eating and its management. *British Journal of Psychology, 141,* 631-633.

Friedman, E. J. (1984). Death from ipecac intoxication in a patient with anorexia nervosa. *American Journal of Psychiatry, 141,* 702-703.

Garfinkel, P. E., & Garner, D. M. (1982). *Anorexia nervosa: A multidimensional perspective:* New York: Brunner/Mazel.

Garner, D. M., & Garfinkel, P. E. (Eds.) (1985). *Handbook of psychotherapy for anorexia nervosa and bulimia.* New York: Guilford.

Garner, D. M., Olmsted, M. P., & Polivy, J. (1983). *Eating Disorder Inventory (EDI).* Odessa, FL: Psychological Assessment Resources.

Goodwin, J. (1988). Eating disorders as a response to multimodal child abuse. Presented at the Fifth International Conference on Multiple Personality and Dissociative States, Chicago.

Griffith, R. A. (1989). Hypnobehavioral treatment for bulimia nervosa: Preliminary findings. *Australian Journal of Clinical and Experimental Hypnosis, 17,* 79-87.

Griffith, R. A., Touyz, S. W., Mitchel, P. B., & Bacon, W. (1987). The treatment of bulimia nervosa. *Australian and New Zealand Journal of Psychiatry, 21,* 5-15.

Gross, M. (1982a). *Anorexia nervosa: A comprehensive approach.* Lexington, MA: Collamor.

Gross, M. (1982b). Hypnotherapy in anorexia nervosa. In M. Gross (Ed.), *Anorexia nervosa: A comprehensive approach* (pp. 119-127). Lexington, MA: Collamor.

Gross, M. (1983a). Hypnoanalytic approach to bulimia. *Medical Hypno-analysis, 4,* 77-82.

Gross, M. (1983b). Correcting perceptual abnormalities, anorexia nervosa and obesity by use of hypnosis. *Journal of the American Society of Psychosomatic Dentistry and Medicine, 30,* 142-150.

Gross, M. (1984). Hypnosis in the therapy of anorexia nervosa. *American Journal of Clinical Hypnosis, 26,* 175-181.

Gross, M. (1986). Use of hypnosis in eating disorders. In F. E. F. Larocca (Ed.), *Eating disorders* (pp. 109-118). San Francisco: Jossey-Bass.

Hall, J. R., & McGill, J. C. (1986). Hypnobehavioral treatment of self-destructive behavior: Trichotillomania and bulimia in the same patient. *American Journal of Clinical Hypnosis, 29,* 39-46.

Halmi, K. A. (1983). Anorexia nervosa and bulimia. *Psychosomatics, 2,* 111-129.

Halmi, K. A., Falk, J. R., & Schwartz, E. (1981). Binge-eating and vomiting: A survey of a college population. *Psychological Medicine, 11,* 697-706.

Hammond, C. (1987). "The red balloon technique." *Newsletter of the American Society of Clinical Hypnosis, 28*(2). From the Editor's notebook, p. 3.

Hartland, J. (1965). The value of ego-strengthening procedures prior to direct symptom removal under hypnosis. *American Journal of Clinical Hypnosis, 8,* 89-93.

Hartland, J. (1971a). *Medical and dental hypnosis* (pp. 197-207). Baltimore: Williams & Wilkins.

Hartland, J. (1971b). Further observations on the use of ego-strengthening techniques. *American Journal of Clinical Hypnosis, 14,* 1-8.

Herzog, D. B., & Copeland, P. N. (1985). Eating disorders. *New England Journal of Medicine, 313,* 295-303.

Hsu, L. K. G. (1980). Outcome of anorexia nervosa: A review of the literature (1954–1978). *Archives of General Psychiatry, 37,* 1041-1046.

Janet, P. (1907). The major symptoms of hysteria. London: MacMillan (second edition, 1920; facsimile of this edition published by Hafner, New York, 1965).

Janet, P. (1919). *Les medications psychologiques.* Paris: Felix Alcan. [English edition: *Psychological Healing* (Vol. 2). New York: Macmillan, 1925.]

Kroger, W., & Fezler, W. (1976). *Hypnosis and behavior modification: Imagery conditioning.* Philadelphia: Lippincott.

Kroger, W. S. (1977). *Clinical and experimental hypnosis* (2nd ed.). Philadelphia: J. B. Lippincott Company.

Larocca, F. (Ed.) (1984a). Symposium on eating disorders. *The Psychiatric Clinics of North America.* Philadelphia: Saunders.

Larocca, F. (1984b). Post-traumatic anorexia nervosa. Presented at the International Conference on Anorexia Nervosa and Related Disorders, Swansea, Wales.

Lindon, N. (1980). Multi-component behaviour therapy in a case of compulsive binge eating followed by vomiting. *Journal of Behavior Therapy and Experimental Psychology, 11,* 297-300.

Long, C. G., & Cordle, C. J. (1982). Psychological treatment of binge eating and self-induced vomiting. *British Journal of Medical Psychology, 55,* 139-145.

McFarlane, A. C., McFarlane, C. M., & Gilchrist, P. N. (1988). Post-traumatic bulimia and anorexia nervosa. *International Journal of Eating Disorders, 7,* 705-708.

Meichenbaum, D. (1977). *Cognitive-behavior modification.* New York: Plenum.

Meignant, P. (1948). Anorexie mentale guerie par narcoanalyse. *Revue Medicale de Nancy, 73,* 180.

Minuchin, S., Rosman, B., & Baker, L. (1978). *Psychosomatic families; Anorexia nervosa in context.* Cambridge, MA: Harvard University Press.

Mizes, J. S., & Fleece, E. L. (1986). On the use of progressive relaxation in the treatment of bulimia: A single-subject design study. *International Journal of Eating Disorders, 5,* 169-176.

Moor, S. L., & Rakes, S. M. (1982). Binge-eating: Therapeutic response to diphenylhydantoin: Case report. *Journal of Clinical Psychiatry, 43*, 385-386.

Mott, T. (1982). The role of hypnosis in psychotherapy. *American Journal of Clinical Hypnosis, 24*(4), 241-248.

Newey, A. B. (1986). Ego-state therapy with depression. In B. Zilbergeld, M. G. Edelstein, & D. L. Araoz (Eds.), *Hypnosis: Questions and answers* (pp. 197-203). New York: Norton.

Pettinati, H. M., Horne, R. J., & Staats, J. M. (1982). Hypnotizability of anorexia and bulimia patients (abstract). *International Journal of Clinical Hypnosis, 30*, 332.

Pettinati, H. M., Horne, R. J., & Staats, J. M. (1985). Hypnotizability in patients with anorexia nervosa and bulimia. *Archives of General Psychiatry, 42*, 1014-1016.

Pettinati, H. M., Kogan, L. G., Margolis, C., Shrier, L., & Wade, J. H. (1989). Hypnosis, hypnotizability, and the bulimic patient. In L. M. Hornyak & E. K. Baker (Eds.), *Experimental Therapies for Eating Disorders* (34-59). New York: The Guilford Press.

Pope, H. G., Hudson, J. I., & Mialet, J. P. (1985). Bulimia in the late nineteenth century: The observations of Pierre Janet. *Psychological Medicine, 15*, 739-743.

Riley, K. C. (1988). Measurement of dissociation. *Journal of Nervous and Mental Disease, 176*, 449-450.

Sanders, S. (1986). The perceptual alteration scale: A scale measuring dissociation. *American Journal of Clinical Hypnosis, 29*, 95-102.

Scouras, P. (1959). Anorexie mentale d'origine complexuelle. Action combinee de l'electrochoc et de la narco-analyse. *Encephale, 39*, 545-553.

Spiegel, H., & Bridger, A. A. (1970). *Manual for hypnotic induction profile*. New York: Soni Medica.

Spiegel, H., & Debetz, B. (1978). Restructuring eating behavior with self-hypnosis. *International Journal of Obesity, 2*, 287-288.

Spiegel, H., & Spiegel, D. (1978). *Trance and treatment: Clinical uses of hypnosis*. New York: Basic Books.

Stanton, H. (1975). Ego-enhancement through positive suggestion. *Australian Journal of Clinical Hypnosis, 3*, 32-35.

Stanton, H. (1979). Increasing internal control through hypnotic ego-enhancement. *Australian Journal of Clinical and Experimental Hypnosis, 7*, 219-223.

Stanton, H. (1989). Ego-enhancement: A five-step approach. *American Journal of Clinical Hypnosis, 31*, 192-198.

Steiger, H. (1989). An integrated psychotherapy for eating disorder patients. *American Journal of Psychotherapy, XLIII*, 229-237.

Stevens, E. V., & Salisbury, J. D. (1984). Group therapy for bulimic adults. *American Journal of Orthopsychiatry, 54*, 156-161.

Thakur, K. S. (1980). Treatment of anorexia nervosa with hypnotherapy. In H. T. Wain (Ed.), *Clinical hypnosis in medicine* (pp. 147-163). Philadelphia: Lippincott.

Thakur, K. (1984). Hypnotherapy for anorexia nervosa and accompanying somatic disorders. In W. Wester and A. Smith (Eds.), *Clinical hypnosis: A multidisciplinary approach* (476-496). Philadelphia: J. B. Lippincott Company.

Theander, S. (1985). Outcome and progress in anorexia nervosa and bulimia: Some results of previous investigations compared with those of a Swedish long-term study. *Journal of Psychiatric Research, 19,* 493-508.

Tolstrup, K., Brinch, M., Isager, T., Nielson, S., Nystrup, J., Severin, B., & Oleson, N. S. (1985). Long-term outcome of 151 cases of anorexia nervosa. The Copenhagen anorexia follow-up study. *Acta Psychiatrica Scandinavica, 71,* 380-387.

Toner, B. B., Garfinkel, P. E., & Garner, D. M. (1986). Long-term follow-up of anorexia nervosa. *Psychosomatic Medicine, 48,* 520-529.

Torem, M. S. (1982). The use of hypnosis in medical practice. *Dayton Medicine, 38,* 29-32.

Torem, M. S. (1984). Anorexia nervosa and multiple dissociated ego states. Presented at the First International Conference on Multiple Personality and Dissociative States, Chicago.

Torem, M. S. (1985). Hypnosis in medical practice. *Physician & Patient,* 35-44.

Torem, M. S. (1986a). The clinical interview in the diagnosis of MPD. Presented at the First Ohio Conference of MPD and Dissociative States, Akron.

Torem, M. S. (1986b). Eating disorders and dissociative states. In F. E. F. Larocca (Ed.), *Eating disorders: Effective care and treatment* (pp. 141-150). St. Louis: Ishiyaky EuroAmerica.

Torem, M. S. (1986c). Dissociative states presenting as an eating disorder. *American Journal of Clinical Hypnosis, 29,* 137-142.

Torem, M. S. (1986d). Hypnosis in psychosomatic medicine. Presented as part of a postgraduate course on hypnosis in clinical practice sponsored by the Cleveland Clinic Foundation.

Torem, M. S. (1987a). Hypnosis in the treatment of depression. In W. C. Wester (Ed.), *Clinical hypnosis: A case management approach* (pp. 288-301). Cincinnati, OH: BSCI Publications.

Torem, M. S. (1987b). Ego-state therapy for eating disorders. *American Journal of Clinical Hypnosis, 20,* 94-103.

Torem, M. S. (1988a). Covert multiplicity underlying eating disorders. Presented at the 11th International Congress of Hypnosis and Psychosomatic Medicine, Leiden, The Hague, the Netherlands.

Torem, M. S. (1988b). A modified ego-strengthening technique as a crisis intervention for the MPD patient. *Trauma & Recovery, 1*(2), 7-12.

Torem, M. S. (1989a). Eating disorders in MPD patients. Presented at the annual meeting of the American Society of Clinical Hypnosis, Nashville, TN.

Torem, M. S. (1989b). Ego-state hypnotherapy for dissociative eating disorders. *Hypnos, 16,* 52-63.

Torem, M. S., & Curdue, K. (1988). PTSD presenting as an eating disorder. *Stress Medicine, 4,* 139-142.

Torem, M. S. (1990). Covert multiple personalities underlying eating disorders. *American Journal of Psychotherapy, 44,* 357–368.

Vandereycken, W., Depreitere, L., & Probst, M. (1987). Body-oriented therapy for patients with anorexia nervosa. *American Journal of Psychotherapy, 41,* 252-259.

Vandereycken, W., & Meermann, R. (1984). *Anorexia nervosa: A clinician's guide to treatment*. New York: Walter de Gruyter.

Vanderlinden, J., & Vandereycken, W. (1988). The use of hypnotherapy in the treatment of eating disorders. *International Journal of Eating Disorders, 7,* 673-679.

Walch, S. L. (1976). The red balloon technique of hypnotherapy: A clinical note. *International Journal of Clinical and Experimental Hypnosis, 24*(1), 10-12.

Watkins, H. H. (1978). Ego-state therapy. In J. G. Watkins (Ed.), *The therapeutic self* (pp. 360-398). New York: Human Sciences Press.

Watkins, H. H. (1980). The silent abreaction. *International Journal of Clinical and Experimental Hypnosis, 28,* 101-113.

Watkins, H. H. (1984). Ego-state therapy. In R. J. Corsini (Ed.), *Encyclopedia of psychology* (Vol. 1) (pp. 420-421). New York: Wiley.

Watkins, J. G. (1971). The affect bridge: A hypnoanalytic technique. *International Journal of Clinical and Experimental Hypnosis, 19,* 21-27.

Watkins, J. G. (1978). *The therapeutic self*. New York: Human Sciences Press.

Watkins, J. G., & Watkins, H. H. (1979-1980). Ego states and hidden observers. *Journal of Altered States of Consciousness, 5,* 3-18.

Watkins, J. G., & Watkins, H. H. (1979). The theory and practice of ego-state therapy. In H. Grayson (Ed.), *Short term approaches to psychotherapy* (pp. 176-220). New York: Human Sciences Press.

Watkins, J. G., & Watkins, H. H. (1981). Ego-state therapy. In R. J. Corsini (Ed.), *Handbook of innovative psychotherapies* (pp. 252-270). New York: Wiley.

Watkins, J. G., & Watkins, H. H. (1982). Ego-state therapy. In L. E. Abt & I. R. Stuart (Eds.), *The newer therapies: A sourcebook* (pp. 136-155). New York: Van Nostrand Reinhold.

Watkins, J. G., & Watkins, H. H. (1985). Ego-states and multiple personalities. Presented at the 10th International Congress on Hypnosis and Psychosomatic Medicine, Toronto, Canada.

Webb, W. (1988). A clinical review of developments in the diagnosis and treatment of anorexia nervosa and bulimia. *Psychiatric Medicine, 6*(2), 24-39.

Willi, J., & Grossman, S. (1983). Epidemiology of anorexia nervosa in a defined region of Switzerland. *American Journal of Psychiatry, 140,* 564-567.

Yapko, M. D. (1983). A comparative analysis of direct and indirect hypnotic communication styles. *American Journal of Clinical Hypnosis, 25,* 270-276.

Yapko, M. D. (1984). *Trancework: An introduction to clinical hypnosis*. New York: Irvington Press.

Yapko, M. D. (1986). Hypnotic and strategic interventions in the treatment of anorexia nervosa. *American Journal of Clinical Hypnosis, 28,* 224-232.

Zung, W. W. K. (1965). A self-rating depression scale. *Archives of General Psychiatry, 12,* 63-70.

Zung, W. W. K. (1971). A rating instrument for anxiety disorders. *Psychosomatics, 12,* 371-379.

16 Enuresis and Encopresis in a Pediatric Practice

Franz Baumann, M.D.

ENURESIS

Enuresis or urinary incontinence remains the single most common behavioral problem confronting the pediatrician (Olness & Gardner, 1988). Diurnal (daytime) incontinence is likely to be a urological, organic problem. Nocturnal incontinence is the common "bed-wetting" complaint seen in 10–20 percent of school-age children. We differentiate between "primary" nocturnal enuresis (never dry at night) and "onset" enuresis (when a previously dry child begins to have wet beds—usually after a precipitating traumatic event).

I feel certain that nocturnal enuresis never is a conscious or willful act. It is more likely to be the result of dream activity and of the arousal factor from the first deep stage of sleep to the next, much lighter one. It is not a sign of mental or emotional "weakness" or deficit or of physical incompetence. Stress, anxiety, and allergy may play a role. Obviously, enuresis can lead to secondary loss of self-esteem. Maturation causes about 15 percent of all children per year to "outgrow" the symptom, with or without therapy. Thus, there are fewer cases of enuresis in high school and college than in first grade—a fact that may console some distraught parents.

Of the numerous medications in use, only one has had a success rate exceeding that attributable to the maturation factor. The drug imipramine (Tofranil) is marketed as an antidepressant. One of the side effects has been described by several of my patients as a "weird feeling." This medication works only during its administration, with symptoms usually recurring when the drug is discontinued.

There have been a number of reports of success with variations of the "bed buzzer," an instrument that produces a loud sound when moisture establishes an electrical contact. It is supposed to awaken the child, although after the fact; it also awakens the parents, siblings, and even neighbors, often before the patient responds. Several "programs" or "enuresis clinics" are based on the use of this equipment. This approach involves much training—but primarily of the parents.

My practice over the past 30 years has involved the treatment of innumerable enuretic children, the majority of whom were referred by other pediatricians, or by neurologists, urologists, or parents of former enuretics. Most of the patients had not responded to previous treatment with medication and bed alarms. Some had had family counseling. All parents knew I was using hypnosis.

Parental Instruction

The first visit usually consists of an interview with a parent or both parents only. After taking the history, instructions are dictated to the parents. They are advised to arouse the child after he has slept for two to two and a half hours by tapping him gently on the shoulder. During this time, they are to say, for example, "Johnnie, it's time to wake up" over and over again. When he finally responds, the next statement is, "Johnnie, *now* it's time to *walk* to the toilet." Once he gets up and starts to walk without help, he must turn on the lights and lift up the toilet seat before he may urinate. He then flushes, lowers the seat, turns off the lights, and goes back to bed. At that time—the magic hypnotic moment—the parents are to tuck him in, kiss him goodnight a second time, and make the following statement, "Johnnie, you have already urinated (peed, gone number one, etc.) and probably won't have to do it again until you *wake up* in the morning and *walk* to the toilet." The following morning, the parents and child check the bed. There are three possible findings:

- If it is dry, they say, exuberantly: "Johnnie, your bed is dry. Doesn't that make *you* feel good?" (Full reward.)
- If it is half dry (only a wet area with dampness or wet spot), they say: "You must have felt it coming and you were able to stop it. Isn't that great?" (One half of the reward.)
- If it is not dry (is wet), they say: "Well, accidents do happen, but don't worry about it because pretty soon you will be having dry beds anyway." (No reward; referred to as an unpaid night.)

The usual full reward could be two stars on the calendar or money. The ultimate reward, of course, will be the ability to sleep over, to go camping, and to face sleep without fear.

Child's First Visit

After testing the urine, rapport is established by having the patient talk about school, home, friends, and his favorite things or being in his favorite places. He might select watching television, playing soccer, or being on a ride at Disneyland; there is no limit to his imagination. It is very important that he and not the therapist selects the place and activity. The induction of hypnosis thus consists basically of asking the child what he would like to be doing and to pretend doing it. This induction requires only moments and demonstrates the magic skill of childhood. The hypnotic state can be recognized by the fluttering of the eyelids (if the eyes are closed) or the staring of the eyes, deep breathing, and fixed facial features, much as in adult patients. Finger movements are then chosen for "yes," "no," and "I don't want to answer." This is rehearsed with a few questions of no importance.

The first therapeutic question is, "Will it make you happy to wake up dry?" The finger signal usually says "yes." At that time I suggest, "You can. You can respond to the shoulder tap to *wake up* completely so you know what you are doing, to *walk* to the toilet, to urinate (pee), and to go back to sleep knowing you won't need to urinate (pee) until you *wake up* in the morning to *walk* to the toilet." The key words *wake up* and *walk* are repeated over and over again. The patient and I both wonder at that point whether he will be the boss of his bladder before the end of next month or by Christmas or Easter, or maybe even right away. We might rehearse a happy sleep-over or a summer-camp experience. Younger children frequently respond to a simple imagination, such as a faucet they can turn off before going to sleep or lying down.

The child is invited to practice self-hypnosis five or 10 times in the office situation and must promise to do this at home at a self-selected time, such as before dinner. During self-hypnosis, he is to talk to his bladder and tell it to let him know when it is time to *wake up* and *walk* to the toilet. This is something the bladder does all the time during the day. In fact, he's told to strengthen the "bladder muscle" during the day by doing an exercise consisting of stopping the urinating flow momentarily and then emptying his bladder completely. Every morning, he is to enter the description of the bed on his pocket calendar in code—for example, 50 cents for a dry bed, 25 cents for a half-dry bed, or zero for an accident. He will bring this calendar with him to my office for future visits so we can share his accomplishment. (Appointments are now made two to three weeks apart.)

Follow-up Visits

The basic instructions are repeated at each subsequent visit. Every success is praised and utilized for "ego building," no matter how infrequent or small these successes are. Parents are taught to be positive; for example, "*When* (not if) you have dry beds all the time, we can take a long trip." Punishment and derogatory remarks must be avoided. There is no need for restriction of fluid intake. If there is a history of food allergy, or colic—especially to cow's milk—that food should be avoided.

Results

The results vary greatly (Baumann, 1981). A few patients respond completely after only one visit. Others may have to return six to eight times. If there is no significant response after six to eight visits, the parents are told that the child is not yet ready. The patient, however, is told to continue practicing self-hypnosis every day. Overall, there are hardly any failures with this approach. It is, of course, difficult to attribute success to the therapy alone, simply because maturity is gained during the elapsed time.

In older patients (teenagers), the help of the parents is not needed unless requested by the patient. There, preference usually is a self-taped message or a radio alarm clock that the patient will set.

Special Note

This simple approach of combining principles of hypnosis and behavior therapy is appropriate only when there is no organic disease. Diurnal enuresis, increased urinary frequency with or without increased fluid intake, urinary burning or pain, dribbling, and bloody or discolored urine require prompt medical intervention. Referrals should be accepted only with the assurance that the child is physically normal and healthy and has no fecal difficulty.

ENCOPRESIS

The function of the colon is to reabsorb fluid from its content. Therefore, when a stool remains in the colon for a long time, it becomes hard—that is, dehydrated—and also usually increases in diameter. This leads to a fecal impaction. I further speculate that when one of these constipated or dehydrated hard stools finally was expelled, it probably caused a great deal of discomfort or even a painful fissure. One can then assume that the child held back further evacuation because he did not want to hurt himself. This, of course, would then further aggravate a vicious cycle of constipation, dehydration, impaction, and lack of well-being.

I am making a case for a physical reason for the original state of chronic constipation and fecal impaction as a form of holding back that is not necessarily deeply rooted. The soiling process may be due to rubbing off of a protruding fecal mass or to diarrhea around a high fecal mass, perhaps in the sigmoidal region. It seems that the origin is more physical than I was trained to believe. Many mothers see soiling as a direct attack on themselves and seek psychological help. In recent years, I have come to feel that physical examination, digital evacuation under local anesthesia with hypnotic relaxation and analgesia, and adjustment of the diet with total omission of milk products and the addition of high-fiber foods such as bran must precede any psychological approach. The relief parents feel when learning that not all of this is psychological and "their fault" is often very dramatic.

Hypnosis is a very powerful tool but it is definitely not strong enough to evacuate a large fecal impaction. I have seen children lose up to seven pounds of body weight after having been "cleaned out" the first time by means of digital removal of a fecal mass followed by a Fleet enema. The usual amount, of course, is much less, ranging from one half to two pounds and sometimes as much as three at the first visit.

In both enuresis and encopresis, the basic message must be to "become the boss," that is, the boss of your pee (urine) or poo (stool). The improvement in general physical appearance is often very dramatic. The Pediatric Allergy Department at the University of California, San Francisco, School of Medicine, described a condition called "tension fatigue syndrome" in children a number of years ago that often was due to food intolerance. In many instances, the single main offender was milk and, of course, anything containing milk or made from milk products. Obviously, cheese, ice cream, yogurt, and the like are milk products, but milk is also used in many candies and cold cuts and in most breads. It is the hidden ingredient under different names such as casein or caseinate or whey in numerous foods, and parents must be taught to recognize this. It seems that even small quantities of dairy products are capable of producing constipation with consequences as I have described.

Dr. Frank Hinman and I have written a number of papers that were published in the *Journal of Urology* (Hinman & Baumann, 1973; Baumann & Hinman, 1974; Hinman & Baumann, 1976). It would appear in some instances that pressure of a fecal mass can produce serious urinary-tract disease such as hydroureters and hydronephrosis. Treatment of the encopresis as outlined may reverse that process and perhaps prevent permanent kidney damage. Where does hypnosis come in? I believe I am using it in the examining room in teaching children to learn to feel, to get in touch with their body, and to recognize their body's needs. I also believe I am using it in projecting beyond the crisis of the moment to the point where children can feel, act, and behave normally, handling their defecation with ease and comfort. It is simply a way of communicating positively with all concerned. It really is a part of everyday handling of children and their parents.

The point to be made is that encopresis is not just a psychological pattern; it requires a total approach and, as I see it, should not be handled without examining children and treating them physically at the same time. (Owens-Stively, 1986). I do believe that more serious psychological problems associated with encopresis are secondary to that condition.

REFERENCES

Baumann, F. (1981). Urinary and fecal incontinence. In H. J. Wain (Ed.), *Theoretical and clinical aspects of hypnosis*, (pp. 107-123). Miami: Symopia Specialist.

Baumann, F. W., & Hinman, F. (1974). Treatment of incontinent boys with non-obstructive disease. *Journal of Urology, 111*, 114-116.

Hinman, F., & Baumann, F. W. (1973). Vesical and ereteral damage from voiding dysfunction in boys without neurologic or obstructive disease. *Journal of Urology, 109*, 722.

Hinman, F., & Baumann, F. W. (1976). Complications of vesicoureteral operations from incoordination of micturition. *Journal of Urology, 116*, 638-643.

Olness, K., & Gardner, G. (1988). *Hypnosis and hypnotherapy with children* (pp. 134-144). Philadelphia: Grune & Stratton.

Owens-Stively, J. (1986). *Childhood constipation and soiling: A practical guide for parents and children*. Minneapolis: Minneapolis Children's Medical Center.

Name Index

264

Subject Index